CAMBRIDGE STUDIES IN INTERNATIONAL RELATIONS: 80

Regions of War and Peace

Cambridge Studies in International Relations is a joint initiative of Cambridge University Press and the British International Studies Association (BISA). The series will include a wide range of material, from undergraduate textbooks and surveys to research-based monographs and collaborative volumes. The aim of the series is to publish the best new scholarship in International Studies from Europe, North America, and the rest of the world.

CAMBRIDGE STUDIES IN INTERNATIONAL RELATIONS

80 *Douglas Lemke*
Regions of war and peace

79 *Richard Shapcott*
Justice, community and dialogue in international relations

78 *Philip E. Steinberg*
The social construction of the ocean

77 *Christine Sylvester*
Feminist international relations
An unfinished journey

76 *Kenneth A. Schultz*
Democracy and coercive diplomacy

75 *David Houghton*
US foreign policy and the Iran hostage crisis

74 *Cecilia Albin*
Justice and fairness in international negotiation

73 *Martin Shaw*
Theory of the global state
Globality as an unfinished revolution

72 *Frank C. Zagare and D. Marc Kilgour*
Perfect deterrence

71 *Robert O'Brien, Anne Marie Goetz, Jan Aart Scholte and Marc Williams*
Contesting global governance
Multilateral economic institutions and global social movements

70 *Roland Bleiker*
Popular dissent, human agency and global politics

69 *Bill McSweeney*
Security, identity and interests
A sociology of international relations

Series list continues at the end of the book

Regions of War and Peace

Douglas Lemke

PUBLISHED BY THE PRESS SYNDICATE OF THE UNIVERSITY OF CAMBRIDGE
The Pitt Building, Trumpington Street, Cambridge, United Kingdom

CAMBRIDGE UNIVERSITY PRESS
The Edinburgh Building, Cambridge CB2 2RU, UK
40 West 20th Street, New York, NY 10011-4211, USA
477 Williamstown Road, Port Melbourne, VIC 3207, Australia
Ruiz de Alarcón 13, 28014 Madrid, Spain
Dock House, The Waterfront, Cape Town 8001, South Africa

http://www.cambridge.org

First published 2002

Printed in the United Kingdom at the University Press, Cambridge

Typeface Palatino 10/12.5 pt *System* LaTeX 2_ε [TB]

A catalogue record for this book is available from the British Library

ISBN 0 521 80985 1 (hardback)
ISBN 0 521 00772 0 (paperback)

To Jacek Kugler in grateful recognition of the enormous intellectual debts I owe him.

Contents

Acknowledgments

I have been working on this project in fits and starts for eight years. Over the years I have benefited from advice offered by various colleagues in myriad settings. I apologize to anyone I have missed, and hope I have kept omissions to a minimum. For helpful comments from the floor at presentations or for insightful responses to my questions, I am grateful to Chris Achen, Stuart Bremer, Bill Claggett, Dan Geller, Paul Hensel, Paul Huth, Harold Jacobson, Pat James, Will Moore, Jim Morrow, Chuck Myers, Ifie Okwuje, John Oneal, Ken Organski, T. V. Paul, Aimee Shouse, J. David Singer, Harvey Starr, Rick Stoll, Frank Wayman, Frank Zagare, and Bill Zimmerman.

A number of especially good friends and colleagues read the entire manuscript and gave me invaluable detailed comments. For those I am grateful to Dan Ponder, Bill Reed, John Vasquez, and Suzanne Werner. Dan deserves extra thanks for cheerfully (and insightfully) putting up with my constant requests for feedback on so many aspects of this project.

Two readers deserve special recognition. Bruce Bueno de Mesquita provided a set of detailed criticisms. As if that were not enough, he went further and actually suggested ways to deal with each objection he raised! The book is a lot better for his observations. Had I time or ability to follow up on all of them, the book might have approached perfection. Jacek Kugler has helped me with every step of this project. He could almost be listed as a co-author. From the initial conceptualization through the data collection and the interpretation of the results to the construction of subsidiary analyses and finally with the revisions, Jacek has been an irreplaceable resource.

John Haslam at Cambridge University Press and his staff have been a delight. The reviewers John selected took great pains to offer penetrating criticisms of my project, but also to indicate where they saw strengths. Their insight and encouragement has been very appreciated. It was a most pleasant experience to discover we share similar evaluations of the status quo.

Finally, for putting up with so many years of inattentive forgetfulness while I worked on and re-worked this book, I express loving appreciation to my wife Jill.

1 Introduction

Earth's billions of people reside in nearly two hundred countries characterized by varying levels of development, governed by numerous forms of political organization, and adhering to the traditions of widely disparate cultures. Could it possibly be that these obviously different peoples conform to common patterns in when, how and why they go to war against others? One might be tempted to immediately answer "no" or at least "doubtful." But others might answer "of course," perhaps citing similarities such as taboos against incest that are common in virtually every culture and society. In this book I ask whether general knowledge about when wars are likely to occur is possible. In an attempt to understand war onset generally, I consider patterns of war and peace among the great powers, as well as in four minor power regions of the globe.[1]

The research project culminating in this book began as a relatively straightforward effort to determine whether a well-established theory of great power interactions could be modified to help understand interactions among minor powers. The theory modified is power transition theory, which posits a hierarchical international system and emphasizes the importance of relative power relationships and the incentives and disincentives states face in their considerations of acting to change the formal and informal rules that govern their interactions. In order to extend the theory to minor powers, careful consideration must be paid to identifying the international sub-systems within which such states interact. This leads to a new operational definition of regional sub-systems. Armed with this notion of what constitutes a region, I press ahead with

[1] Throughout this book I use antiquated terms such as "great powers" or "minor powers" even though they have gone out of style, because there are no widely accepted replacements.

the application of power transition theory to analysis of minor power interactions and find that in spite of considerable similarity between what transpires within these regional sub-systems and within the overall international system, there are nevertheless some differences. Thus my extension of power transition theory to minor power regions requires the definition of regional sub-systems and then raises a follow-up question of why, despite some basic similarity, persistent differences distinguish some of those regions.

In writing the book I thus begin with one, but quickly come to have three tasks. First, modify power transition theory so that it applies to minor as well as great power interactions. Second, define minor power regional sub-systems and then analyze the modified version of power transition theory within those regional sub-systems. Third, attempt to account for the fact that, in spite of a reasonable amount of similarity across the regions, there still are some persistent differences. Although I list these three tasks sequentially, they are interrelated pieces of the puzzle of when and why wars break out between states. The conditions which my version of power transition theory suggests make war more likely do appear to affect when wars occur. A plausible case that these conditions say something about why the wars break out when they do can be made. But there remains an unanswered question of why these conditions are more important in some regions than others. I believe the question remains because the processes of political and economic development not only affect when and why wars break out between states, but also because the developmental process cannot be separated from the wars themselves. Thus, there are persistent differences across regions of the international system because the processes of political and economic development are not evenly achieved around the globe.

My conclusion is that we can understand a significant amount of the war and peace interactions of both great powers and minor powers by paying attention to the hypothesized causes of war suggested by my modification of power transition theory. However, the rest of the story about war and peace interactions remains hidden unless we allow for the cross-regional differences I uncover. I think these differences indicate that at later stages of development, states are more likely to wage war given the conditions central to power transition theory. The more developed states are, the more applicable power transition theory is to their behavior. In a sense, then, the usefulness of power transition theory and my extension increases as national development progresses. The fundamental, and I think fascinating, resulting question is what accounts for the poorer fit of the theory at early stages of development?[2] I begin to address this question toward the end of this book, but necessarily provide only a very crude first attempt. Even that crude first analysis, however, suggests how we might better proceed in the future as we try to address the question.

Issues at stake in this book

The overall task undertaken in this book is to extend knowledge about great power interaction so as to help understand and anticipate minor power interactions. In addressing this task a trio of intellectual issues is raised. The first has to do with the fact that almost all of what we "know" in world politics research is based on the historical experiences and intellectual culture of the West generally, and of the great powers more specifically. We have a great power bias not only in our empirical analyses of world politics, but also in our theorizing. This underlying bias could render the aggregate task of my book quite difficult. The second intellectual issue involves the epistemological question of whether we can aggregate the disparate experiences of different cultures, different time periods, different resource endowments, into one unified analysis. Some political scientists focus exclusively on the "parts" of the international system while others focus on the "whole." The two foci are largely antithetical, or at least are often presented as being so. I treat the epistemological debate as an empirical question, and discover support for those who espouse a "parts" epistemology *and* for those who subscribe to studying the "whole". Finally, a third intellectual issue is why we should care whether the Third World resembles the First? This may seem a rather dismissive reaction to my effort, but as summarized below, there is a growing body of literature within the field of realist security studies that specifically debates whether the Third World matters.

Western/great power bias in "what we know"

Much (maybe most) of the extant empirical and theoretical research on international conflict is informed by the history of great power

[2] I only provide evidence in this book that power transition theory's applicability seems to increase with development, and thus I limit my claims to it. However, I think the interrelationship between development and war makes it very likely that the applicability of other theories varies as development progresses. If this hunch of mine is correct, the key in the future will be to think about incorporating developmental processes into explanations of state behavior. Obviously this will be a harder task with some theories than with others.

(largely Western and European) interactions. Theories are created with this history in mind, and many statistical analyses draw heavily on data reflecting the interactions of the great powers. For example, the first quantitative investigation of the relationship between power distribution and war focused exclusively on the great powers (Singer, Bremer, and Stuckey 1972). More recently, empirical evaluations within the expected utility theory tradition conducted post-*The War Trap* focus on a set of strictly European dyadic observations (*inter alia*, Bueno de Mesquita 1985a; Bueno de Mesquita and Lalman 1992; and Bueno de Mesquita, Morrow, and Zorick 1997).[3] Various theories have been offered either based explicitly on, or otherwise created to explain, great power interactions. As evidence, consider that Gulick's (1955) definitive history of the balance of power is *Europe's Classical Balance of Power*; in his introduction to structural realism Waltz (1979: 73) claims: "A general theory of international politics is necessarily based on the great powers," and, according to its earlier proponents, Organski's power transition theory "can be tested fairly only if we locate conflicts whose outcomes will affect the very structure and operation of the international system" (Organski and Kugler 1980: 45). Most likely these would be conflicts among the great powers.

The centrality of great power interactions to research in world politics has not diminished. Recent titles include William R. Thompson's (1988) *On Global War*, Benjamin Miller's (1995) *When Opponents Cooperate: Great Power Conflict and Collaboration in World Politics*, and George Modelski and William R. Thompson's (1996) *Leading Sectors and World Powers*. Perhaps the clearest statement of this preoccupation is provided by the title of Jack Levy's (1983) *War in the Modern Great Power System*. There is no corresponding *War in the Modern Minor Power System*. Preoccupation with great power politics is understandable; most international relations researchers are from the Western world, if not specifically from one of the great power states. Thus, the history they analyze and explain is, in a very real sense, their own. At the same time, the great powers have existed as political units for a long period of

[3] I mention the expected utility theory research program because it is one of the most sophisticated bodies of theory and evidence currently available about world politics (see Bueno de Mesquita 1989 or Morrow 2000 for supporting arguments). In making the reference in the text, however, I appreciate that expected utility *theory* offers a general argument. It is only the *empirical evaluations* after *The War Trap* that are restricted to European interactions. For a recent global evaluation of expected utility theory, see Bennett and Stam (2000).

time and have been more highly developed than states from other parts of the world, and thus data about them are more readily accessible. Finally, interactions among these heavyweights have been enormously consequential for themselves and for the rest of the world. If scholarly attention has to be restricted to a sub-set of states, this clearly is an important one.

Hopefully, those who write books about great power politics understand that they are restricting themselves. A few explicitly recognize these restrictions. In his analysis of territorial disputes since World War II, Paul Huth (1996: 6) writes: "At present, the scholarly literature on the causes of war in the twentieth century is oriented toward the major powers, in general, and European international politics in particular ... international conflict behavior outside of Europe has not been studied extensively." Kalevi Holsti, summarizing his critique of extant international relations research, agrees (1996: 205): "The world from which these theoretical devices and approaches have derived is the European experience of war since 1648 and the Cold War. They have also drawn heavily upon the experiences of the great powers ..." Similarly, in the introduction to her edited volume, Stephanie Neuman (1998: 2) writes: "mainstream IR Theory – (classical) realism, neorealism, and neoliberalism – is essentially Eurocentric theory, originating largely in the United States and founded, almost exclusively, on what happens or happened in the West ... Few look to the Third World to seek evidence for their arguments." I think it likely Neuman would agree that it is also true that few look to the Third World to develop their arguments in the first place. Finally, Jeffrey Herbst (2000: 23) complains about "the problem that almost the entire study of international relations is really an extended series of case studies of Europe."

So what? If the great powers have been especially consequential in their interactions, and if many of the above researchers consciously understand that their arguments and evidence are restricted only to great powers, what is the harm of a great power bias? There are a number of ways in which great power bias may be harmful. First, which states are designated great powers is somewhat subjective. Is Japan a great power after post-World War II economic recovery? Japan's economy has attained enormous size (third or second largest in the world depending on how GDPs are compared), but the Japanese military establishment is relatively small. Saddam Hussein's Iraq in 1990 had one of the largest armies in the world, but was not considered a great power. If Japan is excluded because of insufficient military resources, and Iraq is excluded (presumably) because of insufficient economic resources, then it must be the combination of economic size and military resources that defines the great powers. Most current lists of great powers continue to include France. This seems odd because France's military and economy are roughly comparable in size to those of a number of states definitely not included as great powers (such as Turkey). Perhaps once a state attains great power status it remains a great power forever. However, if this is true it is difficult to explain why Spain, Portugal, Holland, Austria, or Italy are no longer listed among the great powers. Arguably possession of nuclear weapons is a defining characteristic of great power status. If true, then India and Pakistan unambiguously established themselves as great powers in 1998. But, if true then it also becomes impossible to identify great powers before the first successful atomic explosion in 1945. A similar problem exists if we identify great power status with veto power on the UN Security Council. It is not so clear who the great powers really are. Thus any restriction to "the great powers" is an arbitrary restriction. We cannot be sure that all of the theorists and empiricists referred to above make the same arbitrary restrictions, and thus we cannot conclude that there is any cumulative progress in the corpus of great-power-specific research.

A second problem introduced by restricting analysis to the great powers (assuming a definitive list of great powers existed) is that there may be something odd about great powers compared to the rest of the world's states which we thereby exclude ourselves from knowing if we only study the great powers. Medical researchers at West Virginia University might restrict themselves to analyses of residents of the Mountaineer State. In so doing they would likely draw a sample of individuals heavily representative of coal-miners (relative to samples that might be drawn elsewhere). If they then found that smoking had no effect on whether West Virginians develop lung cancer (presumably because being a coal-miner is such a risk factor for lung cancer that miners who do not smoke suffer lung cancer as frequently as miners who do), such results would surely be of interest in various corporate boardrooms in North Carolina – and presumably would be "true" for the sample studied – but would not provide a revealing picture of the causes of lung cancer generally. The medical researchers at WVU might restrict themselves out of practical necessity (the West Virginian subjects are close at hand and thus easy, like the great powers, to study), but the consequence of doing so could be very misleading.

If, as seems often the case, those who conduct their research under the shadow of the great power bias do not take such considerations into account, the consequences can be very profound. With the availability of desktop computers of staggering computational capability, the most common case selection procedure in recent quantitative studies has become to include gargantuan quantities (over a million in some analyses) of annual observations of all dyads observed over some time period, such as 1816 to 1992 (or to include all "relevant dyads" similarly observed). Thus, most current quantitative research on world politics includes interactions among the non-great powers and between the great powers, as well as between the great and non-great. However, these analyses almost always evaluate hypotheses, generated from theories or from loosely theoretical arguments, about great power interactions without consideration that what makes the arguments "work" for the great powers might prevent them from "working" for minor powers. To quote Holsti (1996: 14) once again: "Are we to assume that the ideas and practices that drove interstate wars between Prussian, Saxon, Austrian, and French dynasts in the eighteenth century must repeat themselves in twenty-first-century Africa?" Apparently we are. In the introduction to her edited volume quoted above, Neuman (1998: 17) goes on to admit that the contributors to her book generally: "find the claim for universalism by mainstream IR theorists annoying . . . " What annoys the contributors is that little or no effort is made to address very basic questions such as Holsti's.

These complaints against traditional empirical conflict analysis might strike many as contrary to the spirit of the enterprise. For many practitioners, the discipline of international relations is designed to uncover general relationships between political phenomena around the world. Thus, the idea that one set of variables is associated with war in Region A but a very different set may be associated with war in Region B suggests general relationships do not exist. Consequently, it is common in international relations research to assume away this potential. Given the advances in knowledge that empirical international relations studies have offered in recent decades, this assumption might be warranted. However, there is a large group of scholars who might inform and thus improve international relations research above and beyond what has been achieved by assuming universality: area specialists. Area specialists explicitly focus attention on one part of the world. Each sub-set of area specialists with the same state or region of focus is as guilty of potential bias as are the great-power-centric analysts. However, the *field* of area studies, taken as a whole, suggests a strong caution against unexamined assumptions of universality.

Square pegs and round holes: can we combine great powers and minor powers?

As just mentioned, a currently prevailing tendency in international conflict research is to analyze the behavior of all dyads of states with respect to hypotheses drawn from models and/or theories heavily informed by great power behavior. This assumes implicitly that all of the dyads are similar enough to make such aggregation ("pooling," in the jargon of statistics) acceptable. Colloquially this is an assumption that the procedure does not cram square pegs into round holes. In terms of the wider discipline of political science, this assumes generalists are correct and area specialists are wrong.

The previous sentence caricatures both political science generalists (whom I refer to as "generalists") and area specialists (whom I refer to as "specialists") as holding polar-opposite epistemologies on whether political scientists should study the whole as the sum of its parts (the generalist position) or each individual part as disparate pieces of an inconsistent whole (the specialist position). I am not aware of any generalist or specialist who holds such polarised opinions about epistemology, but the caricatured distinction is often made. I repeat it here because it serves a useful heuristic purpose for introducing how and why I aggregate regional parts into a global whole.

According to Robert H. Bates (1997: 166) the distinction between the two epistemological camps is caricaturized as follows:

> Within political science, area specialists are multidisciplinary by inclination and training. In addition to knowing the politics of a region or nation, they seek also to master its history, literature, and languages. They not only absorb the work of humanists but also that of other social scientists. Area specialists invoke the standard employed by the ethnographer: serious scholarship, they believe, must be based upon field research... Those who consider themselves "social scientists" seek to identify lawful regularities, which, by implication, must not be context bound... social scientists strive to develop general theories and to identify, and test, hypotheses derived from them. Social scientists will attack with confidence political data extracted from South Africa in the same manner as that from the United States and eagerly address cross-national data sets, thereby manifesting their rejection of the presumption that political regularities are area-bound.

Chalmers Johnson (1997: 172) draws the distinction quite clearly by suggesting that genuine area studies require that:

> for a researcher to break free of his or her own culture, he or she must immerse oneself in one's subject, learning the language, living with the people, and getting to understand the society so thoroughly as a participant that it problematizes one's own place as an objective observer.

Since it is impossible to gain this sort of knowledge for more than a country or two, general knowledge across countries is impossible. Finally, Ian Lustick (1997: 175) summarizes the distinction thus:

> the nomothetic (generalist) side argues that knowledge of specific cases is possible only on the basis of general claims – "covering laws," as it were – whether derived in a process of logical inference or inspired on the basis of empirical observation. The idiographic (specialist) side responds that each case is unique and that knowledge of it can be acquired only through direct immersion in the subject matter.

Clearly these caricatured positions are polar opposites. Again, I admit I am unaware of any individual dogmatically arguing that general knowledge is or is not possible. However, there are convincing arguments to be made both ways. What's more, a number of scholars operating within the sub-field of international conflict studies offer arguments consistent with the specialist position staked out above.

Raymond Cohen (1994) offers a plausible argument that the well-known democratic peace applies only to the Western Europe/North Atlantic group of states by critiquing the other areas of alleged democratic pacificity. His argument thus suggests that something specific to this large and admittedly consequential region accounts for the observed pacificity of democratic dyads. Aggregating all the world's dyads and "pretending" the democratic peace phenomenon is general obscures the fact that the Western Europe/North Atlantic group of states accounts for the finding about democracies remaining at peace with one another, and thus prevents discovery of whatever it is about this specific area that causes the democratic peace.

John Mueller (1989) explains how World War I fundamentally changed attitudes toward warfare in the West, and that since then war among such states has been basically obsolete.[4] Kalevi Holsti (1996)

[4] Singer and Wildavsky (1993) also argue war has become obsolete within the developed West but is still common in the developing world.

argues that wars prior to 1945 were Clausewitzian in type, that they were consciously selected policy options designed to affect relations with other states. After 1945, however, war is fundamentally different. What Holsti calls "wars of the third kind" (wars fought within states or because of political weaknesses internal to states) have replaced the earlier types of warfare. According to both authors, cross-temporal aggregations of data are thus inappropriate unless they take into account how attitudes toward war or the nature of war have changed with the passage of time. Mueller's argument might suggest that aggregation of the West, where war is obsolete, with the non-West, where war is still an option, is as inappropriate as temporal aggregation.

There are also a number of quantitative international conflict researchers who explicitly reject aggregating observations of minor powers and great powers. Both Midlarsky (1990) and Thompson (1990) argue that great power wars must not be combined in analyses with minor power wars because great power wars have system-transforming consequences which make them fundamentally different from minor power wars. In so doing they are repeating Levy's (1983: 4) earlier claim that "Wars in which the great powers participate should be analyzed apart from wars in general because of the importance of the great powers and the distinctiveness of their behavior . . ."

At the other end of the spectrum are those who argue such regional or temporal distinctions are red herrings. In addition to the generalist position staked out by Bates (1997), and the general tendency within international conflict research to employ an all-dyads case selection procedure, a number of specific researchers have espoused the generalist argument. Przeworski and Teune (1970: 4) begin their primer on social science inquiry with the admission that: "The pivotal assumption of this analysis is that social science research, including comparative inquiry, should and can lead to general statements about social phenomena." Reacting to claims such as those of Levy, Midlarsky, and Thompson from the previous paragraph, Bueno de Mesquita (1990a) argues that focusing exclusively on great power wars is a use of *ex post facto* knowledge to select on the dependent variable. He concludes "There currently is no compelling basis for believing that big wars are qualitatively different in their causes from lesser disputes" (p. 169). In a separate article Bueno de Mesquita provides a detailed account of a relatively minor war that he argues had system-transforming consequences (Bueno de Mesquita 1990b).

My predisposition and training encourage me to lean in favor of the generalist's perspective rather than the specialist's. And yet, when one reads Ayoob's book (1995), Holsti's book (1996), or the essays contributed to the Neuman volume (1998), one is repeatedly struck by how plausibly expressed are the concerns that political relations are different in the developing world. The newness of Third World states, the incomplete control of Third World governments over their own people and territory, the pervasive problems of poverty and lack of physical and political infrastructure, all combine to make a rather convincing argument that the international situation confronting Third World leaders is, or at least appears to be, different from the one confronting leaders in great power states.

Those generalists who employ an "all-dyads" approach can point to their results and conclude "no noticeable difference" across great power and minor power dyads. But this conclusion is likely based on *not having looked for a difference* since the operating assumption in such research is that there is no difference. At a minimum, the "all-dyads" researchers should look at a sub-set of their data, that which excludes the great powers. Do the relationships between joint democracy and peace (for example) persist when one only considers Third World dyads? Few or none have bothered even to ask such questions.

In terms of hypothesis testing, to the extent that this is a mistake it is a conservative one. If over-aggregation of dyads into global analyses is inappropriate, then any results actually found in the "all-dyads" studies are likely to be *even stronger* in the appropriate sub-group. But theoretically, this conservative hypothesis-testing mistake could be a major error. Specifically, if we really only have a theory about what the great powers do, then the appropriate referent group for analysis is simply the great powers. It might be that the relationship hypothesized for the great powers is operative in the Far East too, but we do not understand why this should be so based on our theory. What we need to do is enrich our theories by building context into them. For example, if we hypothesize that great powers fight wars to preserve a balance within their international system, then the way to generalize this to minor powers is not to include every minor power dyad in a global analysis. Rather, the correct way to generalize this theory to the minor powers is to think about what minor power international systems are, and to include dyads from these minor power systems in a unified, albeit not necessarily global, analysis with the great powers. If support for this unified analysis were uncovered, it would mean states in the great power system and in minor power international systems fight wars to preserve balances.[5]

In spite of my training and intellectual predisposition, I am persuaded the distinction between generalists and specialists can be treated as an empirical question. In summarizing her edited volume's central critique, Neuman (1998: 17) writes: "The criticism leveled here is not meant to imply that the whole body of IR Theory is irredeemably flawed. Rather it holds that the question of relevance itself needs to be empirically tested." In this book I react to what I call the "square-pegs-in-round-holes" issue by taking up Neuman's challenge: I treat the epistemological debate as an empirical question.

I do this in two ways. First, consistent with the argument made two paragraphs above, I try to build context into my elaboration of power transition theory. I think systematically about minor power systems, and only include cases I think relevant to my revision of the theory. Next, the first step in my statistical analyses is to determine whether pooling minor and great power observations into a unified analysis is statistically appropriate. The likelihood ratio tests conducted in chapter 5 and in the appendix are thus empirical tests of whether or not the minor power dyads are "square pegs" with respect to the "round hole" my theory expects these pegs to fit. Finally, I also allow for the possibility there might be differences specific to a given region by including a set of variables representing each minor power region I study. The inclusion of these regional variables could improve the overall fit of the statistical model to the data on war onsets, and/or some or all of them could be statistically significant. Either of these outcomes would be interpreted as support for the specialists. Finding that the group of regional variables collectively does not improve the fit of the model, or that none of them individually is statistically significant would be interpreted as support for the generalists.

As it turns out, I find that the generalists and specialists are both partially right. There is a general similarity across great and minor powers (as generalists would expect) but there are also characteristics of regions

[5] Additionally, correct specification of the relevant domain of cases applicable to the theory being evaluated will have the benefit of facilitating comparison across theories. If we restrict analysis of a given theory to the correct set of cases about which the theory speaks, we know the empirical domain of the theory. We can then compare this empirical domain to that of competitor theories. One criterion by which we judge a theory superior to a competitor concerns its empirical domain. If theory X's domain subsumes theory Y's, X is a superior theory. However, only if we correctly specify the empirical domain of our theories is such progressive comparison possible.

that make them differ (as specialists would expect). Further exploration of what these region-specific differences might be is offered in a subsequent empirical chapter. This exploration is made possible by allowing for the possibility that there is something to the specialist epistemology. As is so often the case when intelligent people disagree, the "truth" appears to lie in between.

Does the Third World matter?

If the truth lies between the specialists and generalists, then there are some similarities and some differences across various regions in terms of when wars occur. This means we might partly address questions of how similar the Third World is to the great powers, as well as how and why it might differ. In so doing, though, we might be asked why any of this information is important. We might be asked whether the Third World matters.

This question is normatively offensive. Of course the Third World matters. Most of humanity lives in the Third World. Almost all of mankind's ancient civilizations arose in the Third World and thus our species' cultural heritage springs from what we now call the Third World. Most of the material resources that facilitate the easy life those in the developed world enjoy are delivered to the developed world from the Third World. Obviously the Third World matters.

And yet, this obviously true normative reaction belies the possibility of a dispassionate appraisal of how important, specifically to those not in the Third World, knowledge about the Third World might be. Such a dispassionate assessment is at the heart of a debate within the exclusively realist security studies literature about whether the Third World matters. The number of studies touching on this debate is large, but the handful of citations I think best includes David (1989, 1992/1993), Van Evera (1990), Hudson *et al.* (1991), and Desch (1996). The unifying question in this debate is the extent to which the United States (and other great powers) should concern themselves with affairs in the Third World. Van Evera argues the Third World is largely irrelevant to the great powers. At the opposite extreme, Hudson and her co-authors argue that the Third World is more important than Europe. A somewhat more constrained, but clearly pro-Third World view is offered by David, while Desch summarizes both sides and concludes that some areas in the Third World are very important to the great powers, but primarily as military bases.

This literature is relevant to my study because I believe the empirical analyses in subsequent chapters of this book suggest the variables central to my analysis indicate when wars in the Third World are more likely. This means clues exist which might be used to anticipate and possibly diminish the prospect for war in the developing world. If the Third World matters to the great powers either in military strategic terms or in economic terms, or even if only to scholars in terms of understanding what makes war more likely, this is useful information.

I think it reasonably easy to reject nearly out of hand the statement that the Third World does not matter to the First at all. Even Van Evera, the most strident of those skeptical of the Third World's importance, is more accurately represented as suggesting that, since America's security resources are limited, it must pick and choose where it exerts influence. In Van Evera's opinion the main threats to the United States do not arise in the Third World, and thus it should not squander resources there. This is, however, clearly a debatable position (and is vigorously challenged by David and by Hudson *et al.*). I would also stress that it is not based on any empirical analysis by Van Evera. Consequently I think the specific question of whether the Third World matters to American security interests is unanswered. If the answer to this specific question is "yes," the findings of this book are important.

More broadly, a wide range of scholars operating in other sub-fields of international relations research have suggested that the Third World is likely to remain the main locus of interstate conflict for the foreseeable future. This is certainly a conclusion common to Mueller (1989), Singer and Wildavsky (1993), and Holsti (1996). If this conclusion is correct, then the findings of this book are again important.

Finally, any scholar interested in understanding the causes of war should be interested in explanations of war that account for a larger proportion of the world's actors. The realist security studies authors summarized above are basically concerned with questions specific to what America's foreign policy should be. The rest of us, concerned with international conflict more broadly, must seek as wide an understanding of war as possible. Whether this means we develop knowledge of how war differs from place to place, or we develop knowledge about how similar war patterns are around the world, a broader understanding of war must be our goal. Upon this criterion the findings of this book are important.

The tasks of this book, the extension of power transition theory to include minor power interactions, the development of a new definition of what regional sub-systems of the overall international system are, and the investigation of persistent cross-regional differences in the onset of war, raise important intellectual issues about how biased our knowledge of world politics is by the experiences of the great powers, whether we can meaningfully speak about a "global whole" tying otherwise distinct regions together, and whether the outcome of these efforts is useful. I believe all three are addressed in ways that establish the importance of the project reported in this volume. At a minimum, however, those interested in these issues should care about how, and how well, I address my tasks.

Plan of the book

The various tasks comprising this book's subject matter are intricately linked. Nevertheless, the book considers them sequentially. The idea is first to build the argument, then to take the steps necessary to evaluate the argument, and finally to consider the subsidiary question of cross-regional differences. Chapters 2–7 thus move from the general to the specific and then back to the general (with chapter 8 offering a summary, some implications, and directions for future research).

Chapter 2 describes and summarizes the theoretical origins of my effort. I draw on power transition theory. This theory has been around long enough, and has been discussed by sufficient past writers, that there are a number of misunderstandings of it from which I wish to disencumber myself. Thus, chapter 2 lays out power transition theory as *I* understand it, and highlights the strengths, while admitting the weaknesses, which convince *me* it is sufficiently well established to justify elaboration.

Having presented the theoretical origins of my project, I turn in chapter 3 to my revision of power transition theory. The revision I propose, the multiple hierarchy model, suggests the international power hierarchy has nested within it localized power hierarchies operating within minor power regions of the overall international system. Within these local hierarchies, interactions parallel those among the great powers atop the overall international hierarchy. After presenting my multiple hierarchy model I describe past thinking about regional subsystems in order to demonstrate that many others have come to similar conceptualizations, and to indicate how my work differs from these predecessors.

Chapter 4 offers a technical discussion of what a local hierarchy is. My operational definition of local hierarchies focuses on the ability to interact militarily, and calculates how power degrades as states attempt to project it beyond their borders. At some point the costs of power projection become too high to justify efforts to exert military influence any further. Beyond that point, states are not reachable militarily. Basically, my definition of local hierarchies calculates the area of the surface of the globe within which states can exert military influence, and calls the overlapping areas local hierarchies.

In chapter 4 I also discuss how I measure the two explanatory variables central to power transition theory and the multiple hierarchy model: national power and status quo evaluations. Considerations of national power are reasonably straightforward on account of a great deal of previous research by many other scholars. In contrast, evaluations of the status quo have received much less attention. Consequently there is arguably much more room to disagree with the measure of dissatisfaction than with the measure of relative power. Realizing this, and quite frankly realizing how readers may be dissatisfied with my operational definition of local hierarchies, I include a great deal of justification, elaboration, and, as possible, validation of the operational decisions I make. Chapter 4 is a long chapter because I find questions of measurement absolutely central to how we know what we know in the study of war and peace. There are no obvious measures of any of our concepts,[6] and thus it is incumbent upon us to be thoughtful in observation and measurement. Chapter 4 is long because of my attempts to be thoughtful.

In chapter 5 I present statistical evaluation of the multiple hierarchy model's hypothesis about factors that make war more likely to occur. All the statistical models reported support the hypothesis to varying extents. I include a set of variables representing the four minor power regions in my statistical models. The region-specific variables are included in order to capture differences potentially existing across the regions or in comparisons of them with the great powers. What these region-specific variables allow me to do is represent in my statistical evaluation the debate over epistemology between area specialists and generalists caricatured above. If these variables improve the fit of the model and/or are statistically significant, there is evidence the area specialists are correct and the world is not composed of uniform parts. Some of the region-specific variables are always statistically significant. This offers some evidence that the area specialists are justified in highlighting the importance of local context. Perhaps more importantly, the existence of these statistically significant regional variables allows me to estimate

[6] Political scientists seem in strong agreement on this point. Bernstein *et al.* (2000) title their essay on the difficulty of predicting political phenomena "God Gave Physics the Easy Problems." Similarly, Buzan (1991: 200) aptly reminds us: "Politics has never been a tidy subject."

the impact of changes in power and dissatisfaction with the status quo on the conditional probability of war within each region. When I do this I find the substantive effect of these important explanatory variables diminishes sharply as consideration shifts from the great powers through the Middle and Far East to South America and Africa. Inclusion of a set of control variables that could logically attenuate the relationship between the explanatory variables and the probability of war does not diminish support for the multiple hierarchy model's hypothesis nor affect the importance of the region-specific variables.

In chapter 6 I reanalyze my central propositions with a major modification to the dataset. Specifically, the analyses in chapter 6 differ from those in chapter 5 by incorporating great powers as actors within the minor power local hierarchies. This is an important analysis of how sensitive the results are to whether I "allow" great powers to interfere in local hierarchies. This reanalysis also lets me investigate whether variation in the opportunities great powers have had to interfere with local hierarchies causes the regional variations uncovered in chapter 5.

In the chapter 5 analyses the regional variable most statistically and substantively important represents Africa. This variable is also the most negative, suggesting Africa is the most peaceful region of the five I study. I refer to this odd finding as the "African Peace," and structure my subsequent discussion of what might cause the regions to differ around it.

In chapter 7 I follow up the empirical findings in chapter 5 with a discussion of the African Peace and of the larger question of why the region-specific variables matter. In essence, I try to account for the finding of important regional differences. I investigate whether the finding may be coincidental, caused by systematic measurement error, or due to some more readily understandable omitted variables. I offer a new set of analyses attempting to capture the important conditions systematically present or absent in some regions with conceptual variables. I thus try to replace the statistical significance of the region variables with conceptual variables such as underdevelopment and political instability. When I include additional variables in my statistical estimations, the substantive significance of the Africa variable is reduced (i.e., Africa appears less different), but the statistical significance of the Africa variable remains (i.e., Africa still is different). I close chapter 7 with a somewhat more impressionistic consideration of why the regional differences are so persistent.

In summary, chapters 2 and 3 describe power transition and the conceptual modifications I make to it in order to render it applicable to minor power interactions. This is the first task of the book. The second task is undertaken in chapters 4 and 5 where I present what I mean by a local hierarchy or regional sub-system, and evaluate the multiple hierarchy model within these local hierarchies. In chapter 6 I undertake sensitivity analyses by reanalyzing the multiple hierarchy model with a larger set of cases constructed to allow for great power interference in minor power local hierarchies. Finally, in chapter 7 I address the question of persistent differences in how well the multiple hierarchy model accounts for interactions across the regions. This is the book's third task. Along the way I provide a great deal of commentary on and consideration of the three intellectual issues discussed in the first section of this chapter. I also try to anticipate the many objections I understand others might have against the many choices I make along the way. I am aware of the grounds for criticism from which an effort as broad as mine can be attacked. However, I am asking some big questions, and with big questions there is always a lot of room for disagreement. I trust the disagreement will be productive.

Conclusions

The commentary provided by this introductory chapter might lead some to believe that no past international conflict researcher has paid attention to the question of whether or not his or her argument applies globally *and* locally. The extent to which this question has been ignored is impressive, but imperfect. One of the many reasons Bueno de Mesquita's *The War Trap* continues to be read is that in it he addresses exactly this question. In his statistical evaluation of hypotheses drawn from his expected utility theory, Bueno de Mesquita investigates the "cultural objection" (1981: 137–140), "the belief that politics in one place differs in idiosyncratic ways from the politics in other areas" (p. 137). This is especially interesting in terms of Bueno de Mesquita's rational choice model because one of the specialist critiques often raised against generalists (and specifically so by Johnson 1997), is that in other cultures rational expected utility maximization does not occur. If these specialist critiques of generalist arguments are correct, Bueno de Mesquita should be especially unlikely to find support for his hypotheses, such as that positive expected utility for war is common among war initiators. Nevertheless, Bueno de Mesquita demonstrates that if one looks individually at Europe, the Middle East, the Americas, or Asia, the initiators overwhelmingly have positive expected utility for war, whilst the targets equally overwhelmingly have negative expected utility for war. In fact, the strongest relationship is not found in the Western, European region but rather in the Middle East (the relationship between expected utility and whether a state is the initiator or target is also stronger in Asia than in Europe). Bueno de Mesquita thus breaks down his sample into regional sub-sets and reinvestigates his hypotheses, specifically asking whether they apply in disparate regional contexts. One might quibble with some of the specific decisions he makes in doing this, such as which states are assigned to which regions, but he is nevertheless to be highlighted as unique in addressing the empirical question of regional applicability. I am unaware of anyone other than Bueno de Mesquita who has published research similarly breaking their sample into regional sub-sets and addressing this question.[7]

Throughout the chapters to follow I adapt and then apply a great power theory to analysis of minor power interactions. I make every effort to do so with sensitivity to the problems to which my application may fall victim. Critical readers might nevertheless find the application naïve, or at least ill-advised. Those strictly adhering to the specialist perspective might be especially prone to deny the value of my effort, or to conclude *a priori* that the application is doomed because even though statistical regularities are uncovered, they may be trivial or otherwise of very little substantive importance. I try to address such concerns in more detail in the chapters to follow, and especially in chapter 7, but would beg the forbearance of these readers for the following reason. Since I attempt to be so sensitive to the potential pitfalls possibly preventing the application from succeeding, one might view my effort to extend power transition theory as being more likely to succeed than other such efforts at extension (such as Bueno de Mesquita's). The test of whether my revised power transition model applies is thus a relatively easy test. If the application does not work, we have evidence of how difficult such minor power extensions of great power arguments are. We also, I think, would learn something about how our theories, our research designs, and even the organization of our datasets do not reflect reality in the underdeveloped world. This would then constitute a sort of negative knowledge, a knowledge that efforts like mine do not easily work. Imaginative researchers might be able to make very good use of this negative knowledge in subsequently explaining *why* my effort was

[7] Although, for examples of thoughtful treatments of great power–minor power considerations in empirical analyses, see Goldsmith (1987), Papadakis and Starr (1987) and Rasler and Thompson (1999).

less than successful. I do not believe my effort fails. But I will admit that the application of power transition theory to minor powers provides an incomplete picture of war onsets. Several interesting directions for future research are nevertheless identified.

At a minimum, I think research such as I undertake in this volume is very important for scientific progress in the study of war and peace. Many researchers within this sub-field accept Lakatosian standards for identification of what is progressive scientifically. Lakatos's methodology of scientific research programs was first used to evaluate IR theory in the 1980s (see Bueno de Mesquita 1985b, 1989; Kugler and Organski 1989) by scholars applying it to their own research. Recently John Vasquez (1997, 1998) has applied Lakatosian standards to realist theory, and found it sorely wanting. According to Lakatos a scientific research program is progressive, among other things, if it is extended and updated in a way which allows users of the theory to understand the occurrence of additional phenomena while still understanding the occurrence of previously explained phenomena. This is referred to as excess empirical content. Like many researchers within the sub-field of international war studies, I accept Lakatos's standards for scientific progress. I believe the effort reported here is evidence of scientific progress within the power transition research program.[8] In this book I begin with the resource of a widely supported, established theory of great power politics. I then enlarge this theory's empirical domain to offer an hypothesis about war and peace interactions within minor power regional subsystems. I evaluate whether this hypothesis is empirically corroborated. I find that it is, but that the corroboration itself suggests, if only by hints, clues and impressions, that much more theoretical elaboration may be available by linking the process of political and economic development to the occurrences and purposes of war. The intertwining of these issues and questions made the book fun to write; I hope it will prove not only interesting, but also fun to read.

[8] For an independent assessment that applies Lakatos's methodology to evaluating how progressive power transition theory research has been, see DiCicco and Levy (1999).

2 Theoretical origins

As described in chapter 1, one of the motivations of this project is the effort to extend knowledge about the conditions under which great powers (and the developed world more generally) fight wars, so as to determine whether that knowledge can increase our understanding of the conditions under which developing states fight wars. I suspect few would object to such a motivation, but some might not agree with the specific body of existing knowledge I use as the basis for my extension. In this book I extend and adapt power transition theory, a theory developed to account for the incidence of wars fought for control of the international system among the very strongest of states. Some might question why I would focus on any structural theory of international behavior when strategic theories have gained such popularity and offered so many insights. Others might question why I would specifically select power transition theory as the best candidate among structural theories. In order to address such potential concerns, I describe power transition theory in some depth. Having summarized the theory, I suggest it is the best candidate structural theory because it has achieved so much empirical support and offered clues about a variety of international phenomena beyond war and peace. I then address concerns that strategic theories may offer a more promising avenue for extensions such as I attempt. Throughout this presentation it is not my intention to suggest power transition theory is the best theory of international politics or that it does not suffer from some potentially serious explanatory gaps. I am well aware that power transition theory is imperfect. However, I am unaware of any better alternative.

What is power transition theory?

Power transition theory was introduced in 1958 by A. F. K. Organski. In the initial presentation of the theory, Organski describes a hierarchical international system in which states are differentiated by their power resources. Employing the metaphor of a pyramid, Organski illustrates how there are many weak but few strong states. The very strongest of states is called the "dominant power."[1] This dominant power is an especially privileged leader of the international system, generally rising to its position of influence by emerging victorious from an earlier great power war (for more extensive summaries and discussions than are offered below, see Organski 1958, 1968; Organski and Kugler 1980; Kugler and Organski 1989; and Kugler and Lemke 1996, 2000).

Relations within power transition theory's power hierarchy are not anarchical despite the absence of formal rules and enforced international laws. In contrast to realist balance-of-power theories, power transition describes international behavior as falling into established patterns or international orders enforceable by the dominant power. Organski labeled these ordered, albeit informal, patterns the "status quo" (Organski 1958: 325). This status quo concerns economic, diplomatic, and military relations between states.

The dominant power establishes and maintains the international status quo in order to further its own long-term interests. In order to secure more net gains (Kugler and Organski 1989: 172), more value, from its international interactions, the dominant power creates self-serving patterns of interaction. The patterns it creates and defends are the international projection of the political and economic resource allocation patterns it employs domestically (as argued by Lemke and Reed 1996: 146). The gains provided to the dominant power from this status quo are more than material. A status quo that is the international projection of domestic patterns of resource allocation is advantageous to the dominant power both directly and indirectly. Directly, the projection of what has proven successful domestically is likely to provide a stream of material benefits to the dominant power from its subsequent international interactions. The status quo can benefit the dominant power indirectly as well. The projection of what has proven successful domestically is likely to reinforce the legitimacy of the dominant power's governing regime, thereby enhancing domestic stability. It is also likely to legitimize (if only partially) its leadership of the international system, and thus pacify much of its external relations as well.

For example, a dominant power enjoying comparative advantage in commerce with other nations will likely establish a liberal international

[1] In this book the terms "dominant power" and "dominant state" are interchangeable.

economic order. Doing so will protect the profits it can anticipate from international trade, preserve its access to international sources of financial capital, and deny these very resources to potential opponents of the dominant power – those who might organize their domestic resource allocation patterns differently. From this perspective it is not surprising that financial capital is available in the modern international system, a system in which the United States is the dominant power, along lines favored by the United States. The United States was instrumental, via its endorsement of weighted voting rules based on economic resources contributed to the international bodies that disperse financial capital, in constructing the international economic order (see Block 1977 and Woods 1990). Consequently, the International Monetary Fund and the World Bank tend to extend credits to states provided they adjust their domestic economic relations to conform with Western economic principles. This encourages these states to be more integrated into the global economy, supervised by the dominant power. Further, other sources of capital, such as the global bond market, also reward states for being good credit risks, and for adhering to Western, capitalist economic principles. States which attempt to carry out economic relations in line with different political or economic priorities, for example states espousing communism, isolation from the world market, etc., are denied access to important economic resources.

In addition to economic relations, the dominant power is anticipated to externalize its domestic political and military practices as well. Consequently we should expect democratic dominant powers to favor international political organizations which operate along representative lines, and we should expect dominant alliance structures to be defensive in nature, since the military goal of the dominant power is to preserve the existing situation. The rules which compose the status quo are diplomatic/political and military as well as economic. Once established, the dominant power works to preserve this status quo because it expects to profit directly and indirectly over the long run by doing so. The more other states are similar in domestic composition and international outlook to the dominant power, the more they too will benefit from the status quo. These benefiting states are "satisfied with the status quo" (Organski 1958: 326–333).

Were all of the states of the world satisfied with the status quo, power transition theory hypothesizes, international wars would be especially unlikely to occur. However, it is unlikely all members of the world will share the same outlook on the status quo; thus there exists a second category of states, those which are "dissatisfied with the status quo." States may be dissatisfied with the status quo for a number of reasons. It is possible the existing informal rules of international politics are explicitly constructed to isolate and/or deny value to the dissatisfied state. It could more simply be the case that some states are dissatisfied because they had little or no say in the construction of the existing status quo, and enjoy no direct or indirect benefits from it. Still other states may be dissatisfied because they employ different domestic institutions for the allocation of values in their society from those used by the dominant power. Consequently, such a state would be unlikely to benefit from the existing status quo, and in fact would likely expect to benefit greatly if the status quo could be altered to reflect its established resource allocation patterns.

The example of a dissatisfied state provided by the Soviet Union's experience is especially apt. Within the Soviet Union resources were allocated by order of the Communist Party. Officially sanctioned market allocations were exceedingly rare or nonexistent. Thus standards of efficiency and profitability which strongly influence resource allocation in the West would not direct resources to the non-market and unprofitable Soviet system. Consequently, Soviet development was not aided by much foreign investment. Quite the contrary, the Western satisfied states actively denied resources to the Soviets, even intervening against the Soviet government in Russia's civil war after World War I. Subsequent Soviet development thus occurred *in spite of* the status quo. As impressive as such development was (at least through the mid 1970s), any Soviet leader could have very plausibly expected that a different sort of international status quo, especially one dictated by a Soviet-style dominant power, would have allowed Soviet development to occur more rapidly, to attain greater levels of development, perhaps even to avoid stagnation and eventual decline after the late 1970s. Similar images of imperial Germany's inability to enjoy its "place in the sun" (e.g., Taylor 1954, esp. pp. 428, 438) exemplify the concept of dissatisfied states.[2]

[2] I could not invent a more dramatic example of a dominant power deliberately structuring international relations to deny resources to a challenger than is offered by Michael Mastanduno's (1992) discussion of CoCom. CoCom refers to the Coordinating Committee for export controls from NATO member-states. Since the NATO states were among the most technologically sophisticated in the world, and since the aim of CoCom was to deny advanced technologies to the Soviet Union, CoCom was essentially an anti-Soviet technology-denying regime (Mastanduno specifically refers to it as "a system of economic discrimination targeted against communist states" p.6). It had profound consequences

The general concern about dissatisfied states is that they may have what Starr (1978) cogently labels the "willingness" to change the international status quo. If they are especially dissatisfied, what Lemke and Werner (1996) call "committed to change," they have the willingness to wage war with the dominant state to effect this change in the status quo. The critical question is whether or not the dissatisfied states enjoy the "opportunity" (also from Starr 1978) for war with the dominant state. Here Organski's original pyramid metaphor for the hierarchy of power re-emerges in importance. Since the international status quo is defended by the dominant power, only the very strongest of great powers can plausibly threaten to change the status quo. The argument accompanying the power pyramid implies that only if the dissatisfied state is roughly equal in power to the dominant state should it perceive that it has the opportunity to act upon its willingness for war. Thus, power transition theory's war hypothesis is that wars among great powers are most likely to be fought for control of the international status quo when a power transition occurs between the dominant state and a dissatisfied challenger. In the absence of a transition between contenders with disparate evaluations of the international status quo, power transition theory anticipates a high likelihood of peace atop the global power pyramid.

Thus, in direct contrast to balance-of-power hypotheses about the power relationships associated with the outbreak of war, power transition theory posits that periods of rough equality, or parity, of power are war-prone. So long as the dominant state is preponderant it is able to defend the status quo against all dissatisfied states. The weak dissatisfied states realize that they do not have the wherewithal successfully to challenge the dominant state for control of the international system, and peace (albeit not harmony) is likely to prevail.

The critically important variables associated with war and peace within power transition theory are thus relative power relations and status quo evaluations. Among satisfied states and between states with appreciable differences in relative power, peace is generally expected. However, when a dissatisfied state rises in power such that it is roughly or actually the equal of the dominant state, its demands for change to

for subsequent Soviet development. Perhaps the most dramatic denial of technology to the Soviets by CoCom was communications. So far behind did Soviet communications lag, that as late as 1987 Moscow's telephone network could accommodate only sixteen long-distance calls simultaneously. Since all Soviet long-distance phone calls were routed through Moscow (so they could be monitored), as late as the 1980s the entire Soviet Union could receive only sixteen long-distance phone calls at a time!

the status quo move from being passive to explicit. Should the dominant state resist these demands, the probability of war increases dramatically. Such wars are anticipated to be especially violent, since the stakes are so large. A great deal of empirical evidence (summarized in the third section of this chapter) suggests that parity is a dangerous condition; this is consistent with power transition's expectations.[3]

One might reasonably wonder how dissatisfied states could ever achieve a position of parity with the dominant state. If the dominant state begins its "reign" as the strongest state in the international system, and if it is subsequently enriched by the status quo it establishes, how could it ever fall from its premier position? Further, if to be dissatisfied is to be systematically disadvantaged in international interactions, how could a dissatisfied state enjoy such growth that it becomes as strong as the dominant state? The answers to these questions are based upon power transition theory's description of national power as primarily domestically derived. An important, oft overlooked element of power transition theory's intellectual history (exemplified by Organski 1958: chs. 5–8; Organski and Organski 1961; Organski 1965; Organski with Lamborn 1972; Organski and Kugler 1977; and Organski *et al.* 1984) is the focus on domestic, and primarily demographic, sources of national power. Unlike balance-of-power theories that highlight the important contribution of a state's allies to its power, power transition theory argues the ultimate basis of power is the demographic potential of a state. Those governments which prove effective in organizing this potential, by both penetrating their societies and extracting resources therefrom, will be the governments of developed powerful states. In fact, the term "power transition" initially referred to the *domestic* process by which a state's population was mobilized and the state went from "potentially" powerful to a condition of "power maturity" (Organski 1958: 300–306). If the ultimate source of national power is domestic and demographic, then a larger state with a larger population can develop and come to rival even the dominant state in terms of power.

[3] This is not especially hard to understand. Since war requires that one side attacks and the other resists, it is more likely to occur when both sides perceive fighting as preferable to giving in. This in turn is more likely to be the case when neither side expects to lose. Neither side should be especially likely to expect to lose if they are roughly equal in power. Rough equality of power is thus associated with uncertainty about who the likely victor in a war would be. Thus parity is associated with a higher probability of war than is preponderance because under conditions of preponderance everyone expects the stronger side to win. Consequently the weaker side does not initiate war. Since the preponderant state in question is the dominant power, and since it is satisfied with its own status quo by definition, it does not initiate war either.

Again, the example of Soviet development is especially apt. The Soviet Union underwent fabulous modernization and development between the 1920s and 1970s. However, this growth was achieved only at the cost of tremendous domestic suffering as agriculture was collectivized, heavy industry was forcibly constructed, and domestic opponents were liquidated. It is a simple task to imagine an "easier" path to development had the international status quo been favorably disposed to aid the Soviets in their efforts to develop. Instead, the status quo systematically directed resources away from the Soviet Union, and the more painful path had to be taken. Surely Soviet leaders might have expected growth to be easier and faster had the international status quo been amenable to them. That it was not did not prevent Soviet growth. However, it did affect the route to development which the Soviet Union traveled.

In sum, power transition theory posits a hierarchical international system within which states are characterized by their levels of power as well as by their evaluations of the international status quo. Atop the international power hierarchy sits the dominant power, the most powerful state in the system. It supervises the informal patterns and rules of interstate interaction labeled the "status quo." This supervision runs the gamut from the status quo's initial creation through subsequent efforts to preserve it. The dominant state undertakes these tasks because it benefits from the status quo thus in existence. To the extent that other states are similar to the dominant state, they too benefit from the status quo and are satisfied with it. States disadvantaged by the status quo are dissatisfied, and if their efforts at development are successful, such that they come to rival the dominant state in power, the probability of wars among the great powers for control of the international system is expected to rise dramatically.

Problems with the theory

As mentioned in the chapter's opening paragraph, I do not labor under the false belief that the story power transition theory tells about great power relations, and specifically about the conditions under which they fight wars, is complete or otherwise unassailable. Rather, I am well aware the account offered by the theory suffers from various problems, ranging from simple inconsistencies in past research to substantial omissions and conceptual opacity, that, if not corrected, could stall progress within power transition theory research. In this section I outline four of the more common objections to power transition theory, offering what correctives exist but with frank recognition that such concerns are important and that the latter two are not yet satisfactorily resolved.

The "accuracy problem"

A first complaint questions how closely power transition theory's expectations about the outbreak of war have squared with the actual narrative of history. This complaint is essentially a concern that power transition theory does not tell a very accurate story. John Vasquez (1993: 103–104) specifically takes power transition theory to task because neither of the World Wars began as an attack by the rising dissatisfied challenger (Germany) against the declining dominant power (Britain). Instead, both began as wars involving other dyads which then spread and consequentially came to include the dominant power in direct conflict with the challenger.

In response I suggest that power transition theory, like all theories, offers only a stylized account of the world. Reality is too complicated for all of its nuances to be encompassed within any comprehensible theoretical structure. All theorizing involves simplification. Thus we should not be too surprised when power transition's general expectations about world politics do not square exactly with the specific diplomatic record. For example, World War I, according to power transition theory, was a clash pitting Britain and its allies against Germany and its allies. Clearly this is not how the diplomatic dispute between Austria-Hungary and Serbia which evolved into the war originated. But in a larger sense, was it not exactly the tensions atop the great power hierarchy, specifically between England as hegemon and Germany as the rising state seeking its "place in the sun," that made the July Crisis a major crisis? When we consider its implications for the international system, World War I very much was a competition between Britain and Germany with allies arranged accordingly. Similarly, World War II began when Germany invaded Poland and the British (and French) no longer were willing to idly watch German aggression. But why was Chamberlain's visit to Munich the centerpiece of pre-WWII crisis diplomacy? Why was that so much more consequential a part of the historical record of the origins of the war than the actions of other actors, clearly more directly involved at earlier stages in actual fighting? It may be Anglocentrism in English-language historical sources; but I suggest instead that it represents an acceptance of power transition theory's broad brushstrokes about world wars as valid.

The "timing problem"

A second complaint might be called the timing problem. It is represented by questions of the timing of wars relative to power transitions between great powers. In his original statement of power transition theory, Organski suggests dissatisfied challengers are most likely to initiate war prior to actually catching up with or overtaking the dominant state (Organski 1958: 333). He offers this claim because it helps him understand why the challengers he has in mind (Germany in the two twentieth-century world wars and France in the Wars of the French Revolution and Napoleon) proved unsuccessful in their bids to overturn the then existing status quo. In contrast to Organski's intuitive presentation, Organski and Kugler report empirically that wars are disproportionately likely to occur *after* the challenger has overtaken the dominant power via an international power transition (see Organski and Kugler 1980: 59 and specifically their figure 1.2).[4] Thus we have a situation in which the original proponents of power transition theory directly contradict themselves (although Organski and Kugler suggest their empirical finding takes evidentiary precedence over Organski's earlier conceptual claim).

Critics of power transition theory have occasionally used this contradiction to suggest weaknesses in the theory. However, Thompson (1983: 99) redirects attention usefully to the fact that power transition theory is consistent with wars either before or after power overtakings. Rather than suggesting power transition theory is non-falsifiable with respect to the likely timing of wars relative to power overtakings, Thompson's observation redirects attention to how we should empirically evaluate power transitions and war occurrences. Specifically, what is important in the relative power → war equation is that there be some uncertainty about who will win any war fought. If one actor "knows" it will win a putative war, presumably the other actor "knows" it will lose. When the first actor makes a demand, the second should thus be expected to concede since it expects to lose anyway. Organski's critique of balance-of-power expectations about wars occurring among unequal states is persuasive exactly because of the likely importance of uncertainty about who will win. If both sides can reasonably expect *not* to

[4] According to Organski and Kugler, the challengers tended to lose in their bids to overturn the international status quo not because they attacked *too* early, but because the dominant powers these challengers faced were able to construct powerful coalitions of allies to resist the challenger's attack.

lose, war must be more likely. Both sides are likely to think that victory is possible when they are roughly equal in power. Thus, the critique of balance of power based on uncertainty which Organski incorporates into power transition theory suggests that what is likely to lead to war is rough equality, or parity, of power. Two states are roughly equal just before the actual overtaking and at the point of overtaking, as well as just after the overtaking. At any of these times war should be more likely than in periods when there is a clear difference in national power. Consequently, power transition theory's expectation is only that *parity* is associated with a marked increase in the probability of war.

Another reason we should be suspicious of hypotheses about a specific relationship between the exact overtaking and the timing of war between a dissatisfied challenger and the dominant state is that the data we are likely to use in observing whether such a relationship exists traditionally have not been available to national decision-makers. Thus, they would be unable to know a transition occurs exactly at the point we as analysts discover it did. We therefore create unrealistic demands for our statistical models to satisfy. For example, since gross national product or Correlates of War material capabilities data were not available to British and German leaders in the first decades of the twentieth century, it would have been impossible for them to monitor these indices in order to initiate World War I at exactly the right moment. Even if German and British leaders had an understandably heartfelt desire to prove the yet-to-be-born Organski right in his contention that dissatisfied challengers attack before the actual overtaking, they would have to have been clairvoyant to time the outbreak of war in August 1914 such that years later when David Singer and his colleagues collected what became the Correlates of War (COW) composite capabilities index the relative power of Germany would be trending toward that of Britain, but not yet overtaking it (in fact, Germany's share of the COW power index overtook Britain's several years *before* World War I). In short, the data we use are generally unavailable to the decision-makers choosing between war and peace. To expect that these decision-makers time their decisions precisely, as would be indicated years, decades, or centuries later by then-unavailable statistical indicators assumes a false equivalence between what was of interest to decision-makers, our theoretical constructs of those interests, and our empirical measures of them. The data are messy, so general relationships may be the best we can expect.

That said, however, I wish to be very clear that I think our power data are reasonably valid. I think the data that go into measuring COW-style material capabilities or the vast economic resources represented by GNP or GDP are very important to leaders and they take pains to try to gauge these very same things when they consider the costs and benefits of given foreign policy choices. Thus, I think that although the data are not perfectly representative of actual power calculations made by decision-makers, they are reasonable approximations and are suitable for evaluation of all but very specific hypotheses. I simply mean to suggest that how scholars measure power and how leaders gauge relative power are likely to be imprecise and unlikely to be identical.

Consequently, I agree with Thompson that we should not consider power transition theory to offer specific hypotheses about the exact timing of war. We should expect a general relationship between parity and an increase in the probability of war, conditioned of course by the caveat that parity is only expected to be dangerous when one of the states in the dyad is the dominant power and the other is dissatisfied with the status quo. It is exactly such a hypothesis that Lemke and Werner (1996) evaluate and substantiate with multiple indicators of power, and with dichotomous as well as continuous measures of parity. In my opinion, the "timing problem" is not really a problem for power transition theory.[5]

The "powerful-therefore-satisfied problem"

Much more troublesome is what might be referred to as the powerful-therefore-satisfied problem. This problem represents a concern that catching up with the dominant power should make a state satisfied with the status quo. Recent statements of this concern (e.g., de Soysa, Oneal, and Park 1997; but see also Powell 1999: ch. 4) suggest the process of becoming as powerful as the dominant state must mean the rising

[5] An alternate, and in some ways opposite, reaction to the "timing" problem is offered by Frank Wayman (1996). Wayman suggests that rather than being overly specific in expectations about the timing of war relative to power shifts, power transition researchers have not been specific enough in describing and cataloging power shifts. Wayman logically argues that the general phenomenon of shifting power creates incentives for war among both rising and declining states, and so a larger category of power shifts should be studied. He then offers just such a study, focusing on the presence and absence of power shifts among great powers. Wayman gauges Organski's notion of status quo dissatisfaction by indicating whether the great powers were enduring rivals. He finds power transitions do increase the risk of war generally, and specifically among enduring rivals, but that another kind of power shift, what he calls "rapid approaches," is even more dangerous. Summarizing his empirical results, Wayman writes: "Organski and Kugler have merely established a specific instance of a more general pattern. The general pattern is that change – any change in relative capabilities, not just power transitions – produces war." (1996: 157) It would be interesting to replicate Wayman's great power analysis using my minor power hierarchies to see if the general category of power shifts is similarly bellicose among minor power dyads.

state is a very successful one. Why would such a state remain dissatisfied with the status quo? Would it not be likely that being powerful and being satisfied are very nearly, if not exactly, the same thing? If so, then the problem for power transition theory is that it would lead us to expect there never would be a situation in which a *dissatisfied* state catches up with the dominant state because by the time it achieved such a premier position it would be or become satisfied. Power transition theory would thus predict that wars between great powers never occur, flatly contradicting its other hypothesis about the conditions under which great powers wage war with each other.

Lemke and Reed (1998) comment on de Soysa, Oneal, and Park's presentation of the "powerful-therefore-satisfied problem," admitting its plausibility but suggesting it does not follow from a careful reading of power transition theory. Specifically, it is possible for a state to rise in power, even to the point of becoming the most powerful state in the world, yet remain dissatisfied with the international status quo, because the state in question might have experienced such dramatic growth *in spite of* the current status quo. Lemke and Reed offer the example of Soviet growth initiated under Stalin. The Soviet Union, as mentioned above, experienced tremendous economic advance and did so in relatively short order. However, all of this growth originated domestically. American growth in the middle of the nineteenth century was similar in scope to Soviet growth in the middle of the twentieth century, but American growth occurred under the favorable shadow of substantial investment from Europe, was promoted energetically by valuable trade links between the United States and more developed continental economies, and thus was actively abetted by the British-imposed nineteenth-century status quo. In contrast, Soviet growth occurred without foreign economic assistance, virtually without foreign trade, and occasionally with the active antagonism, via interventions in the early Soviet period or CoCom restrictions during the Cold War, of status quo supporters. Consequently the Soviets would be expected to resent the British and then American status quo under which they suffered. Had the international status quo been established by a Soviet-style state, it is very likely Soviet growth projects would have been actively assisted by other members of the international system. It is possible to be powerful *and* dissatisfied, as power transition theorists have always argued. Lemke and Reed close their comment with an empirical demonstration that status quo evaluations and national power levels (measured either as COW capabilities or GDP) or status quo evaluations and changes in national power, are not systematically related to each other. Lemke and Reed conclude the powerful are not disproportionately likely to be satisfied, and the weak are not disproportionately likely to be dissatisfied.

However, this does not mean the "powerful-therefore-satisfied problem" is easily dismissed, for as Oneal, de Soysa, and Park (1998) aptly rejoin, it is not exactly clear which states will be satisfied and, most importantly, it is not clear – based on the theory – why some states are satisfied while others are dissatisfied. Oneal, de Soysa, and Park's concern is clearly evident in the following passage: "The theory's proponents need to show that a rising challenger would have grown more rapidly, according to standard economic theory, if it had not been for the influence of the dominant state. Some evidence of how the hegemon thwarted the challenger's potential would also increase confidence in the theory." (1998: 518) Assertions, even if illuminated by an apt historical example, are not satisfactory substitutes for demonstrated empirical regularities.

Thus, the "powerful-therefore-satisfied problem" is not so much a direct challenge to the account of world politics power transition theory offers; it does not mean power transition theory is logically inconsistent or otherwise falsified, but it certainly does highlight one of the most glaring conceptual opacities in the theory – what does it mean to be satisfied? How are satisfied states "benefited" by the status quo, and how are dissatisfied states "harmed" by the status quo? As yet there are no definitive empirical answers to these questions. Thus, this remains a very important direction for continued research.

The "prevention problem"

A fourth concern is represented by the prevention problem. According to power transition theory, wars to change the international status quo are most likely to occur among great powers when a power transition brings a dissatisfied challenger into parity with the dominant state. The probability a dissatisfied challenger will initiate a war to change the status quo when it is dramatically inferior to the dominant state is hypothesized to be very low, specifically because leaders of a weak challenging state are expected to anticipate their effort will be unsuccessful given their power disadvantage. Instead, they are more likely to bide their time until their loss to the dominant power is not certain. This depiction represents dissatisfied challengers as reasonably efficient foreign policy practitioners. They are hypothesized to be unlikely to waste resources frivolously in struggles they are likely to lose. Rather, they are likely to wait until the odds on success improve. There is little in this view of challenger behavior that poses a problem. But, in contrast to the reasonably efficient foreign policy practitioners at the helm of dissatisfied challengers, the leaders of dominant states seem rather myopic. They presumably can extrapolate challenger growth trends and must anticipate rising dissatisfied states are an increasing threat to the status quo and thus to themselves. And yet, power transition theory hypothesizes wars are disproportionately likely to occur under parity, implying dominant states will tend *not* to wage preventive war against dissatisfied challengers in an effort to stall their growth and thus stave off future, more serious and costly, challenges to the status quo.

How dominant states can ignore the preventive motivation for war is increasingly difficult to understand when we consider the many incentives conventional wisdom associates with waging preventive war (Vagts 1956; Morgenthau 1960: 211; Levy 1987; and Schweller 1992). It is almost as though power transition theory presents rising states as patient and forward-thinking actors while dominant states are unable to anticipate the likely future course of relations with those rising, and perhaps dissatisfied, states.

To be sure, this "prevention problem" is not an insurmountable one for power transition theory. The British did not wage preventive war against the main rising states of the nineteenth century (Germany, Russia, and the United States), the United States did not wage preventive war against the Soviet Union and does not appear likely to do so against a currently rapidly rising People's Republic of China. If Reiter's (1995) claims about preemptive wars almost never occurring can be translated into a similar claim about preventive wars almost never occurring, then the "prevention problem" may be an anomaly of great power politics generally rather than specifically for power transition theory.[6] At a minimum, however, it seems odd that dominant powers would tend not to prevent dissatisfied states from achieving parity with them. Thus, this problem also persists as a clear area within which conceptual, and hopefully empirical, elaboration of power transition theory would be helpful.[7]

[6] The distinction between preemptive and preventive wars concerns the imminence of the threat being addressed. In preemptive wars the "preemptor" initiates war under the immediate concern its adversary is about to attack, whereas in preventive war the "preventor" initiates under the perhaps long-term concern its adversary will eventually attack.

[7] Of course, it is possible the problem of identifying who is dissatisfied *causes* the prevention problem. If the dominant power is unsure whether the rising state is satisfied or

The four problems presented in this section are not exhaustive of concerns about power transition theory. However, they are four of the more common complaints about the theory, and thus recommend themselves as important for consideration. Neither individually nor cumulatively do they suggest power transition theory is a poor base of knowledge from which to begin the process of generalizing from great power relations to those of minor powers. The "accuracy problem" reminds us that power transition theory is a crude tool, ill-suited for anticipation of the exact details of international politics. The "timing problem" suggests power transition researchers should not be overly specific in their hypotheses about when wars will occur, but rather should only anticipate parity is associated with war (and primarily so where there is dissatisfaction of the challenging state). The "powerful-therefore-satisfied problem" suggests power transition theorists have thus far failed to be explicit about how the status quo benefits satisfied states or denies benefits to dissatisfied states. The "prevention problem" suggests an interesting asymmetry may exist between the farsightedness of challengers and the myopia of dominant states.

None of these problems suggests we should doubt power transition theory's hypotheses about the causes of war. None of these problems suggests power transition theory is internally inconsistent or otherwise false. Rather, they point to fruitful arenas for future theory elaboration. This is indicative of a fertile and productive research tradition, rather than of insurmountable problems. This is a part of my justification for using power transition theory as the starting point from which I generalize to minor power conflict relations. The rest of my justification is that there is a wide range of empirical support suggesting power transition theory offers a reasonably persuasive account of the causes of war. This empirical support is summarized in the next section.

Empirical evidence about power transition theory

There is no definitive empirical evaluation of power transition theory. Rather, there is a wide range of studies employing different spatial and temporal domains, different model specifications, different statistical

dissatisfied, it is probably more likely to resist the preventive motivation for war. Powell (1996) offers a discussion of this issue in his formal consideration of appeasement, and deduces that some amount of appeasement is always an equilibrium solution to the strategic problem of relative decline.

techniques, and different operational definitions of relative power and status quo evaluations. The general findings of these various studies are persistently consistent with power transition theory's expectation of parity and disparate evaluations of the status quo as likely causes of war. Technically speaking, this hypothesis only applies to dyads including the dominant power. Of the many studies summarized below, only Lemke and Werner (1996) restricts analysis to just dyads including the dominant power. Thus, only Lemke and Werner (1996) offers a direct test of power transition theory's hypothesis. The other studies should be interpreted as suggestive and consistent with power transition theory's expectations, but not as direct tests of the theory's war hypothesis.

A vast number of studies have demonstrated power parity (variously measured) is associated with war among great powers, major powers, or all dyads, and preponderance (again, variously measured) is similarly associated with an absence of war. Organski and Kugler (1980) demonstrate for the very strongest of great powers that power equality is strongly associated with great power war. Houweling and Siccama (1988), Kim (1989), and Gochman (1990) extend this finding to the slightly larger population of all major powers. Geller (1993, 1998) extends it to the population of interstate rivals. A related body of studies demonstrate power inequality, especially power preponderance within a dyad, is associated with the absence of war (see Weede 1976 for the earliest finding, but Bremer 1992 for perhaps the most persuasive demonstration of this relationship). Only a sampling of the wide range of studies is mentioned here (interested readers are referred to the more exhaustive summary in Kugler and Lemke 2000), but other researchers come to the same conclusion about the robustness of the parity→war and/or preponderance→peace relationship. For example, in their comprehensive survey of the empirical literature on international conflict, Geller and Singer (1998: 75–76) conclude: "conditions of approximate parity and shifts toward parity are consistently and significantly associated with conflict and war ..."[8]

A small but growing body of studies investigate the importance of status quo evaluations on war occurrence. Ray (1995) offers a case study

[8] A large number of studies include relative power variables as controls when investigating other hypotheses. Those finding parity associated with war, or preponderance associated with peace, include Bremer (1992, 1993), Huth, Bennett, and Gelpi (1992), Huth and Russett (1993), Maoz and Russett (1993), Davis and Moore (1997), and Oneal and Russett (1997).

comparison of two crises in 1898, arguing that negative evaluations of the status quo caused war in one case while satisfaction with the status quo prevented it in the other. Rousseau *et al.* (1996) report the international crisis actor dissatisfied with the status quo in dispute is much more likely to be the first party to escalate hostilities. Gelpi (1997) reports dissatisfied states are more likely to give in to pressures to divert attention from domestic woes by initiating foreign conflicts. None of these studies conceptualizes status quo evaluations in exactly the same way as power transition theory, and thus they are suggestive at best, although consistent with power transition expectations.

However, more directly applicable to power transition theory's war hypothesis are studies by Kim (1991, 1992, 1996) and Werner and Kugler (1996) which find that disparate evaluations of the status quo are very dangerous among great power dyads. Lemke and Werner (1996) report that for dyads including the dominant power, disparate status quo evaluations have a greater positive effect on the probability of war than does power parity.

All of the studies cited here offer evidence of parity and status quo dissatisfaction being dangerous conditions increasing the probability of war. Only the Lemke and Werner (1996) study evaluates the importance of these variables within the population of dyads including the dominant power. Unfortunately, they fail to evaluate correctly the statistical importance of the interaction between parity and status quo evaluations, because only the multiplicative interaction term is included in their models. Consequently, no definitive evaluation of the theory has been offered. Nevertheless, the range of studies and research designs that suggest parity and dissatisfaction are dangerous is certainly indicative of empirical support for power transition theory. I am aware of no other structural theory of the causes of war which has enjoyed such robust empirical support across so many spatial and temporal domains, operational definitions, or model specifications.

Empirical validation is only one criterion by which we judge a particular theory to be superior to competing explanations. Another criterion involves excess content: theories that can account for a wider range of behaviors are superior to those limited to fewer types of behavior. In this regard, power transition theory is indeed impressive. Power transition arguments have been employed to offer insights into questions of nuclear deterrence (Kugler and Zagare 1990; Kugler 1996), the democratic peace (Lemke and Reed 1996), the existence of interstate rivalry (Lemke and

Reed 2001b), and to offer predictions about likely threats to great power peace in the post-Cold War world (Lemke 1997; Tammen *et al.* 2000).

Power transition theory is attractive because it is logically coherent, enjoys substantial empirical support, and offers implications for a wide range of interstate behaviors and for disparate subsidiary literatures in world politics. For these reasons I derive my theoretical origin from the literature on power transition theory. I am convinced I am building on a reasonably sound foundation in this endeavor; yet one significant question remains: why employ any structural theory of world politics when strategic explanations have been so productive in recent decades? Even if power transition theory is the best candidate among structural theories, why employ a structural theory at all? I address this question in the next section.

Why power transition theory instead of a strategic theory?

Strategic theories of world politics have gained great popularity, probably because of the successes of Bruce Bueno de Mesquita with his expected utility theory of war (1981) and its later extension in game-theoretic form (Bueno de Mesquita and Lalman 1992). Bueno de Mesquita's work is the tip of the iceberg, as subsequent scholars have offered myriad strategic theories about many aspects of world politics (see Morrow 2000 for a summary of formal strategic work in world politics).

By "strategic" theory, I mean theoretical arguments and models explicitly designed to represent the strategic calculations of leaders when they decide to undertake a given foreign policy. It seems obvious that leaders of states calculate the likely consequences of the decision to initiate war against another state. They must consider whether they are likely to win, whether third parties will involve themselves, and whether they might not be able to extort concessions from their would-be opponent without all the costs associated with actually going to war. The expected results of these calculations must affect whether the foreign policy is enacted. What is more, these calculations likely involve expectations of what the leaders of the other states are similarly calculating. Thus, the foreign policies chosen are the result of strategically interdependent choice. By strategic theory I mean any theoretical argument or model that explicitly incorporates such calculations.

In contrast, structural theories focus on physical realities without explicit consideration of how decision-makers calculate how they should react to those physical realities. Power transition theory is a structural theory because it hypothesizes that given certain structural regularities in the relations between a pair of states, certain foreign policies are expected to be observed. Thus, all satisfied states are expected (with a very high probability) to be at peace with each other. Further, a dyad with a dissatisfied state at parity with the dominant power is expected (with a very high probability) to experience war. No explicit consideration is given to the thought processes of the leaders of any of these states; they are simply expected to conform to the structurally induced pattern (probabilistically, of course). Power transition theory does not deny such strategic calculations are made, and there is an implicit strategic calculation implied by the expectation that states are more likely to fight at parity because under such equality both are more likely to expect they will not lose. The record of empirical success that power transition theory enjoys suggests the absence of any explicit strategic calculations does not impinge on power transition theory's usefulness in anticipating what leaders of states will do internationally. And yet, although power transition theory does contain implicit and non-formal strategic elements, it is essentially a structural theory and, arguably, many useful insights would be gained if explicitly strategic considerations were incorporated into the theory.[9]

I am convinced good theories accurately reflect the activities and thought processes of the actors theorized about. I am persuaded this means good theories must (eventually) explicitly consider the strategic calculations of these actors. In spite of the fact that power transition does not include these explicit strategic considerations, I think it is still enormously useful for extensions such as presented here. There are two reasons for this. First, the structural focus of power transition theory provides a backdrop within which the strategic calculations central to

[9] Readers interested in an example of non-obvious insights are referred to Alastair Smith's (1995) game-theoretic model of alliance choices. A conventional non-strategic literature (exemplified by Sabrosky 1980) "demonstrated" alliances are an unreliable way to guarantee a state's security, since most of the time allies do not honor their promises when one member of the alliance finds itself attacked. Smith's strategic model of alliance choices persuasively suggests such past research errs by ignoring that attackers likely target states with no allies or with alliances deemed unlikely to be honored. His empirical follow-up article (Smith 1996a) suggests this is true. Conceptually, Smith's work instructs us to reconsider how alliance choices are strategically linked. Would-be attackers do not attack states with allies likely to honor their commitments while would-be targets with unreliable allies are less likely to resist attacks. Thus, the strategic calculations of would-be attackers, would-be targets, and would-be honorable allies *stop* opportunities occuring for allies to honor their commitments. Gartner and Siverson (1996) offer a similarly dramatic strategic reinterpretation of the extant literature on war diffusion.

formal modeling are made and thus we are benefited by knowing as much as possible about the structural backdrop and how widely applicable it is. Second, there are explicitly strategic models similar to power transition theory offering the same or similar war hypotheses as the traditionally structural version of the theory (Alt, Calvert, and Humes 1988; Kim and Morrow 1992; Powell 1996; Alsharabati 1997).

In his memoirs, William Somerset Maugham wrote:

> The metaphor of chess, though frayed and shop-worn, is here wonderfully apposite. The pieces were provided and I had to accept the mode of action that was characteristic of each one; I had to accept the moves of the persons I played with; but it has seemed to me that I had the power to make on my side, in accordance perhaps with my likes and dislikes and the ideal that I set before me, moves that I freely willed. (Maugham 1938: 281)

Maugham perceived he had room in his life within which to make strategic choices, to choose between options with due consideration paid to the likely course of decisions made by others. However, he also felt constrained in these choices by the structures of society around him. One might expect a playwright to have chosen the metaphor of society providing the physical constraints of a stage, set, etc., and his life the dialog and actions portrayed within the confines of the stage and set, but his use of the chessboard metaphor is striking here, perhaps more so since security studies and analyses of war often also use chess as a metaphor.

Maugham's chessboard is similar to Shepsle and Weingast's (1981) notion of structure-induced equilibria. Shepsle and Weingast respond to Tullock's "Why so much stability?" question of how the expectations of social choice models for pure majority rule institutions (cycling majorities and rampant instability) can be so at odds with observed legislative reality. They suggest the structure of legislative institutions such as the US House of Representatives induces stability and equilibria. Specifically, in the House of Representatives amendments to bills are voted on with the initial version of the bill always brought up for reconsideration last. Second, legislation can only be advanced to general consideration after it has passed through committee review. Third, the House Rules Committee can alter the debate and amendment procedure for each bill. Singly or cumulatively such rules affect who has access to the agenda as well as the order in which proposals are considered. This allows the pure-majority-rule pathologies of cycling majorities and instability to be overcome, and stability prevails. Why so much stability? The rules (structure) of the House (institution) constrain the actions and decisions of its members (actors).

James Morrow (1988) applies such consideration to analysis of world politics. He writes: "Generalizing from the literature on democratic institutions and social choice, structure – in the form of rules and institutions . . . allows decisive and consistent social choice." (1988: 85) In world politics the structural elements of the international system include the distribution of power, the nature and durability of alliances, international regimes, etc. Morrow concludes that a theory focusing only on the structures (such as power transition theory) or ignoring those structures altogether will be inadequate. Good theory must consider the preferences of the actors *and* the structures which constrain their efforts to achieve their more preferred outcomes.

I suggest that power transition theory's empirical success demonstrates that the constraints of relative power and the status quo are important structural bounds on behavior in world politics. Relative power and the status quo are akin in world politics to the chessboard, number of pieces and rules of movement from Maugham's metaphor. They constrain the behavior of actors in world politics much as the deliberative rules of the U.S. House of Representatives constrain the instability that pure majority rule would otherwise produce. These structural elements are thus important building blocks that strategic theories should consider if they would satisfy Morrow's (1988) reasonable demands for good theory. Further, evaluations of the status quo (whether a state is satisfied or dissatisfied) clearly are statements of preferences. However, if power transition theory's important structural considerations are limited only to interactions among the very strongest of states, then we might reconsider how generally important these structural constraints really are. Most strategic theories aim at generality. If relative power and the status quo are structures constraining relatively few actors, strategic theorists might profitably avoid inclusion of them as the structural elements in their models. Consequently, I see an important implication of the empirical analysis in this book being that strategic theorists would be well served by incorporating relative power and the status quo as the structural constraints in their models. Power transition theory is generalizable to regional interactions (as demonstrated in later chapters), and thus relative power and the status quo do not constrain behavior only among the very strongest of states.

In contrast to the previous paragraph, Robert Powell (1999, esp. chs. 3–4) argues that power transition is neither useful nor accurate as a theory of international politics because its main expectations do not follow logically from its underlying assumptions. He specifically suggests (pp. 141–2) that war is not deduced to be more likely at or around transition points and thus that parity is not especially dangerous. Further, he claims past evidence in favor of power transition theory is discredited because of research design flaws. If he is right, then continued investigation of international politics based on power transition theory is pointless and the wealth of empirical evidence in favor of the theory suspect. Although Powell's book, and the three models contained therein, are potentially useful opening claims in a modeling dialog, there are a number of problems with his evidence and models. Consequently, we should not reject power transition theory based on his preliminary and incomplete efforts.

The first problem is that Powell makes a number of assumptions in building his models which are inconsistent with power transition theory.[10] As a result, Powell's models' failure to identify the greatest risk of war as being at or around parity is not a problem for power transition theory. Rather, this suggests Powell's models are inconsistent with power transition theory, and, consequently, whether power transition theory or Powell's models are correct depends on whether his assumptions or power transition's lead to empirically accurate deductions.

These assumptions vary quite a bit. Powell implicitly assumes the anticipated costs of waging war for both rising and declining states are independent of the distribution of power. In addition, he explicitly assumes (p. 91) that, once waged, the costs of war are constant for the rest of time. Both of these assumptions are very important to his deductions about when war is most likely to occur. Powell repeatedly demonstrates that high costs decrease the likelihood of war. If the costs of war are related to the distribution of power, then relaxing Powell's assumption about expected war costs would very likely modify all of his deductions about the distribution of power and the probability of war. Constant and uniform costs that must be paid after war is waged affect decisions about when to wage war because in Powell's models the rising and declining states must think about future streams of utility from different courses of

[10] Critiquing assumptions is frowned on in many circles. I disagree with the likes of Friedman and Waltz, agreeing instead with Bueno de Mesquita (1981: 10) who writes: "When assumptions are made without sensitivity and knowledge of 'real' experiences, the result is likely to be a trivial theory about an unreal world."

action. Since all of Powell's deductions about the timing of war depend on his assumption about permanent and constant war costs, they too would change if this assumption were relaxed.

Neither of Powell's assumptions about the costs of war are consistent with power transition theory. In fact, it is precisely the expectation a state will lose and thus suffer high costs without any compensation that deters dissatisfied weak challengers from waging war prior to achieving parity. At parity the expected benefits of waging war increase, and consequently the net costs of waging war decrease. Thus power transition theory assumes that the expected costs of war change as relative power shifts. This directly contradicts Powell's assumption of war costs being independent of the distribution of power.

Moreover, research on the Phoenix Factor (Kugler 1973; Organski and Kugler 1977; Kugler and Arbetman 1989b), related closely to other power transition theory research, demonstrates empirically that the costs of war not only diminish over time, but actually vanish in the reasonably short time-span of two decades (Olson [1982] offers similar cautions against assuming constant non-diminishing war costs). It seems clear that in order to model power transition theory Powell's assumptions about the expected costs of war must be changed.

There are also substantial differences between power transition theory and Powell's models in terms of what is the status quo and what it means to be dissatisfied. Powell defines dissatisfaction as concomitant with a willingness to fight, and since power increases improve a state's prospects in war, rising power, *ceteris paribus*, engenders dissatisfaction. According to Powell (1999: 91) "a state is dissatisfied if it is willing to use force to try to revise the status quo." This definition is an important central element of his models, but while it has some initial plausibility in a conversational sense, it differs fundamentally from power transition's notion of dissatisfaction. Power transition's dissatisfied states are those not benefiting from the status quo or who at least believe they would benefit more from a revised status quo. Their willingness to use force to achieve a different status quo is immaterial to whether or not they are satisfied or dissatisfied within the confines of power transition theory. It is for precisely this reason Organski described "weak and dissatisfied" states (those who, although they dislike the status quo, do not challenge the dominant power because they know they would lose) in the first place (1958: ch. 12). Similarly, it is quite conceivable, within power transition theory, for a satisfied state enjoying growth in power to remain satisfied, and peaceful, even if the benefits it enjoys from the international status quo do not change. This is impossible in Powell's models but not in power transition theory because of different notions of what the status quo is across the two bodies of work.

Neither of these disagreements between power transition theory and Powell's formal models is proof Powell is wrong. Certainly none of this is proof power transition theory is right. Powell himself (1999: ch. 1) writes of a "modeling dialogue" in which modelers and empirical analysts react to each other's work. Even in the absence of empirical analysis, modelers themselves often envision a series of models beginning with one the modeler might believe is wrong. The dialog is heuristic, with increasingly more practical payoffs as more and more accurate and powerful models develop. In this regard Powell's version of the strategic situation facing rising and declining states is a potentially useful opening offer in a modeling dialog. I believe this opening offer misses important structural elements central to power transition theory, and if he incorporated them by changing his assumptions, his deductions would change too. Whether or not that is the case will have to wait future conversations in the modeling dialog, but there is some evidence I am right (or at least not yet wrong).

This evidence is offered by other formal modelers who reach different conclusions. For example, perfect deterrence theory, which is based on a set of assumptions consistent with power transition, finds parity relationships to be particularly tenuous (Zagare and Kilgour 2000). In addition, Kim and Morrow (1992) offer a game-theoretic model of the strategic interaction between a state declining in power and another rising in power. Kim and Morrow's model applies to overtakings among and between any two states, and is thus more general than power transition theory. However, they deduce from it a number of propositions very similar to power transition theory. For example, Kim and Morrow deduce that war should be more likely if the two states are roughly equal in power and if the rising state is dissatisfied with its relations with the declining state (1992: 908). These are power transition theory's war hypotheses (at least as I present them above). Kim and Morrow's model of the "logic of overtaking" (as they call it) produces additional deductions about the importance of transition points, rates of growth, and risk propensities. The evidence I present in this book suggests Kim and Morrow included important structural constraints in their model, and at least two of the hypotheses of their model are supported among developing states (they evaluate the hypotheses of their model only for great powers over the 1816–1975 time-period).

The existence of contradictory models proves nothing. In the end, theories must be judged by the empirical accuracy of their conclusions. On this score, Powell's models do not withstand scrutiny. Indeed, the weight of empirical evidence on war and power distributions (discussed at length in the previous section) directly contradicts Powell's conclusions. Powell is aware of this contradiction, but seems untroubled by it. Specifically, he suggests the weight of empirical evidence misleads because research design flaws compromise past research on power transition theory and consequently the general evidence about power distributions and war does not yield consistent conclusions.

Powell claims (1999: 146n) that in addition to a weak logical foundation, power transition theory has weak empirical legs. He specifically criticizes past evaluations of power transition theory for including too much in their analyses. He suggests power transition theory can only be tested fairly by evaluating dyads in which the distribution of power is expected to change. This is incorrect. Power transition theory hypothesizes that while the dominant power is preponderant, war is unlikely. The theory thus makes a specific prediction about the behavior of unequal dyads in which power is not changing, and consequently there is no justification for excluding the information contained in such cases from analyses of the theory.

Powell also complains about the procedures used to evaluate power transition theory in the past being suspect because they ignore strategic interaction with third parties. This is true, but is an odd criticism for him to make as his models also ignore strategic interaction outside of the dyad in question. Presumably, whatever pathology this introduces into past research on power transition theory compromises and renders suspect his work too.

Finally, Powell repeatedly suggests his deductions are consistent with an alleged absence of widely accepted empirical findings linking parity and war. This is an interpretation of past research that is difficult or impossible to substantiate. His summary of studies coming to different conclusions about the relationship between parity and war (see, for instance, Powell 1999: 109) conflates systemic with dyadic work, and only lists studies from the 1970s and early 1980s as those finding parity associated with peace. The overwhelming majority of dyadic analyses in the past two decades disproportionately find parity associated with war and preponderance associated with peace (see the studies listed in note 8 above and summarized in Kugler and Lemke [2000]). Moreover, the selfsame Geller and Singer volume Powell repeatedly cites as evidence of no strong empirical relationship between parity and war informs us of "a growing and cumulative body of evidence pointing to the salience of both static and dynamic capability balances for the occurrence and initiation of militarized disputes and warfare. Specifically, conditions of approximate parity and shifts toward parity are consistently and significantly associated with conflict and war irrespective of population" (1998: 75–76).

In sum, power transition theory is not internally logically inconsistent. Powell's models are based on assumptions which contradict power transition theory. When the theory's assumptions are faithfully represented (as in Kim and Morrow's [1992] and Zagare and Kilgour's [2000] works), parity is deduced to be dangerous. What is more, power transition's conclusions are simply much more empirically accurate than Powell's. The evidence presented in subsequent chapters further solidifies this claim. And yet, this should not be read as a rejection of formal models of power transition theory or of the strategic situations facing states. In spite of its empirical success and range of associated hypotheses, power transition theory is imperfect. These imperfections are not only easier to diagnose, but also easier to fix, if formal tools are included in the continuing development and evaluation of power transition theory.

Conclusions

The theoretical origin of this book is power transition theory. Power transition theory provides a persuasive and empirically validated account of the conditions under which great powers are more likely to engage each other in war. In addition to its central hypotheses about war's occurrence, it also offers insights into other behaviors such as why democracies have been so peaceful among themselves for the past two centuries, why some great powers become interstate rivals, etc. It is thus a robust and empirically rich theory. That said, it does suffer from a number of problems (accuracy, timing, powerful-therefore-satisfied, and prevention), which need to be addressed if the theory's usefulness is to continue. Problems notwithstanding, the theory offers helpful indications to strategic theorists in spite of the fact that in its traditional form it offers no rational choice formal model. It offers these useful indications by highlighting important structural constraints which affect the strategic calculations of decision-makers.

The result of all these considerations is a claim that power transition theory offers a very useful base of knowledge which might be extended to attempt to understand when, where, and why developing states go to war with each other. I attempt this extension in this book in an effort to see how successful it can be. The result of this effort tells us much about the structural constraints conditioning the strategic calculations of decision-makers in charge of developing states as well as of those at the helm of the great powers. The extension begins in the next chapter.

3 Theoretical revision: the multiple hierarchy model

Because of its internal coherence, long history of empirical validation, and wide range of excess empirical content compared to competitor theories of world politics, I center my efforts in this book around a theoretical revision of power transition theory intended to permit analysis of minor power international relations. I call my revision of power transition theory the "multiple hierarchy model." Power transition theory describes the international system as an international hierarchy of power. My revision recasts the international system as a series of parallel power hierarchies, each of which functions similarly to the others and to the overall international power hierarchy. The revision highlights the existence of sub-systems within the overall international system. In purely technical terms this may seem a modest revision. But I very much hope the reader will not dismiss my revision as too modest to be of interest. Oaks grow from acorns, after all, and I suggest the discussion hinted at in chapter 1, and returned to in chapters 5 through 7, augurs well that a rather mighty theoretical oak will grow from the acorn of the multiple hierarchy model. In the following pages I describe in detail what the multiple hierarchy model is, how it differs from traditional power transition theory, and what specific hypothesis follows from it. I then trace some of the intellectual history of the notion of sub-systems, subordinate state systems, and regional systems in an effort to provide some sense of the plausibility of a theoretical revision along these lines. The chapter closes with a discussion of the operational requirements for an evaluation of the multiple hierarchy model, and therein foreshadows chapter 4.

The multiple hierarchy model

The structure of the international system

Recall from the discussion in chapter 2 that Organski's conceptual description of the international system offers a diagram of it as a pyramid in which height represents power, and thus the dominant state is at the apex. Similarly, width in the pyramid represents the number of states at different power levels: many weak and few powerful states. This pyramid conceptually represents the international hierarchy of power.

The multiple hierarchy model begins with the same diagrammatic depiction of the international system, but then nests smaller pyramids of power within the overall international power pyramid. These smaller pyramids represent local hierarchies of power within the international system. They are thus local/regional systems, or sub-hierarchies, of the overall international system or overall international power hierarchy. In a similar structure to the overall international power hierarchy, each of these local hierarchies has a local dominant state supervising local relations, by establishing and striving to preserve a local status quo. Just as with the global system and the overall dominant state, local dominant states bother to create and defend the local status quo because they anticipate gains from doing so. There are thus localized parallels to the relative power and status quo evaluation concerns which power transition theory highlights for the overall international system.

The expectations about peace and war within local hierarchies are very similar to those about peace and war in the overall international power hierarchy. When the local dominant power is preponderant, there is a high probability peace will obtain within the local hierarchy. However, when a power transition upsets the power hierarchy and a locally dissatisfied state rises to parity with the local dominant state, the expectation is of the probability of war increasing substantially within the local hierarchy.

These local hierarchies are often geographically very small. They encapsulate local relations between geographically proximate states. As described in the next chapter, for example, the African continent is made up of as many as nine local hierarchies with from two to eight states in each. The overall international power hierarchy may be thought of as the chessboard upon which great powers operate. The local hierarchies are the parallel smaller chessboards within which proximate small powers interact. Martin Wight (1946) was among the first to attempt definitions of "great powers" and "small powers." He noted as important that "At the Paris Conference in 1919 the distinction was made between Powers with general interests and Powers with limited interests." (1946: 18) The former type of powers are great powers, while the latter are small or minor powers. In the multiple hierarchy model the "limited interests" of small or minor powers are geographically limited. Great powers have geographically general interests which lead them to be active politico-militarily around the globe. The limited geographical interests of the small powers, combined with their relative impotence and inability to exert influence around the globe, lead them to be active politico-militarily within the local hierarchy in which they are located.[1]

It is very important to stress that the multiple hierarchy model offers hypotheses about war and peace within the overall global hierarchy as well as within the various local hierarchies. The original empirical content of power transition theory is subsumed by the multiple hierarchy model. In the multiple hierarchy model the great powers are described as interacting with each other within the construct of the overall international power hierarchy. The dominant state of this overall international power hierarchy is power transition theory's dominant state. When a dissatisfied challenger within this overall hierarchy achieves parity with the dominant state, the probability of war is hypothesized to increase. The first contribution of the multiple hierarchy model, then, is to extend these expectations to relations between developing states within local hierarchies.[2] The intent is to work toward a single theoretical argument about the causes of war among great powers as well as among minor powers.

Great power interference in local hierarchies

Of course, it is possible for great powers, perhaps most frequently the dominant power, to interfere with relations within local hierarchies. Since at least the time of Thucydides, it has been conventional wisdom that the strong do as they will while the weak suffer what they must. Great powers are strong while minor powers are weak, so great powers could anticipate some level of success in any effort to interfere in local

[1] Similar representations of minor powers as locally constrained are reflected in Papadakis and Starr's claim: "since the small-state capacity for international interaction is limited, it is most likely that their interactions will be regionally located" (1987: 429); and in Rothstein's recognition: "the Small Power is forced into an intense concentration on short-run and local matters" (1968: 25).

[2] Similarly, Jack Levy (1983: 10) writes: "The great power system may be a subsystem of the larger international system, but in fundamental respects it is a dominant subsystem."

hierarchies. Although no specific hypothesis about great power interference within local hierarchies is drawn from the multiple hierarchy model at this point, such interference is possible but does not contradict the model. When the dominant power or another great power feels strongly about the issues at stake in a dispute within a local hierarchy, interference might be expected. However, *in the absence of such strong interest by external great powers*, the local hierarchies are expected to function in a manner parallel to the overall international power hierarchy. When great powers do not interfere, parity and dissatisfaction with the local status quo are expected to increase the probability of war within local hierarchies.

What would great power interference look like? The most obvious form of such interference in minor power local hierarchies would be overt military intervention. Of course, it is reasonable to assume minor powers would take steps to prevent such interference, perhaps by adjusting policies to forestall such dramatic great power action. If this reasonable expectation were valid, then it would be more likely for great powers to interfere indirectly, aiding one or another local hierarchy member by transferring economic or military resources, by providing intelligence, etc. Such interference would be hard to observe but perhaps all the more common as a consequence.

Do the great powers interfere with local hierarchy relations much? If we restrict interference to overt military intervention, the answer is a perhaps surprisingly loud "no." Great powers almost never intervene militarily in minor power interstate conflicts and disputes. There are surely some obvious exceptions (such as American participation in the conflict between North and South Vietnam or UN participation in the conflict between North and South Korea), but by and large great powers do not intervene in minor power affairs. Hensel (1994: 295n2) reports that in the entire population of "militarized interstate disputes" initiated by Latin American states against each other, there is not a single instance of a great power subsequently becoming a party to the dispute. More generally, Tammen *et al.* (2000: ch. 3) claim that in the global population of more than two thousand disputes initially involving only minor powers, great powers subsequently intervened only seventy times. Given that each great power could intervene in each of these minor power disputes, this is a tiny fraction of the "opportunities" for such great power intervention. In terms of disputes underway between minor powers, great powers generally turn a blind eye militarily.

Of course, the great powers might not actively intervene simply because they can more effectively intervene covertly, or indirectly, or because their covert/indirect interventions tend to prevent disputes from occurring in the first place. Such interference may be quite common. But a problem arises: we have no way to gauge whether covert intervention is common or not, because by its nature it is hidden. There is no existing dataset on covert operations by the great powers against minor powers. There are similarly no datasets about informal pressure by great powers on minor powers.[3]

As mentioned above, the multiple hierarchy model hypothesizes that in the absence of great power interference, minor power local hierarchies function as parallel smaller international systems. If great powers do not interfere, the local hierarchies are hypothesized to behave according to the model. If great powers do interfere, the multiple hierarchy model does not apply because it assumes great power indifference. Statistically, the potential of great power interference is not an insurmountable problem either. If great powers do consistently interfere in covert or indirect ways they may prevent wars from occurring when they otherwise would, or cause them to occur when they otherwise would not. Either way, it would seem unlikely the great powers would intervene in such a way that minor power wars in local hierarchies would occur under conditions of parity and dissatisfaction. Put simply, if great power interference is common it would be likely to obscure any consistent pattern between structural characteristics such as relative power or status quo evaluations and the occurrence of war between minor powers. Great power interference would be the "cause" of such wars, and the correlates of such interference would be great power intentions, preferences, etc., rather than the structure of local relations between the minor powers. Consequently, great power interference, if and when it occurs, will deflate statistical estimates of a relationship between war and dissatisfaction and parity within local hierarchies *unless* great power intentions and preferences strongly correlate with the structure of local relations. I find strong statistical relationships between parity, dissatisfaction and war within local hierarchies in chapter 5, even though I include no provision for great power interference.

But concerns about great power interference clearly are not adequately silenced by statistically significant coefficient estimates. Rather

[3] It would be interesting to interview area specialists as a data source about "known" but unpublished instances of great power covert interference in local relations.

than rely on an untested assumption of non-interference, I replicate and extend the analyses from chapter 5 in chapter 6. In those replications and extensions I allow for great power interference by reconstructing my dataset to allow great powers to be actors within local hierarchies. Details are provided in chapter 6.

In constructing the dataset upon which the analyses in chapter 5 are based, I assume states predominantly pay attention to the highest-level power hierarchy within which they may be able to operate. In a sense, this assumption is simply a statement that states are snobs. If they have the resources to be active in the overall global hierarchy, they will do so with more interest than they pay to the local hierarchy from which they emerge and within which most of their past international activity has been carried out. Arguably, the United States initially was able to interact politico-militarily only within a North American local hierarchy. The course of American economic and political development allowed the United States to extend its influence over time, ultimately to the global overall power hierarchy dominated by the great powers. Concomitant with American development was the expansion of its international milieu. The United States has certainly not abandoned interest in North American interstate relations,[4] but these have become only a part of America's foreign policy. Prussian development in the nineteenth century changed its foreign policy from being primarily Central European to being global after the unification of Germany in 1871. China today may similarly be "outgrowing" East Asia. A perhaps more acceptable way to express this "states are snobs" assumption is simply to suggest that as states move from minor power to great power status, their control over local relations becomes solidified to such an extent, or their fears and worries about what their local neighbors do diminishes to such an extent, that they can largely overlook the interactions of their neighbors.[5]

What is the local status quo?

Another question asks with what issues a local status quo might be concerned? If the global dominant state of the overall international power

[4] US obsession with Castro is an interesting example of a great power paying close attention to local concerns. Note, however, that in this case Soviet influence on Cuba introduces a global element to the otherwise local concern.

[5] In an interesting prediction of Soviet foreign policy in the 1980s, Bill Zimmerman (1981: 101–103) wrote that as Soviet global influence waxed, Soviet activity in, and concern about, Eastern Europe would wane.

hierarchy establishes and defends patterns of interaction globally, then a local dominant state would be courting trouble if it established a local status quo at odds with the global dominant power's preferences (since such a local status quo might "invite" interference by the global dominant power). It seems likely the local dominant state would prefer to avoid such great power interference, and therefore the local status quo of most local hierarchies would revolve around issues of local concern. Local issues of diplomacy, economics and/or security politics not addressed by the global status quo would most likely compose the substance of a given local status quo.

The most obvious such issue of primarily local concern is likely to be rules governing the control of territory. The exact boundaries of developing states were often poorly delimited by colonial administrators. Rectifying such uncertainty, by assigning specific territories to specific local actors, would likely matter little if at all to the great powers atop the global power hierarchy. So long as the resources of such territories continue to be exported to world markets the great powers are unlikely to care from whom they buy them. For example, the territorial boundaries of Chile, Peru, and Bolivia were dramatically redrawn in the 1880s. These three countries border each other in the Atacama desert region, a territory rich in nitrates, copper, and other minerals. Peru had traditionally been the strongest state in this Pacific Coast local hierarchy, and not surprisingly controlled most of the poorly defined border region either directly, or indirectly through its ally, Bolivia. By the 1870s Chilean development had progressed and Chile achieved parity with Peru. The decisive War of the Pacific (1879–1883) was waged between Chile and a Peru–Bolivia alliance, with Chile emerging clearly victorious. As part of the peace settlement Chile redrew the local status quo arrangements about territorial control, thereby denying Bolivia access to the sea and demanding substantial territorial concessions from Peru. This dramatic change in the local status quo clearly benefited Chile, the new local dominant state, at the expense of Peru and, especially, Bolivia. Since the Chileans were interested in exporting for profit the mineral wealth of the Atacama, the great powers raised no objections and did not interfere with the war nor with subsequent relations in this local hierarchy.

This example may be representative of the local status quos the multiple hierarchy model describes as existing around the globe. If local dominant states are interested in benefiting themselves but are constrained by the existence of a global status quo maintained and defended by the much-stronger global dominant power, designing rules to govern which states have access to territory may be the most likely issue around which a local status quo is created. Local dominant powers are posited to be entrepreneurial just like the global dominant power. They are interested in types of international interactions they can carve out of the international system as their own, so they can achieve benefits thereby. The plausibility of a claim that this potential is likely to be realized in specifically territorial matters is increased by the fact that of all the local hierarchy relations empirically analyzed in chapter 5, in every case where minor power wars occurred there was a pre-existing territorial disagreement between the belligerents (more discussion of this is offered in the next two chapters). If the local status quo commonly concerns rules about territorial control or access, then we should expect wars within local hierarchies to be disproportionately about control of or access to territory. This seems to be the case.

However, I do not mean to imply all local status quos revolve around territorial arrangements, or territory only matters in terms of minerals within it. It is probably more useful to think of territorial arrangements within local hierarchies in a very broad fashion. For example, the territorial component of local status quos may also concern rules about which states have access to navigable waterways and other transit routes, who has access to water for irrigation, who has control of more easily defended geologic formations so borders are secure, who enjoys access to holy sites or otherwise culturally important places, etc. Further, it will likely prove useful to think of local status quos as rules governing nonterritorial issues as well. It is possible for local status quos to be characterized by differing attitudes between local dominant powers and local challengers about ethnic, military, economic, and even ideological matters.

An example is potentially offered by recent relations within Central Asia. Since the dissolution of the Soviet empire, a Central Asian local hierarchy may be emerging (see Anderson 1997 for an interesting discussion). The five former Soviet Republics (Kazakhstan, Kyrgyzstan, Tajikistan, Turkmenistan, and Uzbekistan) and the state of Afghanistan jointly compose what I suspect is the heart of this new local system. These six countries vary dramatically in terms of ethnic composition, economic development, and the degree of secularization of their societies. No clear local dominant power has yet emerged, but it seems obvious that whichever state emerges as locally dominant will affect the character of Central Asian interstate relations. Uzbekistan is the most populous of the five former Soviet states, and its leaders have made statements about potential Uzbek leadership of the region (see Anderson 1997, esp. pp. 197–201). Should Uzbekistan emerge as the local dominant power the local status quo would likely be decidedly different, specifically with respect to rules about the influence of secular and religious interests in politics, than it would be if another important regional actor, Afghanistan, emerges as locally dominant.

Ideological local status quos are conceivable as well. One of the local hierarchies from the empirical analyses to follow is that of Southeast Asia. Vietnam emerged as the local dominant power within this small sub-system with its defeat of South Vietnam in the 1970s. For some time communist Vietnam's leaders had been encouraging a communist insurgency in Laos, and in 1977 invaded Cambodia and instituted a similar regime in Phnom Penh. Any local status quo in Southeast Asia under Vietnamese influence involved primarily ideological rules of interaction. A similar example may be offered by South African influence over political relations within and between the states at the southern end of Africa. Under the apartheid regime the political/ideological character of this local hierarchy's status quo would be expected to be very different from the post-apartheid era.

These last two ideological examples again raise interesting subsidiary questions about interference by great powers within local hierarchies. Here I do not mean activities such as American relations within a North American local hierarchy, but rather US intervention in African, Asian, or other local hierarchies. The Southeast Asian and South African local hierarchies were ones within which there clearly was a great deal of external interference by the great powers. Perhaps the ideological nature of the local status quos in these local hierarchies triggered the United States, the Soviet Union, and China (among others) to involve themselves in local hierarchical relations. One wonders if there might be a pattern of types of local status quos that consistently do or do not trigger great power interference.[6]

In summary, the main thrust of the multiple hierarchy model is a conceptualization of multiple international sub-systems, of multiple power

[6] Zimmerman (1972) offers a fascinating account of how Eastern European states struggled to carve out some autonomy and influence within their regional interactions. His account repeatedly emphasizes they were successful, and avoided Soviet repercussions, only when their actions did not have immediate Cold War implications. Similarly, Buzan (1991: 215) writes "Indeed, it has been a notable feature of post-war superpower interventions in the domestic politics of Third World countries that the superpowers were much more interested in manipulating Third World attitudes towards the East–West divide, than in reconditioning the attitudes of Third World states towards each other."

hierarchies, that cumulatively form the international system. Traditional power transition theory arguments focus only on the overall global system, the overall global power hierarchy, and on relations among great powers atop the hierarchy. The hypothesis is that when the great power hierarchy of power is overturned such that a dissatisfied great power challenger achieves parity with the global dominant state, the probability of war increases. The multiple hierarchy model preserves this traditional depiction of the international system and this traditional hypothesis about war among great powers, but extends them by adding the notion of multiple local hierarchies of power nested within the overall international hierarchy. Within each of these local hierarchies there is a local status quo established and maintained by a local dominant state. Should the local power hierarchy be overturned and a dissatisfied local challenger achieves parity with the local dominant state, the probability of war is hypothesized to increase. Local hierarchies operate in parallel fashion to the overall global power hierarchy, so long as great powers do not interfere. The multiple hierarchy model thus offers a consistent theoretical argument about wars among great powers and wars among minor powers.

Past conceptualizations of multiple international systems

This discussion of multiple international systems operating simultaneously is not unique within the literature on international politics (although it is original within the literature dealing specifically with power transition theory). Various researchers have discussed the international system as a set of systems. I review them briefly in order to suggest that extensions like mine are commonly considered plausible. I also do so in order to give credit where credit is due to those earlier scholars who informed my thinking on these matters. A third reason for this review is to allow an opportunity to indicate where my notion of local hierarchies differs from other efforts at sub-systemic classification.

A number of balance-of-power theorists have written about multiple international systems operating simultaneously. Their conceptualizations are very similar in many respects to that of the multiple hierarchy model. For example, Hans Morgenthau wrote:

> We have spoken thus far of the balance of power as if it were one single system comprehending all nations actively engaged in international

> politics. Closer observation, however, reveals that such a system is frequently composed of a number of subsystems which are interrelated with each other, but which maintain within themselves a balance of power of their own. (1948: 146)

Morgenthau continues his discussion by introducing notions of sub-European, Asian, Western Hemisphere and even African balances of power. He includes consideration of how subordinate the various lesser balances of power were to the dominant balance of power (claiming primarily that physical distance greatly enhances the autonomy of lesser balances). All of this is very consistent with the multiple hierarchy model.

In addition to Morgenthau, historians of the balance of power, such as Martin Wight (1946: esp. 12) and Edward Vose Gulick, have also written about multiple international systems, but within an exclusively European international balance. Gulick specifically mentions "smaller, local frameworks, or 'inferiour balances'" (1955: 13) as important parts of the overall balance of power.

More recently, theorists also writing within the balance-of-power theory tradition reiterate Morgenthau's earlier conceptualization of multiple international systems. Hedley Bull writes that "The existence of *local* balances of power has served to protect the independence of states in particular areas from absorption or domination by a *locally preponderant power*" (1977: 106, emphasis added). Kenneth Waltz is often cited for the first line of the following, but the rest is more relevant here:

> A general theory of international politics is necessarily based on the great powers. The theory once written also applies to lesser states that interact insofar as their interactions are insulated from the intervention of the great powers of a system, whether by the relative indifference of the latter or by difficulties of communication and transportation. (1979: 73)

In spite of the fact that these authors variously use the terms lesser-, subordinate-, "inferiour"-, local-, or regional balances, they all seem to be suggesting the same thing; namely, the international balance or international system is a *set* of international systems arranged geographically, or in positions of relative inferiority/superiority, or both. Scholars associated with the balance-of-power tradition have thus offered a conceptualization of the international system much like that advanced by my multiple hierarchy model. Unlike these earlier balance-of-power efforts, however, the various local hierarchies of the multiple hierarchy model are defined operationally and empirically analyzed in the remainder of this book. What is more, the sub-system focus in the multiple hierarchy model is primarily on Third World local hierarchies rather than on regional balances within Europe as in most of the balance-of-power work cited above.

In addition to these conceptual efforts at describing regional systems and inferior/superior sets of systems, a wide range of scholars (mostly outside of the balance-of-power theory tradition) also contribute conceptualizations of systems and sub-systems. In these efforts to divide the international system into meaningful sub-units we are offered conceptualizations of "regions" (Russett 1967; Banks 1969; Cantori and Spiegel 1969; Lebovic 1986), "subordinate state systems" (Brecher 1963; Bowman 1968), "subordinate international systems" (Binder 1958), "international subsystems" (Berton 1969; Hellman 1969; Sigler 1969; Haas 1970), "hierarchical regional systems" (Zimmerman 1972), "regimes" (Krasner 1983), "regional subsystems" (Kaiser 1968; Thompson 1973a), "politically relevant neighborhoods" (Gochman 1991), and "clusters of nations" (Wallace 1975). Most of these conceptualizations lead to lists of sub-units impressionistically culled from a perusal of the international system. In those few instances in which operationalization employs systematic data analysis, the criteria for being labeled a sub-unit include cultural similarities, trade patterns, common membership in international organizations, alliance patterns, and demographic similarities, but most often, simple geographic proximity.[7]

The various regional or country-specific specialists we tend to label as practitioners of "area studies" are implicitly designators of sub-systems within the international system. My impression is that it is uncommon for such area specialists to indicate the criteria justifying their exclusive focus on the region of interest to them. This is not a criticism, and would be inappropriate as such, for area specialists are not engaged in an effort to uncover general patterns across the international system. Their purpose thus differs from that of most practitioners of international politics research. However, the failure of area specialists to delineate what makes their specific regions of interest unique translates into an

[7] Buzan's (1991) regional security complexes are especially relevant to my local hierarchies in terms of conceptual similarity as well as descriptive similarity. I return to them in more detail in the next chapter.

absence of criteria by which we can designate operationally what is a sub-system of the international system. A laughably sad example of the lack of precision in regards to delineation of regional sub-systems is offered by an article entitled "Where is the Middle East?" (Davison 1960). The term "middle east" was coined, apparently, by Alfred Thayer Mahan in 1902, but Mahan identified the Indian subcontinent as the "middle east." In the early 1920s, Winston Churchill, then British Colonial Secretary, "officially" designated the "middle east" as the area between the Bosporus and the eastern frontiers of India. Davison offers an example of Dulles, Eisenhower, and a State Department spokesman all using "middle east" to designate different areas of the world in a single year. These are not academic references, but the confusion crosses from the public realm to the scholarly, and vice versa.

In the next chapter I devote a fair amount of space to the question of defining local hierarchies. I offer explicit criteria for designation of an area as a local hierarchy. What I lose in flexibility I gain in replicability and transparency. I think the trade-off is one that is well worth making. There is a wide range of conceptual discussions of regional sub-systems of the international system. I think these scholars are right to think in systemic *and* sub-systemic terms. I hope I emulate them in this regard. However, most previous efforts fail to offer anything approaching objective guidelines for sub-system classification (I regard Russett 1967, Wallace 1975, and Buzan 1991 as laudable exceptions).

Many readers will likely note most of the references in this section are quite dated. Academic discussion of regions and sub-systems appears to have tapered off after the mid 1970s. I strongly suspect the cause of this decline in attention was failure to specify objective criteria for defining regions and sub-systems. Regardless, with the end of the Cold War there is a resurgence of interest in questions of regions and regionalism (see, *inter alia*, Singer and Wildavsky 1993; Lake and Morgan 1997; Mansfield and Milner 1997, 1999; Kacowicz 1998; Moon 1998; Solingen 1998), but none of these new regional studies offers an answer to the question: "What, *specifically*, is a region?" I attempt to answer such questions in the next chapter.[8]

[8] T. V. Paul (2000) persuasively argues that the conflict dynamics within each non-great power's region are especially important influences on decisions to acquire or forego nuclear arsenals. His book makes clear the impossibility of understanding foreign policy choices without consideration of regional context. Unfortunately, like the other "new regionalism" works referred to above, Paul offers no empirical criterion by which regions might be generally defined.

An alternate application of the multiple hierarchy model

Addressing questions about what is a region allows me to test the multiple hierarchy model and thereby evaluate my reformulation of power transition theory. Using the operational definition of a region from the next chapter to construct a more generalized regional perspective might allow researchers to say something about *other* theories of international relations as well. For example, a regional perspective like the multiple hierarchy model might lead us to recast Cliff Morgan and Glenn Palmer's "two-good" theory of foreign policy.

Morgan and Palmer (1997) argue states are motivated by two types of concerns in foreign policy: concerns about preserving what they already enjoy (security), and concerns about improving their situation by changing other states' behavior or otherwise enlarging the pool of goods they enjoy from international interactions (proaction). Security and proaction are the two goods pursued in the "two-good" theory. Morgan and Palmer claim increases in power allow states to pursue more of both proaction and security, but the mix of proaction and/or security a state will pursue, given an increase in power, depends on whether the state is already powerful or weak. Specifically, powerful states will use increases in power to pursue more proaction than security, while weak states enjoying an increase in power will employ the windfall to enhance their security.[9]

Morgan and Palmer offer an empirical evaluation of their hypothesis that increases in power among the powerful lead to more proaction while increases in power among the less powerful lead to security-enhancing foreign policies. They define militarized interstate dispute initiation as proaction (arguing that initiators are attempting to change something internationally by starting disputes) while militarized response by targets in such disputes represents security-seeking (since such responses clearly represent actions to defend what a state already has). Morgan and Palmer find support for both expectations.

[9] Morgan and Palmer assume the rate at which a state can use increases of power to pursue security-enhancing foreign policies diminishes at higher levels of power. Intuitively we might think that there are larger gains in security to be had among weak states, since they are so insecure in the international system. Morgan and Palmer also assume the ability of a state to use increments of power to pursue proaction increases at higher levels of power. For a follow-up incorporating some domestic political concerns, see Morgan and Palmer (1998).

The multiple hierarchy model or some more generalized regional perspective might recast the two-good theory of foreign policy. This claim is suggested by the way in which Morgan and Palmer evaluate the hypothesis that increases in power among the powerful are likely to be used for proactive foreign policies. They report that increases in power among the more powerful of *great powers* are associated with a greater propensity to initiate militarized interstate disputes (1997: tables II and III). Note that they restrict the empirical domain of this analysis to observations only of great powers. I suspect that if they had studied all states, they would not have found evidence confirming their hypothesis.

In order to explore my suspicion, I undertook a cursory review of the dispute dataset (Jones, Bremer, and Singer 1996) used in the Morgan and Palmer study.[10] Recall their operational definition of proaction is dispute initiation; great powers are especially proactive (according to this definition). The United States initiated 131 disputes between 1816 and 1992. Similarly, other great powers account for many dispute initiations, and are thus also proactive. The United Kingdom accounts for 86 dispute initiations, Germany managed to initiate disputes 95 times during its tenure as a great power, Russia/Soviet Union accounts for 162 disputes, and China is attributed 73 militarized interstate dispute initiations. Reasonably high numbers of disputes were initiated by Italy, Austria, and Japan, but at much lower levels than the first group. This is all consistent with Morgan and Palmer's expectations of proaction by the powerful, since the most powerful of the great powers initiate more disputes than do the less powerful great powers. However, there

[10] In an attempt to adhere to Morgan and Palmer's guidelines as much as possible, I culled cases from the Militarized Interstate Disputes (MID) version 2.1 dataset as follows. First, since dispute initiation is consequential, I consider only originators on side A. Like Morgan and Palmer, I delete cases where there was more than one originator on side A of the dispute. The number of dispute initiations I include (1,975) is larger than their sample size. I am not especially concerned about the disparity in the number of cases because, unlike them, I do not eliminate the first ten years of the 1816–1992 MID time-frame (since I am not including an independent variable of power change over time), and similarly, since I am not including any covariates in this descriptive exploratory analysis, I do not lose any cases on account of missing data on the independent variables. To establish my suspicions definitively, I would need to construct a nation–year dataset of all states and rerun Morgan and Palmer's analyses presented in their tables I, II, and III. I do not do so here because I am only suggesting there may be another way to interpret and apply their two-good theory of foreign policy from a regional perspective. The empirical description offered is thus only intended to elucidate the potential of my regional suggestion for reconsideration of the empirical evidence for their theory.

are patterns within the dispute initiation data which are less consistent with their expectations. For instance, 42 of the disputes initiated by the United States occurred prior to American achievement of great power status in 1898, and in all but two of those 42 cases I am reasonably sure the disputes were initiated regionally within the Western Hemisphere. Peru (with 42 initiations) appears more proactive than Japan (with 38 initiations), Iran ranks higher than most great powers in proaction, with 82 dispute initiations. Iraq has initiated 63 disputes (even though it has only been an independent member of the interstate system since the 1930s). Syria and Egypt have combined for 87 dispute initiations, while Israel has initiated 41 disputes since 1948. Other minor powers (India, Pakistan, Chile, Argentina, North Korea, Thailand, etc.) also have initiated dozens of disputes. When one considers that these minor powers have not been independent states anywhere near as long as the great powers, the dispute-initiating propensity of these particular minor powers becomes even more impressive. I suspect that if one constructed a nation–year dataset and replicated Morgan and Palmer's evaluations of the impact of power changes on the probability of dispute initiation for *all* states rather than just for great powers, one might not be able to claim the powerful are disproportionately likely to seek proaction given an increase in power.

However, if we take a regional perspective our notion of who is a great power may change. Iran is not a great power. But, within a Middle Eastern local hierarchy Iran is definitely a major player. It should not surprise anyone if an increase in national power was employed by Iran to seek proaction *within* the Middle East. In such a scenario Iran would not be using a power windfall to try to change the policies of the great powers, but the Iranians might use such a gain as a gambit to change the behavior of the Saudis.

What we might get from a regional reformulation of the two-good theory of foreign policy is an expectation of minor powers behaving within regions as major powers behave within the overall international system. Minor powers seek proaction locally. The leading states within regions and the leading states at the top of the international power hierarchy are expected, in this regional reformulation of the two-good theory, to use power advances proactively. Lesser global powers and lesser regional powers are expected to use power advances to enhance their security. A list of the twenty most frequent dispute initiators is a list of the great powers and of minor powers who are important actors within regional sub-systems.[11] This reformulation suggests that if we take into account regional concerns we might gain a richer perspective of the foreign policy behavior of both major and minor powers, one that is probably more consistent with the empirical record than is the two-good theory of foreign policy as currently constructed. The two-good theory of foreign policy offers an interesting statement of the goals and behaviors associated with states' foreign policies. However, it might enjoy even greater empirical support if reformulated to take into account regional considerations.[12] I suspect a large number of additional theoretical arguments would be similarly improved by consideration from a regional perspective.

Conclusions: requirements for evaluation of the multiple hierarchy model

The multiple hierarchy model hypothesizes that within power hierarchies (global or local), preponderance by a dominant state decreases the likelihood of war. However, should a dissatisfied challenger achieve parity with the dominant state (again, global or local), the probability of war is hypothesized to increase. Thus, the multiple hierarchy model offers a war hypothesis much like that of traditional power transition theory, but one which offers expectations about wars among developing states as well as among the great powers.

This chapter has described the multiple hierarchy model and offered a number of hypothetical, but hopefully plausible, examples of local hierarchies, of wars fought within them, and of local status quos. In the next chapter I turn from plausible examples to detailed discussion of measurement issues with regard to the central concepts of local hierarchy, dyadic power relations, and status quo evaluations. In chapter 4 I offer operational definitions for each of these concepts, and provide detailed justifications for the measurements I offer. I do so for two reasons. The

[11] The "top twenty" list is as follows (minor powers in bold and number of dispute initiations in parentheses): Russia/Soviet Union (162), United States (131), Germany (95), United Kingdom (86), **Iran (82)**, People's Republic of China (73), **Iraq (63)**, **Syria (53)**, France (53), Italy (50), **Turkey (43)**, **Peru (42)**, **Israel (41)**, **India (40)**, Japan (38), **Egypt (34)**, **Argentina (33)**, **Pakistan (30)**, **Chile (27)**, **Thailand (24)**. One last great power, Austria/Austro-Hungarian Empire, does not make it onto the "top twenty" list, as it initiated only 18 disputes over the 102 years it is commonly considered to have been a great power.

[12] I discuss the two-good theory here not because I think it the only theory likely to be improved by regional considerations, but rather because I happen to like it.

first is, of course, that one must go to such lengths to satisfy a scholarly audience. The second reason, however, is much less Machiavellian: I honestly find such measurement issues fascinating.

Many scholars claim we need to think regionally as well as globally. This refrain is enjoying renewed popularity of late. I offer suggestions in this chapter of how a regional perspective might enrich both power transition theory and the two-good theory of foreign policy. I believe many other theoretical arguments can be similarly improved by incorporation of regional considerations. However, if we are to accept such calls for regional thinking, we have to know what a region is. There is a woeful dearth of objective indicators to help us in this regard. I offer one in the next chapter. It leads me to a very different view of regions than is traditional. Specifically, most "regional" theorists use continents as shorthand for regions. They thus talk about "Africa" or "Latin America" or "Asia" as a region. I find almost no continental regions in the parts of the world I study. I find four "regions" within South America alone, nine "regions" in Africa, etc. If my measurement technique has any validity, it suggests regions are smaller than we traditionally think. If so, then a solution to problems in Africa may need to be nine different solutions.

Similarly, dissatisfied states are expected to be the initiators of conflict in the international system. Scholars outside the power transition theory tradition also use the term "dissatisfied states" (e.g., Ray 1995; Rousseau *et al.* 1996; Gelpi 1997), meaning something conceptually similar to Organski's notion. Raymond Aron (1966: 160–162) writes of "peace by satisfaction," clearly implying that dissatisfied states are less likely to be peaceful than are satisfied states. Other scholars write of revisionist states, frustrated-hence-aggressive states, etc. Clearly the idea of different kinds of states with different attitudes toward the status quo is an important one. If we knew which states were dissatisfied we could attempt to satisfy them, and thereby avert conflicts. But how to measure which states are satisfied and which dissatisfied? There is no definitive answer to this question as yet, and only an unsatisfying solution is proposed in the next chapter. But, merely struggling with this specific vexing measurement issue is rewarding, and thus I discuss it at length in chapter 4.

If we would evaluate the multiple hierarchy model we also need to know when wars occur as well as when they do not occur. This is a much less contentious operationalization, specifically since there are extant data collections, the validity of which is generally widely accepted. Finally, the multiple hierarchy model focuses attention on two important explanatory variables (relative power and status quo evaluations).

Surely war is caused by more than these two important variables. In order to test the robustness of the parity and dissatisfaction and war relationship, I include some control variables. The variables included as controls are strong candidates as suggested by their importance in previous analyses. I justify each and discuss my measurements of them as they become relevant in later chapters.

I have written these paragraphs of introduction to chapter 4 in hopes of conveying to the reader the excitement I feel such measurement questions should generate. I see one of the major contributions of this book as being the struggle with questions such as "What is a region?", or "What is a satisfied or dissatisfied state?" For this reason I think skipping over chapter 4 in a rush for the results in later chapters will miss quite a bit. The devil may not really be in the details, but these deviling details are nevertheless interesting and important in their own right.

4 Identifying local hierarchies and measuring key variables

The multiple hierarchy model requires extensive attention to case definition and variable measurement. I need information about a number of important variables in order to evaluate the model's hypothesis that power parity and dissatisfaction with the relevant status quo increase the probability of war within international hierarchies. In addition to knowing when wars occur or do not occur I need to know what a local hierarchy is, when contenders in such hierarchies are at parity, and whether the challenger is dissatisfied with the status quo. In sum, the evaluation of the hypothesis necessitates operational definitions of local hierarchies as well as of the variables highlighted by the model. Local hierarchies are not a self-evident phenomenon. What it means to be at parity, and even more, what it means to be a dissatisfied actor, are similarly non-obvious. Nevertheless, these are the theoretically important concepts in my analysis, and as such must be operationally defined. In order to clarify the operational definitions I offer, I go to some length justifying my choices and explaining my rationales. I subject my readers to all this detail in an effort to make my procedures as transparent as possible, and thus replicable and, ideally, amenable to subsequent improvement.

Constructing operational definitions of these concepts allows me to evaluate the multiple hierarchy model's central hypothesis about when wars will and will not occur within international hierarchies. However, these concepts are increasingly important to other explanatory efforts in world politics research. Consequently, I hope the measures produced here will prove useful to those investigating other questions as well.

Operational definition of local hierarchies

As described in chapter 3, previous researchers interested in regional or local international systems tend either to cull, impressionistically, a list of such local international systems from perusal of the general international system or alternatively to offer operational definitions of international sub-systems based on a combination of cultural similarities, trade patterns, common IGO membership, alliances, demographic similarities, and geographic proximity. Neither of these tendencies is completely useful in either a general sense or in terms of my specific evaluation of the multiple hierarchy model.

In order to evaluate the multiple hierarchy model I need a definition of local hierarchies such that the members of each local hierarchy consider each other when developing their foreign policies and planning for various military contingencies. Recall that power transition theory at the global level describes great powers fighting for control of the status quo of the overall power hierarchy that is the international system. Great powers, according to the theory, fight for the privilege to write the rules that structure the general tenor of their relations with each other. Since the multiple hierarchy model is an extension of power transition theory to minor powers, it describes minor powers as fighting for control of the status quos of their local hierarchies. Minor powers, according to the model, fight for the privilege to write the rules governing important local elements of their relations with each other.

What is needed, then, is an operational definition of local hierarchies that identifies the members of such international sub-systems as able to interact militarily with each other. The definitions of sub-systems advanced by the qualitative and quantitative efforts of other scholars over the decades are not especially relevant in this sense because they tend to identify sub-systems coterminous with continents. I find it hard to believe Indonesia's foreign military planning takes into consideration likely Pakistani foreign military activities. Both are Asian states, and consequently any definition of international sub-system that identifies "Asia" as a sub-system (as many of the past researchers mentioned in chapter 3 do) would group these two together as members of the same international sub-system. I would accept a claim that Indonesia and Pakistan interact more frequently and in more ways than do Indonesia and Paraguay or Ivory Coast and Pakistan, but would not extend this to meaning Indonesia and Pakistan consider their "Asian" relations to be governed by an "Asian" status quo. I would be surprised to learn that in either Islamabad or Jakarta serious consideration is given to potential military interactions with the other state's forces. I suspect (a suspicion supported below) that Indonesia and Pakistan could not go to war with each other even if they wanted to, and thus that they do not consider each other as militarily relevant.

Nevertheless, past efforts attempting to conceptualize and/or list international sub-systems are, in contrast to the criticisms leveled heretofore, partially useful for my purposes. A common theme running through past efforts is the claim that international sub-system designation should be based upon notions of proximity and interaction (Thompson 1973a). A combination of such notions forms the conceptualization of local hierarchy I offer. Specifically, rather than proximity and observed interaction being central, the essential characteristic of interstate relations assigning states to the same local hierarchy is the ability to interact militarily. Proximity will, of course, increase the probability such military interaction is possible, but the relationship is far from perfect. Two proximate states separated by a body of water when neither possesses a naval force are unable to interact militarily. Two otherwise proximate states bordering one another within an area with high mountains are similarly hampered in any effort to interact militarily. Thus, in identifying local hierarchies proximity matters, but the physical nature of the distance between states conditions the extent to which proximity matters.

Readers may be initially suspicious of the replacement of actual interaction with only the ability to interact. However, I think this an important and useful alteration to past conceptualizations because in situations where one state is especially dissatisfied with the local status quo, it is very likely to be isolationist. There may be little or no actual interaction between this state and the local dominant power. A seething local Cold War type of situation would represent such relations. Any definition of local hierarchies based on actual interaction would fail to place such a pair of states in the same sub-system. For example, aside from the militarized interstate disputes that have occurred, most of Arab–Israeli history has involved no interaction between Israel and her Arab neighbors. The tensions between Israel and Egypt or Syria, for instance, precluded cultural exchanges, governmental interactions, and even trade. Any definition of local hierarchy requiring or expecting sustained actual interaction would potentially fail to include Israel and Egypt in the same sub-system.

Substantial interaction certainly is consistent with joint membership in a local hierarchy, but the absence of such interaction could mean either a pair of states are not members of the same local hierarchy *or* they are members who choose not to interact. Using the ability to interact as the conceptual core of the operational definition of local hierarchies allows me to separate the states unable to interact from those who are able but choose not to interact. In sum, my conceptualization of local hierarchies defines them as groups of states with the ability to interact militarily.

Two states are able to interact militarily to the extent that they can move military resources into each other's territory. If Indian forces can invade Pakistan, and vice versa, regardless of the likely outcome of such invasions, India and Pakistan are able to interact militarily and are consequently part of the same local hierarchy. Technically, so long as one member of a dyad can invade the other, those two states can interact militarily, but initially I focus on joint ability to invade each other as the centerpiece of my operational definition of local hierarchy. This more strict criterion of mutual ability to interact militarily makes membership in one of my local hierarchies the conceptual equivalent of the contender great powers central to analyses of power transition theory among the great powers (see Organski and Kugler 1980: 42–45 and Lemke and Werner 1996: 243–244 for discussions of power transition tests focusing on contender great powers).[1]

Each state has the ability to exert military influence over some portion of the globe's surface. Obviously the more powerful a state is, the larger the area over which it can exert military influence. Similarly, the further from a state's home territory it tries to exert military influence, the harder such efforts become. Power degrades over distance because of the loss-of-strength gradient (Boulding 1962).[2] The weaker a state is to begin with, the rougher the terrain across which military influence is to be exerted, or the less developed the transportation infrastructure between the state and its intended target, the steeper the loss-of-strength gradient. The steeper the loss-of-strength gradient, the smaller the portion of the globe within which the state can exert influence or interact militarily. The "strength" lost over the loss-of-strength gradient could be exclusively military or more generally could be thought of as power. In this book I use the loss-of-strength gradient to degrade general power.

[1] Buzan (1991: 194) similarly distinguishes between mutual and asymmetric security interactions.

[2] I cannot be clearer than Boulding himself, so I quote him: "The general principle applies that each party can be supposed to be at his maximum power at home . . . but that his competitive power, in the sense of his ability to dominate another, declines the farther from home he operates. This is the great principle of *the further the weaker*. The amount by which the competitive power of a party diminishes per mile movement away from home is the *loss-of-power gradient*" (1962: 78–79, emphasis in original). For the remainder of his book, Boulding refers to this as the loss-of-strength gradient, so I do too.

Applying the concept of the loss-of-strength gradient to state efforts to interact militarily (potentially or actually) with other states, we can calculate (making certain assumptions discussed below) the portion of the globe within which a given state can operate. This portion of the globe is the state's "relevant neighborhood." All the states within a focal state's relevant neighborhood are proximate enough that the focal state can "reach" them militarily and thus exert military influence within their territory. When two or more states' relevant neighborhoods overlap, I define them as forming a local hierarchy. Borrowing a term widely used by others (Weede 1976; Maoz and Russett 1993; Lemke 1995; Oneal and Russett 1997; Lemke and Reed 2001a), such mutually reachable pairs of states may be thought of as "relevant dyads," as their joint reachability makes war between them possible.

Local hierarchies are thus sets of dyads with the ability to reach each other militarily; each state within a dyad has the ability to exert military influence within the other's territories. Such states are virtually certain to take each other's likely courses of action into account when formulating military contingency plans. More importantly, when a minor power is dissatisfied with its local relations, its local status quo, the states it will identify as the source of its dissatisfaction or at least against which it may take steps to redress that dissatisfaction, are those against which it can exert military influence, those it can "reach" militarily. All of these considerations are offered as a justification, based on the theoretical story the multiple hierarchy model tells, for this nearly operational definition of local hierarchies.

In moving from a "nearly operational" to a genuinely operational definition of local hierarchy, I build upon Bruce Bueno de Mesquita's formula representing Boulding's loss-of-strength gradient. Bueno de Mesquita (1981: 103–108) operationalizes it as a logarithmic exponent to which a country's share of power is raised. The component parts of this exponent are the distances between the state in question and its dyadic partner, the distance that can be covered per day, and a constant term which prevents the exponent from degrading power immediately (since short transits should be relatively costless). The exact formula is:

$$\text{Adjusted Power} = \text{Power}^{\log[(\text{miles})/(\text{miles per day})+(10-e)]}$$

According to Bueno de Mesquita, "miles" is the distance from the home country's locus of power to the nearest point of its dyadic partner. The "miles per day" that can be achieved vary with time, in order to represent advancing transportation technology. Consultation with military officials and published histories leads Bueno de Mesquita to use 250 miles per day from 1816 through 1918, 375 miles per day from 1919 through 1945, and 500 miles per day thereafter. The logarithmic character of the formula assures that the degradation in power over distance will be monotonic, and that the weaker a state is at home, the steeper the loss-of-strength gradient will be. The exponent is positive because Bueno de Mesquita developed this exponential formula to degrade power *share* (based on Correlates of War composite capabilities index data) rather than raw power total. Were one using a raw power total, inserting a negative sign at the beginning of the exponent would suffice to degrade power as the positive version of the exponent does for *shares* of power.[3]

Bueno de Mesquita's loss-of-strength gradient formula is simple, conceptually appealing, and, not surprisingly, widely used (for example, the expected utility modeling literature sparked by Bueno de Mesquita's 1981 book, as well as research by others, such as Bennett and Stam 1996, Huth 1996, Rousseau *et al.* 1996, etc., all degrade power over distance with Bueno de Mesquita's formula). Wohlstetter (1968) offers a plausible critique of Boulding's contention that power loss over distance is monotonic, but his suggested changes would require collection of data on overseas bases and/or contributions from allies which he argues might abate the loss-of-strength gradient. Such data would not only be quite difficult to collect, but also would be of questionable value since it is not clear that advanced overseas military bases would reverse the loss-of-strength gradient. Consequently, Wohlstetter's complaint might simply reduce to the discovery that the loss-of-strength gradient may become less steep, or even flatten considerably, but then decline thereafter. Such a pattern would still be monotonic, or at least very nearly so.

[3] Mathematically inclined readers may find the decay function Bueno de Mesquita specifies in his loss-of-strength formula odd. Specifically, the combination of the logarithm from the base ten with *e*, the exponent of the natural logarithm, is uncommon. However, Bueno de Mesquita discusses and justifies this seemingly odd functional form as providing the most appealing beginning point at which power begins to degrade as well as a satisfactory rate for it to degrade. If we simply use distances and transit rates with the logarithm from the base ten, power will not begin to degrade until ten days' transit has occurred. That seems too long a delay. In contrast, using the natural logarithm will degrade power scores after *e* (2.71828...) days' worth of travel, which seems reasonable. Unfortunately, employing a natural logarithm will then subsequently degrade power very rapidly. Consequently, Bueno de Mesquita's formula adds 10 to the logarithm from the base ten specification so that power decline is not delayed ten days, but then subtracts *e* from that 10 so that the decline in power begins after a little under three days. Thus, the exponential equation is uncommon in form, but has intuitively appealing results (for his own explanation, see Bueno de Mesquita 1981: 106).

An alternate complaint is offered by Diehl (1985: 1209) and Moul (1988: 254) who criticize Bueno de Mesquita's "miles per day" estimates as overly generous. This latter critique has substantial merit.

The expectation of military transit of 500 miles per day after 1945 cannot apply to the military establishments of Third World states. Lack of transportation infrastructure and power projection capabilities such as large air forces, substantial number of troop-ships, or even paved roads prevent Third World militaries from moving virtually anywhere quickly. A stark but representative example was offered in 1997 by Kabila's rebel insurgency in Zaire. While it is true that Kabila himself moved around the country by jet, his was the only airplane the insurgents possessed. His troops moved by canoe, by foot, and, on very rare occasions when possible, by stealing automobiles from unfortunate civilians. Consequently, Kabila's troops rarely advanced more than fifty miles per day.[4] A developed-world example suggests caution as well. The distance between Washington D.C. and Riyadh, Saudi Arabia (arguably the average beginning and end points of the American deployment for the Gulf War) is roughly 8,500 miles. After Iraqi forces invaded and occupied Kuwait in August 1990, President Bush asked General Schwarzkopf to estimate how long it would take to get American forces in position to defend Saudi Arabia from any continued Iraqi aggression. The General estimated seventeen weeks. Moreover, to have sufficient resources in the area to mount an offensive operation against the Iraqis, Schwarzkopf estimated that eight to twelve months would be required (Woodward 1991: 303). The 8,500 miles and seventeen-week time-frame (for the more limited *defensive* goal) indicates Schwarzkopf's best guess at American transport range being just over seventy miles per day. Obviously, some forces were in position in Saudi Arabia within days, and the eight-to-twelve-month estimate proved too conservative (given that the defensive Desert Shield became the offensive Desert Storm only five months after the beginning of the mobilization). Further, the American mobilization and transportation of forces to the Gulf in 1990–1991 is an extraordinary case in which reserves were called up, and, together with

[4] According to contemporaneous accounts:

> With Mobutu's army in collapse, the rebels' biggest challenge has been the great distances between cities in a country one-third the size of the United States. Throughout most of their seven-month war, rebel forces have moved without motorized vehicles, advancing by foot or in dugout canoes and typically covering anywhere from 20 to 60 miles a day, depending on the terrain. "The only military obstacle now between the rebels and Kinshasa is the state of the roads," said one regional military expert. (French 1997: 2)

regular military units, dispatched literally half-way around the world and sent into a situation where battle with a large entrenched army was viewed as possible at any point. I do not mean to imply that a 500 miles per day transit range is impossible, but rather that it should be seen as an upper limit.

There is thus reason to credit Diehl's and Moul's complaints that Bueno de Mesquita's transit ranges (the "miles per day" part of the formula) are inaccurate. However, accepting the complaint as valid requires the substitution of the 250, 375, and 500 miles per day ranges with more accurate distances. In making this substitution, I take account of the physical characteristics of the distances to be covered between potential adversaries (are there mountains or jungles or plains; if the distance is not over land, are the obstacles rivers or seas?), the transportation infrastructure in existence in the territory in question, the troop transit resources of the states in question, and the speeds at which military or at least quasi-military forces have actually covered distances with similar terrain type and transportation infrastructures.[5]

In effect what this means is that within each of the general minor power regions I study (South America, the Middle East, the Far East, and Africa),[6] I collect data from atlases, compendia of the world's navies, and military histories about terrain, transportation infrastructures, and actual transit ranges of forces that have moved through the same or similar territory with the same or similar transportation infrastructures. This is exactly the type of detail military planners would be likely to consider when contemplating militarized engagement. It is thus exactly the type of detail relevant to calculations about which other states pose threats to one's state, or against which one's state might exert military influence. In short, when military planners consider with which other states military interaction is possible (recall: the conceptual definition of

[5] One is struck by the literary parallel offered in the opening line of James Fenimore Cooper's (1993 [1826]) *The Last of the Mohicans*: "It was a feature peculiar to the colonial wars of North America that the toils and dangers of the wilderness were to be encountered before the adverse hosts could meet." Clearly terrain mattered in those wars, but in no "peculiar" way.

[6] I apologize for the Americo-centric regional designations. I appreciate the fact that the Far East is "Far" or "East" only from a Western perspective (and also appreciate that the West is only the West from an Eastern perspective). I sympathize with non-American readers who wonder why there is so much discussion of "miles per day" when most of the world's military planners (including those at the Pentagon) think in terms of "kilometers per day." I am a typically insular American, and these are the terms which spring to my mind. Perhaps if there is sufficient interest in this work, I will be offered the chance to produce an "international" edition equally offensive to American readers.

local hierarchies is the ability to interact militarily), it is exactly this sort of information upon which they are likely to focus. Logistics, transit, and supply have been incredibly important elements of warfare over the past centuries, and, as the Gulf War shows, they are still important for even the most sophisticated modern military establishments. Boulding and Bueno de Mesquita explicitly recognize this in their thinking about the loss-of-strength gradient. I believe they were right to do so, but would go further and suggest more accurate measurement of such concepts will produce more valid information about which states can interact militarily. In using such detailed information I am approximating what I think are the actual considerations of military planners. Doing so allows me to determine the memberships of local hierarchies which validly represent the security environments, and thus the international sub-systems, within which minor powers carry out their primary foreign relations.[7]

Information about the speed with which military or quasi-military forces can cover, or have covered, various terrain types is widely available, although time-consuming to compile because of the variety of sources. Most useful are military histories of past conflicts. The importance of logistics and of transit more generally are well-enough established that many histories provide detailed information about how far and how fast troops moved. For example, Wilson (1971) provides an appendix of the itinerary of the Long March in which he indicates where the Chinese Communist forces were each day between October 1934 and October 1935 complete with daily mileage figures. Such sources offer invaluable indications of how rapidly a highly motivated group can move over the various terrain types encountered as the Long March unfolded. Similarly excellent summaries of the logistic reality of military transit in the Third World are offered by Lawrence (1927, 1938) for World War I activities in the Middle East, by Karnow (1983) for movement along the Ho Chi Minh Trail, by Morris (1965) for the movements of both British and indigenous military forces in southern Africa, as well as in histories of many other conflicts. From these one can gain specific

[7] A few quantitative researchers in world politics have begun to consider similar concerns directly relevant to military planning. Allan Stam's (1996; see also Bennett and Stam 1998 and Reiter and Stam 1998) inclusion of strategies, and of their appropriateness given the terrain within which most of the battles of a given war are fought, as a variable in his analyses of war outcomes epitomizes a tendency to represent in our statistical models the same sorts of things considered by military planners as they plan, fight, or avoid conflicts with other states. What I attempt to do in defining local hierarchies with detailed information about terrain type and actual military transits is the logistics equivalent of what Stam and his co-authors do with respect to military strategies.

information about individual conflicts. Additionally, one can also then generate general information about how fast military forces can cover different terrain types in different historical periods and given different transportation infrastructures by using each war as an example of likely transit under similar conditions.[8]

Such sources are invaluable, but they only convey information about military movements actually undertaken. In order to identify local hierarchies, I also require information about the likely speed of military movements *not* undertaken. This is needed because of the possibility that such movements were not undertaken specifically because military planners decided the distances were so insurmountable that states could not interact militarily. Whereas I can and do estimate how fast other military forces might move in East Asia based on Wilson's data, there are some parts of the world that have never experienced war (specifically much of Africa and South America), and thus for which military transit histories do not exist.

Often the areas without a history of wars are especially underdeveloped and have no roads or rails. In such instances I am not confident about the use of records of military transits in other parts of the world to estimate how long it would take to march from one state to another. Fortunately, the records of explorers can often be used to fill these gaps. The journals of explorers are well suited to provide this kind of information because their efforts were often quasi-military (if not overtly military). Additionally, such explorations were specifically interested in how long it took to get from one point to another because this affected the feasibility of future colonial and economic operations. The members of such expeditions were usually trained to determine their locations accurately, rendering their estimates of distances covered highly reliable. Finally, the explorers were interested in advancing scientific knowledge about the territories they explored, and thus spared no effort to keep meticulous records. Anyone doubting the relevance of such information for troop movements in the Third World today should compare Stanley's expedition through the Congo from east to west in 1874 with that of Kabila's insurgency in 1997. They not only covered the same territory, but they did so at virtually identical speed.[9]

[8] An argument might be made that I should consider climate as well as terrain. See, for instance, Winter (1998).

[9] I do not mean to imply that I have consulted explorer accounts about distances between all Third World states for which actual military records are unavailable. Rather, there have been sufficient numbers of explorations in the "missing" areas to increase my confidence

As with past research limited to analysis of South American local hierarchies (Lemke 1993, 1995; Lemke and Werner 1996), I use my estimates of transit ranges to replace the "miles per day" component of Bueno de Mesquita's loss-of-strength gradient formula and determine how much of one state's power would be lost in a hypothetical effort to exert military influence against another state. The revised version of Bueno de Mesquita's loss-of-strength gradient formula I use is:

$$\log\left[\sum_i ((\text{miles}_i)/(\text{miles per day}_{j(i)})) + (10 - e)\right]$$

where index i refers to types of terrain to be traversed and index $j(i)$ refers to the transportation technology j used to traverse terrain type i. Note that the transportation technologies available to each state in a dyad for traversing a given terrain type, and hence the "miles per day" for that terrain, may differ.

In order to apply this equation as an exponent to degrade a state's power and determine what part of the earth's surface it can exert military influence over, I need to know the focal state's share of power and the distance it must overcome in order to exert military influence against some potential target. The list of other states against which such influence can be exerted constitutes the focal state's relevant neighborhood.

I use regional shares of power and inter-capital distances. Whether one uses regional share of gross domestic product (GDP) or regional share of the Correlates of War (COW) project's composite capabilities index, very similar relevant neighborhoods are identified (this is because the correlation between GDP and COW power shares is so high). The choice of regional share of power as the indicator of a focal state's capabilities at home is somewhat arbitrary. But were I to use global shares of power instead of regional shares, I would discover that virtually all Third World states have all their power degraded away before even their nearest neighbors can be reached. The reason for this is that the loss-of-strength gradient formula uses a logarithmic transformation and, consequently, weak states have especially steep loss-of-strength gradients. Given the glaring inequality between superpowers like the United States and most or all Third World states, the global power shares of these states are tiny indeed. I agree that most are very constrained in

that the terrain type and lack of transportation infrastructure confronting movement in these parts of the world today are similar to those in at least one or a few of the explorer accounts available. Readers may be surprised by how plentiful explorer accounts are. For Africa alone I have consulted accounts of twenty-nine explorations across all parts of the continent.

terms of the size of their relevant neighborhoods, but reject as obviously untrue the notion that none can exert military influence beyond their borders. Using world shares of power would suggest this is true and thus overly penalize Third World states by creating an unnecessarily small list of local hierarchy members. Share of regional power (where the regions are the selfsame continental designations I criticize above as too general) offers a more intuitively satisfying roster of local hierarchy members.

My decision to use inter-capital distances to define the "miles" part of the loss-of-strength gradient formula is also somewhat arbitrary, but it strikes me as simple, plausible, and easy to measure. National capitals are arbitrarily defined starting and ending points for any putative military mission. However, whatever other start and end points I might choose would also be arbitrary. Inter-capital distances seem least arbitrary to me. In his initial usage of the loss-of-strength gradient formula, Bueno de Mesquita degrades power over the distance from the "sender" state's *locus of power* to the nearest point of the "target" state. It is not obvious what the locus of power of a given sender is. Bueno de Mesquita informs us that: "Until the Spanish-American War, I viewed the locus of American power as being on the Atlantic coast . . . In the case of Russia/ Soviet Union before World War II, the locus of power was in the area from Moscow to its borders with Europe on the west and from Leningrad to Stalingrad in terms of a north-south axis." (1981: 104–105) Where the locus of power is on the Atlantic coast of the United States is not clear (although Bueno de Mesquita suggests Washington D.C. – coincidentally the capital). Where in the area of the two overlapping parts of Russia one might locate Russian power is never disclosed. Some physical point must be used; inter-capital distances are easy to identify and use and arguably relevant to military planning.

According to the multiple hierarchy model, the purpose of wars fought within international power hierarchies is control of the relevant status quo. Being the local or global dominant power grants a state the ability to rewrite rules and establish the status quo to its advantage. There are thus positive incentives to be the dominant power. Presumably, challengers find that current dominant powers resist their efforts to alter the status quo. The current dominant power may have to be conquered by the challenger in order for their struggle to come to a clear conclusion. How is a state conquered? It seems likely to me that a conquered state has its capital city occupied, its government toppled, etc. Thus, the kinds of wars envisioned by the multiple hierarchy model suggest inter-capital distances may be more appropriate and less arbitrary than one might initially think. Inter-capital distances also offer the benefit of making the distance between states symmetric within each dyad.[10]

Returning to considerations of other distances, what if a state has multiple loci of power? What is the locus of power of the United States currently? It would seem to be either the entire United States, or else the demographic and industrial/economic centers of major cities like New York, Atlanta, Los Angeles, and Chicago. Alternately, perhaps it is the site of major American military installations. When calculating the distance between the American locus of power and Nigeria, for instance, which of these various loci should an investigator employ? On the other end of this calculation, why should the Nigerians be especially concerned about American military activity on the Nigeria–Benin border (which appears to me to be the closest point of Nigerian territory to an American locus of power in New York City)? Often the nearest point of the target state is some similarly marginal territory of little or no value to either the target or focal state.

Alternately, I might take advantage of sophisticated computer routines available in Geographic Information Systems and specify the "miles" part of the loss-of-strength gradient formula as the distance between the focal and target states' geographic centroids. This alternate specification of geographic distance would certainly raise questions such as why geographic centroids are appropriate? I would surely be asked whether states usually keep their military forces at their centroids?

The fact is that for most countries in the world the capital city is either the only city or the most important city. The prospect of another state being able to move military forces into this salient area, and thereby disrupting economic and political life, is especially threatening. For my purposes there is no clearly superior alternative to inter-capital distances. A locus of power might be an appealing concept, but it is not amenable to operationalization. Nearest points on or in target states are likely often to be barren, remote, and unimportant. Alternately, a major port may be an important start- or end-point for putative military operations, but

[10] Capitals are salient diplomatic features as well. Herbst (2000: 110) informs us that "the OAU said, in effect, that if an African government is in control of the capital city, then it has the legitimate right to the full protection offered by the modern understanding of sovereignty." Similarly, Coser (1961: 350) writes: "If in the common consciousness of the citizens, the capital symbolizes the very existence of the nation, then its fall will be perceived as defeat and will lead to the acceptance of the terms of the victor."

often the major port *is* the capital city. Further, for land-locked states, what is the major port? Again, no preferable alternative to inter-capital distances emerges.[11]

Using regional power shares and inter-capital distances (and bearing in mind the physical characteristic of those distances and transportation resources available for covering them), I calculate how much of a focal state's power is lost as it hypothetically exerts military influence beyond its borders. I thus calculate what each state's adjusted power is at other states' national capitals. If I find that at some target state's capital this adjusted power is less than 50 percent of the focal state's unadjusted power share (i.e., its power "at home"), I define that target state as not militarily reachable. All other states to which a focal state could extend 50 percent or more of its power constitute the focal state's relevant neighborhood. Wherever relevant neighborhoods of two or more states overlap, local hierarchies are defined to exist.

Admittedly, 50 percent power loss as the cut-off point beyond which targets are not reachable is somewhat arbitrary. I do not know how much power a given focal state is willing to "spend" in travel to a target. It is possible that some especially aggrieved state would be willing to use almost all of its power covering the distance to a hated target. However, I suspect such instances are extremely rare. A focal state's power share will not degrade to zero no matter how remote the target. The logarithmic exponent will make a focal state's power share approach zero asymptotically, but it will not become zero. Thus, mathematically,

[11] Readers may be struck by the fact that some states are not even able to reach contiguous neighbors. One reader suggested that using the distance from one's capital city to the nearest point on the putative foe's border is preferable *prima facie* to inter-capital distances. There may well be something to this, and a replication along these lines, though quite time-consuming, might prove interesting. However, such a change in case identification would introduce potential subsidiary problems. First, capital-to-border distances will not be symmetric within dyads. This means it will be easier for one dyad member to attack the other, independent of differences in their power shares. What, effectively would this mean? It would mean that State A would have an easier time getting its troops to State B's hinterland than does State B itself. What would State A's troops find in this hinterland? Presumably none or few of B's troops. If A's army is to engage B's troops, would it not be quite advantageous for B to withdraw and make A carry the fight to it (as the Russians historically have done against invaders from the West)? Surely A's military planners would take this likely strategy into account when planning the attack against B. In such a case, would A's planners not be more likely to think of the distance from its capital to B's? I agree that the non-relevance of some dyads, such as Chad–Libya, in my dataset is unfortunate and indicates some *prima facie* problems with my case identification procedure, but I think alternatives are worse. I think that Hitler planned to go all the way to Moscow rather than just to Minsk, and that more generally inter-capital distances are representative of strategic considerations.

all states can reach all other states. Even Ivory Coast will find some of its power remains after its forces reach Islamabad, but I cannot imagine Pakistani military considerations are seen as especially important in Yamoussoukro. I must set a limit to distinguish pairs of states that face a real possibility of interacting militarily from those that do not. No choice will be perfect. I choose 50 percent in an effort to minimize errors.

In order to introduce the various local hierarchies, I now turn to somewhat more detailed discussion of the local hierarchies identified in South America, the Middle East, the Far East, and Africa. In so doing, I not only list the actual local hierarchies, but also provide some more information about specific decisions made for each region, as well as some of the sources consulted.[12]

South America

I analyze South American power projection capabilities for the ten states that have been independent sovereign entities throughout the period 1860–1990 (i.e., I do not include Suriname, Guyana, or French Guiana).[13] I calculate each state's relevant neighborhood at ten-year intervals. Ideally the relevant neighborhoods would be calculated annually, but the procedure is tedious and power shares and transportation infrastructures do not change much from year to year (the ten-year interval also applies to my identification of local hierarchies in the other regions described below).

I describe my efforts to identify South American local hierarchies in more detail elsewhere (Lemke 1993, 1995, 1996), so only a cursory description is offered here. I consult the records of travelers and scientific explorations in South America in the nineteenth and early twentieth centuries. These suggest transit ranges of 8 miles per day through jungles,

[12] Observant readers will note that temporal coverage varies across the regions in my study. This unfortunately inconsistent left-censoring is imposed by data availability. I appreciate the fact that South American history pre-dates my 1860 start point, but I have been unable to compile GDP data for South American states prior to this (with a few exceptions – see Lemke 1993: appendix B). Similarly, I think it would be very useful to include Middle Eastern interactions in the 1950s, but find that data are extremely limited. Where possible (see the end of chapter 5), I attempt to evaluate empirical patterns prior to the years included in my dataset.

[13] In South America and the other regions, I employ the standard Correlates of War (COW) project definition of states as international system members (Russett, Singer, and Small 1968), with the exception that I retroactively include Uruguay as a state as early as 1860. A recent reconsideration of this COW list (Gleditsch and Ward 1999) provides numerous thoughtful arguments about what our "states" should be. It would be interesting to replicate my analyses with Gleditsch and Ward's list, and at a minimum we should think carefully about their article.

10 or 20 miles per day through the Andes (depending on altitude), and 30 miles per day over open ground (see Lemke 1993: app. A for a detailed list of sources). When more sophisticated transportation infrastructures such as railroads or, especially after 1970, paved roads are in place, I employ Bueno de Mesquita's estimates of the "miles per day" that can be traversed.

Using regional power shares, inter-capital distances as calculated from historical atlases, the ExpertMaps computer program (I deviate from straight-line distances when a better route offers itself), and the miles per day transit ranges of the previous paragraph, I uncover four persistent groupings of states in local hierarchies in South America. Colombia, Ecuador, and Venezuela are identified as a "Northern Tier" local hierarchy for the entire time-period. Argentina, Brazil, and Uruguay constitute an "Atlantic Coast" local hierarchy, while Chile and Peru constitute the parallel "Pacific Coast" local hierarchy. After 1900 Bolivia and Paraguay are able to interact militarily with each other, and thus they form a "Central" local hierarchy for the final ninety years of the period. After 1970 the transportation infrastructure in South America is developed enough to justify definition of all of South America as one local hierarchy, with Brazil as the South American dominant power. According to my calculations the "tyranny of distance" separating South American states from each other has largely been eroded owing to the shrinking world of advancing technology. I have not made similar calculations across European history, but I presume this same phenomenon occurred there much earlier.

Middle East

As mentioned in chapter 3, there is no consensus as to where the Middle East begins and ends. Some include northern Africa in the Middle East because of the common Islamic faith and other ethnic similarities. Others extend the Middle East through the Horn of Africa as well as into Afghanistan, and presumably would include Central Asia. I define fifteen states as Middle Eastern: Bahrain, Egypt, Iran, Iraq, Israel, Jordan, Kuwait, Lebanon, Oman, Qatar, Saudi Arabia, Syria, Turkey, the United Arab Emirates, and Yemen. The time-period I consider is 1960 to 1990. I understand arguments for inclusion of northern African states in the Middle East (below I describe a "Maghreb" local hierarchy in Africa), and understand that some may argue Turkey is European rather than Middle Eastern and/or that Afghanistan belongs in the Middle East. I do not think that alterations of "Middle Eastern-ness" along these lines would have any noticeable effect on the results reported in the next chapter, and am comfortable with my decisions regarding inclusion.

Above I raised doubts about the United States' ability to move into the Middle East at a rate of 500 miles per day. The American effort to transport troops and fighting material into the Middle East was intercontinental and thus a larger undertaking than would be the dispatch of Arab troops against Israel, or of Saudi troops against some member of its local hierarchy. Consequently I suspect Middle Eastern forces would move at least somewhat faster through the Middle East than American troops moved to the Middle East (recall Schwarzkopf estimated US troop movements at about 70 miles per day). Of perhaps special interest are the movements of T. E. Lawrence's irregular indigenous forces throughout the Middle East (they ranged from Egypt through Palestine and much of Saudi Arabia, throughout Syria, and even into parts of modern-day Turkey and Iraq) during the Arab Revolt in World War I (Lawrence 1927, 1938). My calculations of the distances he reports his forces traversing suggest they averaged, over the two years they were active, just over 37 miles per day. Lawrence and his men moved almost exclusively by camel, but their speed was seen as their greatest asset in their ultimately successful war against their better-equipped and more numerous Turkish enemies. Thus, even though modern Middle Eastern forces would not move by camel, we might still begin with Lawrence's efforts and suggest the transition from camel to internal combustion engine would result in modern military forces moving roughly three times faster, or 100 miles per day. This is admittedly an imprecise estimate, but hopefully a reasonable one.

Using regional power shares, inter-capital distances (again, based on atlases such as Grosvenor 1966 and Garver 1990 and ExpertMaps, and deviating from straight-line routes when such appears advantageous), a figure of 100 miles per day as the possible transit range, and the list of states above, application of the modified loss-of-strength gradient formula produces relevant neighborhoods that form three local hierarchies in the Middle East. Not surprisingly, this procedure uncovers an "Arab–Israeli" local hierarchy comprising Egypt, Iraq, Israel, Jordan, Lebanon, and Syria. A second local hierarchy along the "Northern Rim" of the Middle East includes Iran, Iraq, and Turkey. Finally, an "Arabian Peninsula" local hierarchy emerges after 1971 when many of the states of the peninsula achieved independence. This Arabian Peninsula local hierarchy comprises Bahrain, Kuwait, Qatar, Saudi Arabia, and the United Arab Emirates.

Of special note is the role Saudi Arabia attains in GDP-based calculations of relevant neighborhoods. Because of its vast oil wealth, Saudi Arabia's share of regional GDP is extremely large. If one calculates power with GDP, Saudi Arabia emerges as something of a Middle Eastern hegemon, able to exert military influence in every other state in the Middle East, even though most other regional states cannot "reach" Riyadh. If one calculates power with COW's composite capabilities index, Saudi Arabia does not achieve such distinction. The COW power interpretation of Saudi Arabia's role in the Middle East strikes me as more realistic than the GDP power interpretation. Saudi Arabia is surely a major power in the Middle East (as demonstrated by its status as local dominant power within the Arabian Peninsula), but not a hegemon.

Far East

As with the Middle East, there is no perfect consensus about where the Far East begins or ends. Since there is no immediately obvious characteristic of a state that makes it "Far Eastern," I have decided to err on the side of being too inclusive and designate twenty-five states as such: Afghanistan, Bangladesh, Bhutan, Brunei, Burma/Myanmar, Cambodia, China, India, Indonesia, Japan, Laos, Malaysia, the Maldives, Mongolia, Nepal, North Korea, North Vietnam, Pakistan, Philippines, Singapore, South Korea, South Vietnam, Sri Lanka, Taiwan and Thailand. I consider interactions between these states from 1950 to 1990.

The region designated "Far East" is thus quite vast and encompasses some of the world's densest jungles as well as its highest mountains. In calculating the miles per day that Far Eastern military forces may expect to cover, I have attempted to take these matters into consideration. At a minimum, I am convinced no Far Eastern state is or has been able to transport military forces at a rate of 500 miles per day. Consider the following.

On the first day of the Korean War (June 25, 1950), North Korean forces just reached Seoul (Dupuy and Dupuy 1986). This was a land distance of about 25 miles from the North Korean border but about 130 miles from Pyongyang. If the North Korean forces were able to travel at a rate of 500 miles per day, they should have reached Seoul either one hour or six hours after their advance began (depending on whether they began from the border or their capital city). Obviously the North Koreans were slowed by South Korean resistance, but when would such resistance not be a factor? It would not be a factor, or would be much less of a factor, when an army advances through its own territory. Evidence about such speeds in Asia may be gleaned from a number of sources. In his authoritative history of the war in Vietnam, Karnow (1983) describes travel ranges on the Ho Chi Minh Trail of ten miles per day. More useful, perhaps, are reports about the Chinese Communist Party's Long March of 6,000 miles in 1934–1935. Wilson (1971: Appendix) provides a daily itinerary of the Chinese 1st Army, the main military unit involved in the Long March. Based on his data, I calculate the 1st Army averaged just over 16 miles per day, over a variety of terrain from jungles to mountains to grasslands. Many legs of the Long March were conducted under attack by the KMT, while many other days were spent recuperating from previous forced marches. Thus, it might be more useful to consider the upper limit days, those on which the greatest distances were covered. According to Wilson, on September 23, 1935 the 1st Army covered 80 miles on foot in one day. In his recounting of the Long March, Salisbury (1985: 128) writes that the communists "covered extraordinary distances on foot, forty or fifty miles a day. Sometimes they held that pace for several days running." Salisbury himself retraced the route of the Long March with a small party of Chinese military officials in 1983. With newer roads, automobiles, and airplanes they averaged slightly under 100 miles per day. Maintaining this kind of speed over time, under attack or not, is impressive. But, it is far from 500 miles per day.

In an effort to employ a more realistic set of transit ranges, I suggest that 100 miles per day is an accurate estimate when there are roads, railroads, or navigable waterways. In the absence of a transportation infrastructure, I estimate that military forces are limited to 10 miles per day. I assume Far Eastern militaries will use whatever route offers the least difficulty. The preferred route is likely to depend on whether the state has sufficient naval capabilities to land troops by sea, or on whether there are roads or railroads. I determine which Far Eastern states have navies large enough to transport invasion forces by consulting Gardiner's (1979, 1983) historical compendia of the world's fighting ships. Naval forces with at least ten ships of 1,000 tons or more are designated large enough to allow regional transport of troops by sea.[14] The presence of roads or

[14] This ten ships of at least 1,000 tons may seem especially arbitrary, but careful perusal of Gardiner's books suggests anything smaller is likely to be employed only for limited coastal defenses and not for international transit. Further, the ten ships of at least 1,000 tons criterion provides a convenient breakpoint between states with small naval forces and states with large navies. Finally, there are few cases that fall just below or just above

railways is determined by consulting atlases published at various points in time (Grosvenor 1966; Garver 1990). Once the likely mode of transit is found, I use the ExpertMaps computer program to determine how many miles the chosen route entails.

Application of the loss-of-strength gradient formula indicates a number of local hierarchies in the Far East. The first is a "South Asia" local hierarchy composed of Bangladesh, Bhutan, India, and Pakistan. India is the dominant power within this local hierarchy for the entire time-period under study.

Additional Far Eastern local hierarchies include a "South East Asia" local hierarchy among Cambodia, Laos, South Vietnam (until 1975), Thailand, and Vietnam (formerly, North Vietnam). An "East Asia" local hierarchy is presided over by China as the local dominant power, and also includes Japan, Mongolia, North Korea, South Korea, and Taiwan. An "Asian Archipelago" local hierarchy includes Indonesia, Malaysia, and Singapore. Finally, there are three dyadic relations within the Far East, each of which either includes the only reachable target for one of the dyad's members, or else has a clear history of separate interstate relations within the dyad to justify its consideration as a local hierarchy on its own. Given this limited military horizon, these states are very likely to view each other as the most relevant international "system" of interest. In each of the three cases the dyadic local hierarchy is similar to the South American "Central" local hierarchy of Bolivia and Paraguay in that much stronger external regional actors can, and probably do, exert influence upon one or both members of the dyad. These dyadic local hierarchies comprise the dyads of Afghanistan–Pakistan, Burma/Myanmar–Thailand, and North Korea–South Korea. Designation of the Korean peninsula or Afghanistan–Pakistan as distinct sub-regional local hierarchies seems plausible, especially given the limited ability one or more of these states has to interact with others. Burma–Thailand as a sub-regional local hierarchy is included because it satisfies the same conditions, although it is not as immediately plausible as the other two dyadic systems.[15]

this breakpoint. Although not mentioned in discussion of the other regions, I consulted Gardiner in ruling out naval delivery of troops by South Americans, Middle Easterners, and Africans.

[15] Readers may be surprised by the absence of Russia/Soviet Union as an actor in Far Eastern local hierarchies. Russia is excluded from the Far East because of my coding rules. Specifically, although Russia/Soviet Union possessed sufficient resources to allow

Africa

Compared to the Middle East and the Far East, there is much less difficulty identifying African states. Although some might argue North Africa should be considered part of the Middle East, I make relevant neighborhood calculations for all states physically present on the continent of Africa (but also include the island states of Cape Verde, Comoros, Equatorial Guinea, Madagascar, Mauritius, São Tomé and Príncipe, and the Seychelles) so that a total of fifty-one states are designated "African." I employ the procedure described above to identify nine local hierarchies in Africa over the 1960 to 1990 time-period.

Information about the transportation infrastructure of Africa was gleaned from the previously mentioned atlases and maritime compendia, with the addition that I also consulted van Chi-Bonnardel (1973) for information about African roads and rail lines. I calculate inter-capital distances with the ExpertMaps program for what appear, based on available travel options and geographic obstacles, to be the most direct routes.

As discussed in detail in chapter 6, there have been very few wars and surprisingly few militarized interstate disputes in Africa since post-colonial independence. Consequently, I am unaware of any contemporaneous histories of efforts by African states to move military resources into each other's territories. I make extensive use of explorers, accounts to fill in the gaps, and am reassured that doing so is reasonable by the above-mentioned nearly equal speeds of travel attained by Stanley's

power projection to the Far East, no Far Eastern state could similarly project power back to Moscow. Consequently the two-way reachability component of my definition of local hierarchies is never present, and Russia is excluded. One possible way to correct this potential oversight might be to designate Vladivostok as Russia's capital for Far Eastern purposes. However, this in turn would raise two new problems. First, what proportion of Russia's aggregate capabilities should be designated Far Eastern? Certainly not all, but what fraction? Second, how many other states might have a base of interest in a distant region? Should the United Kingdom's capital be London for Great Power calculations, but Lagos or Mombasa for African purposes and Delhi or Hong Kong for Far Eastern purposes? Rather than open such vexing questions I prefer initially to accept the perhaps questionable designation of Russia/Soviet Union as not being a principal actor in the Far East. This may not be such a questionable designation, however. James L. Richardson writes that Russo-Japanese conflicts in the Far East in the twentieth century were exacerbated by Russia not paying sufficient attention to the Far East on account of the low priority of the region in Russian/Soviet foreign policy (1994: ch. 6, esp. pp. 106, 121). Anyone still unconvinced will find reassurance in chapter 6's replications. In that chapter I relax the two-way reachability assumption somewhat, and consequently Russia becomes an actor within some Asian local hierarchies.

second expedition in the 1870s and by Kabila's insurgents in 1997. I consulted annotated versions of the records left by twenty-seven European explorers in Africa from the mid 1700s through the early twentieth century (Hibbert 1982; Pakenham 1991). In addition, I consulted Morris's (1965) history of military activity in southern Africa in the nineteenth century, and the unannotated accounts of du Chaillu (1861) and Stanley (1890). By averaging the miles per day traveled by different explorers within similar territories it is possible to determine how far military operations are likely to be able to move per day. The major difference between Livingstone's miles per day and those of the Zimbabwean army today is there are now often railroads and paved roads. Where such modern transportation infrastructure exists I estimate armies are able to move 100 miles per day. Where roads and railroads are absent, I estimate armies are able to move at the speed of earlier explorers. In the absence of roads and rails the distances are small indeed. In north-eastern Africa the average speed is 15 miles per day. In western Africa I calculate the average to be 16 miles per day. In the Sahara and around Lake Chad, 19 miles per day is the average. In southern Africa the distance drops to 12 miles per day. In eastern Africa the distances further drop to 8 miles per day, while in the heart of central Africa's jungles, only 4 miles per day on average is achieved.[16]

Nine African local hierarchies are identified. First is the above-promised north African "Maghreb" local hierarchy of Algeria, Libya, Morocco, and Tunisia. It may strike some readers as odd to learn Egypt is not included in this local hierarchy (or alternately in one with Ethiopia or Sudan), but the fact is no African state is calculated as being able to exert military influence within Egypt – not even Libya. This may be an example of a gap between intuition and evidence. However, I suggest it is not surprising upon reconsideration. Egypt *is* physically in Africa.

[16] This may sound like ridiculously slow progress, but consider the following: "the men tramped rapidly westwards, swinging their arms rhythmically, averaging eight or ten miles a day, a record for the period" (Pakenham 1991: 407). Pakenham is here describing a joint European military mission through what later became Tanzania to rescue endangered missionaries in 1891. In such a situation time would surely be of the essence. Similarly, Morris (1965: 621) describes the advance of Lord Chelmsford's main column in the second invasion of the 1879 Zulu War: "With close to 700 wagons and more than 12,000 lumbering oxen he could hardly sprint . . . Four miles, three miles, a heart-lifting five miles and once a whole day crossing a silted drift that had to be firmed with bundles of grass thrown into the riverbed." One might question the relevance of oxen to estimates of the expected speed of African armies today, but recall Kabila's dugout canoes. These distances are also consistent with Herbst's (2000) various discussions of power projection abilities in Africa.

Egypt does have a fair amount of interaction with her African neighbors. But, Egypt's foreign policy is primarily geared toward the Middle East. Historically, Egypt's military threats have been more Middle Eastern than African. Further, when Egypt threatens others, those others are located in the Middle East. Thus, I think the identification of Egypt as a Middle Eastern-directed, albeit physically African, state is valid.

The second local hierarchy is that of "West Africa," and includes the Gambia, Guinea, Guinea Bissau, Mali, Mauritania, Senegal, and Sierra Leone. A "Gulf of Guinea" local hierarchy lists Benin, Burkina Faso, Ghana, Ivory Coast, Liberia, Niger, Nigeria, and Togo as its members. A "Central Lowlands" local hierarchy comprises the Central African Republic and Chad. The "Horn of Africa" local hierarchy has Djibouti, Ethiopia, Somalia, and Sudan, while a "Central Highlands" local hierarchy comprises Burundi and Rwanda. Continuing down the continent from North to South, the "South Atlantic Coast" local hierarchy includes Angola, Cameroon, Congo, Gabon, and Zaire. An "Indian Ocean" local hierarchy is made up of Kenya, Tanzania, and Uganda. Finally, the "Southern Africa" local hierarchy includes Botswana, Lesotho, Malawi, Mozambique, South Africa, Swaziland, Zambia, and Zimbabwe. None of the island states ringing the African continent possesses sufficient naval resources to mount an invasion of its mainland neighbors, and thus none is part of any local hierarchy.

The minor power local hierarchies for all four regions are listed in table 4.1.

Great Power overarching hierarchy

The final hierarchy included in the analyses in subsequent chapters is the global hierarchy in which the great powers contend for control of the overall international system's status quo. The great powers of interest are those actively influencing the international system: those states that are either currently the dominant power or capable of challenging the dominant power within the foreseeable future. Of interest, in short, are the contenders for system leadership (see Organski and Kugler 1980: 42–45 for the initial power transition discussion of contenders). These are the great powers actively engaged in maneuverings related to system leadership. The dominant power and its main challenger clearly are contenders. Additionally, those great powers allied with the dominant state or with the leading challenger are also contenders. Basically, the active powerful core of the great powers are the states of interest in

Table 4.1. *Local hierarchies*

South America (1860–1990)	Middle East (1960–1990)
Northern Tier	**Arab–Israeli**
Colombia*	Egypt*
Ecuador	Iraq
Venezuela*	Israel*
	Jordan
Atlantic Coast	Lebanon
Argentina*	Syria
Brazil*	
Uruguay	**Northern Rim**
	Iran*
Pacific Coast	Iraq
Chile*	Turkey*
Peru*	
	Arabian Peninsula (after 1971)
Central (after 1900)	Bahrain
Bolivia*	Kuwait
Paraguay	Qatar
	Saudi Arabia*
	United Arab Emirates

Notes: Local hierarchies are listed for whole decades, but obviously states did not become members until independence, which often occurred mid-decade.

Asterisks indicate the local dominant power. Some local hierarchies list more than one dominant power. This indicates either that there was an overtaking at some point or that for some time the identity of the dominant power was not clear (e.g., because the area had just emerged from colonial status).

Far East (1950–1990)	Africa (1960–1990)	
South Asia	**Maghreb**	**Horn of Africa**
Bangladesh	Algeria*	Djibouti
Bhutan	Libya	Ethiopia*
India*	Morocco*	Somalia
Pakistan	Tunisia	Sudan*
South East Asia	**West Africa**	**Central Highlands**
Cambodia	Gambia	Burundi
Laos	Guinea	Rwanda*
South Vietnam (until 1975)*	Guinea Bissau	
	Mali	**South Atlantic Coast**
Thailand	Mauritania	Angola
Vietnam* (former N. Vietnam)	Senegal*	Cameroon
	Sierra Leone	Congo
		Gabon
East Asia	**Gulf of Guinea**	Zaire*
China*	Benin	
Japan	Burkina Faso	**Indian Ocean**
Mongolia	Cameroon	Kenya*
North Korea	Ghana	Tanzania*
South Korea	Ivory Coast	Uganda
Taiwan	Liberia	
	Niger	**Southern Africa**
Asian Archipelago	Nigeria*	Botswana
Indonesia*	Togo	Lesotho
Malaysia		Malawi
Singapore	**Central Lowlands**	Mozambique
	Central African Rep.	South Africa*
Dyadic local hierarchies		Swaziland
Afghanistan–Pakistan*	Chad*	Zambia
Burma/Myanmar–Thailand*		Zimbabwe
North Korea–South Korea*		

applications of the multiple hierarchy model at the apex of the overall international power hierarchy.[17]

In an effort to be consistent with past work (Lemke and Werner 1996), I define the set of contenders as follows. First, the dominant state is always a contender. The dominant state of the global hierarchy of power was the United Kingdom until World War II, and the United States thereafter (Organski 1958: 326; Organski and Kugler 1980: 19). Second, the other contenders are defined by ranking, according to their capabilities (measured as GDP, as described below), all states identified by the Correlates of War project as major powers. I then observe where the largest unit drop in capabilities occurs. Great powers above this point are identified as contenders for the overall international power hierarchy. For example, a set of hypothetical great powers and their capabilities might look like: great power A = 100 power units, great power B = 90 power units, great power C = 85 power units, great power D = 40 power units. The largest unit drop is from great power C to great power D. Thus, great powers A, B, and C would be the contenders. Third, it is essential that the great powers identified as contenders be actively engaged in great power interactions. Isolationist great powers, ignoring their opportunities or responsibilities with respect to the international status quo, are not contenders, regardless of how powerful they are. Thus, active involvement in great power interactions, identified by the presence of alliances with other great powers or a relatively recent history of such alliance commitments, is the third criterion for contender status.[18] The states identified

[17] The Great Power overarching global hierarchy represents the overall international system. Conceptually every state in the world is a member of this overall hierarchy, and thus there might be analysis of all dyads including the global dominant power. This would lead to an enormous inflation of cases in which developing states would be paired against the United Kingdom or United States. In all of these instances parity would not obtain, and dissatisfaction also would be unlikely to be observed (given how I measure it). Of course, in virtually all of these cases there would be no war. Statistically this would result in a lot of cases appearing to support the hypothesis about war onsets. However, I suspect in most, if not all, of them the dominant power and the developing state did not really think about the possibility of going to war with each other. This perceived impossibility of war would surely be captured by calculating how much of Ghana's power, for instance, would have been degraded in an effort to transport troops from Accra to Washington, DC. Consequently it seems quite reasonable to apply the traditional power transition theory contender classification to analysis of the multiple hierarchy model when the overall international hierarchy is the focus of consideration.

[18] This third coding rule primarily excludes the US from contender status until after World War II. This exclusion is consistent with past power transition research (Organski and Kugler 1980; Lemke and Werner 1996), but is somewhat controversial (see Vasquez 1993: 99,103). I can certainly understand how readers might see American omission from contender status during World War I and World War II as odd, specifically since America's

as contenders according to these criteria are Britain from 1816, France from 1816, Prussia/Germany 1816–1945, Russia/USSR from 1816, and the United States from 1950.

Assessing the validity of local hierarchies

I apply my revision of Bueno de Mesquita's loss-of-strength gradient formula to minor power regional power shares, given detailed information about distances between national capitals, to identify the relevant neighborhoods of minor powers. Where such relevant neighborhoods overlap with each other, local hierarchies are defined to exist. There are four local hierarchies in South America, three in the Middle East, seven in the Far East, nine in Africa, and one additional power hierarchy among the great powers. In the analyses to follow I study interactions within these power hierarchies for all dyads including the dominant state of that hierarchy.

I have tried to be as transparent as possible in describing the procedures used to arrive at the designation of local hierarchies. However, I understand these procedures involve a certain amount of opacity which might raise concerns among more skeptical readers. In order to allay such fears, I offer some more detail here, via a specific example of where my version of the loss-of-strength gradient formula and Bueno de Mesquita's original version differ, and then by offering a more intuitive discussion of the local hierarchies as recognizable international sub-systems. In a "conceptual explication and propositional inventory" of the then-state-of-the-field in analysis of international sub-systems, Thompson (1973a: 89) encourages researchers to define international sub-systems based on proximity, interaction, and the intuitive recognition of an area as a sub-system. I have combined proximity and interaction into a single component of the ability to interact (heavily influenced by proximity), and offer the paragraphs that follow in defense of the intuitive recognition of the local hierarchies as sub-systems.

First is the specific example of the application of the revised version of the loss-of-strength gradient formula. Suppose one were interested in

contributions to those wars arguably proved decisive to their outcomes. However, in the case of World War I the US avoided participation in the war for years, and then quickly retreated to isolationism as soon as the Central Powers were defeated. The US remained isolationist as a matter of legislative stipulation until World War II broke out in 1939. Such resistance to international interactions is hardly the action of a leading state or would-be leading state. Those somehow unpersuaded by this note will be pleased to see the US included in the Great Power hierarchy from 1900 in chapter 6's replications.

ascertaining how much power would be lost by Argentina in a putative invasion of Colombia in 1880. In 1880 Argentina had a 21 percent share of South American power (this example employs GDP data discussed in Lemke 1993: appendix B). Between Buenos Aires and Bogotá at that time there were 850 miles of open terrain, 725 miles of mountainous terrain, and 1,200 miles of jungle. Since there were no rails or roads linking these countries in 1880, and since neither had naval capacities sufficient to transport troops overseas, the distances that could be traversed were 30 miles per day, 20 miles per day, and 8 miles per day respectively. With Bueno de Mesquita's formula the exponent would be:

$$\log\{(2775/250) + (10 - e)\} = 1.26$$

Since Bueno de Mesquita treats all miles as equivalent, and assigns 250 miles per day as the transit range in 1880, the exponent remains fairly simple. For my adaptation of the formula, Argentina's power share should be raised to:

$$\log\{(850/30) + (725/20) + (1200/8) + (10 - e)\} = 2.35$$

Raising Argentina's 21 percent share of South American power to Bueno de Mesquita's exponent results in an adjusted power share of 14 percent, while using my exponent results in an adjusted power share of 3 percent. According to my coding rules Argentina could not "reach" Colombia in 1880. According to Bueno de Mesquita's transit range Argentina could reach Colombia. Clearly these are large differences in how much power Argentina could expect to retain after transit in any effort to invade Colombia in 1880. I suggest my one-seventh is more plausible than the alternative two-thirds.

As already mentioned, most sub-system classifications tend to refer to continents as sub-systems. My procedure defines sub-systems much more narrowly, and thus produces a longer list of sub-systems (local hierarchies) than do others. For instance, the most systematic data-based effort to define regions (Russett 1967) offers, among other things, five regions of "socio-cultural homogeneity." These five regions comprise Afro-Asia, Western Community, Latin America, Semi-Developed Latins, and Eastern Europe. There are some odd classifications within these five regions. For example, China is "unclassifiable," apparently not sufficiently similar to either the Afro-Asians or Eastern Europeans (largely communist) to be included in their regions. Japan and Argentina are found in the Western Community, rather than in the Afro-Asian or Latin American regions, while the Philippines is located in the Latin American region. One can easily offer persuasive reasons for these classifications (specifically if we take the cultural dimension and the economic development aspect of the social component seriously). However, in terms of militarized interactions, these five regions are clearly too broad to offer an intuitive way to divide the world into sub-systems.

Are my much more geographically constrained "regions" more intuitively appealing sub-systems? I think so. As part of an intriguing discussion of warfare from an anthropological perspective, Quincy Wright (1942: 545) offered a map he titled "Regional Classification of Primitive Peoples." The map divides the world such that indigenous peoples with similar ways of organizing their societies, similar cultural patterns, and similar forms of production are grouped together. Presumably these similarities were caused or reinforced by interaction. There are a number of very close overlaps between Wright's map and my local hierarchies. For instance, in South America the Northern Tier, Pacific Coast, and Central local hierarchies closely correspond to sections 1, 3, and 4 of Wright's map. The Atlantic Coast local hierarchy of South America is represented on his map as sections 5 and 6 of South America. In Africa, his section 1 is my West Africa, his section 2 is my Gulf of Guinea local hierarchy, his section 3 is very nearly identical to my South Atlantic Coast, his section 5 corresponds nearly exactly with my Indian Ocean local hierarchy, while his section 6 is very similar to my Southern Africa. Turning to the Middle East, there are no overlaps, as he has only one section for all of what I consider the Middle East. However, in the rest of Asia (what I call the "Far East"), similarities return. His section 2 is my East Asia, his section 6 is my Afghanistan–Pakistan dyadic system, his section 11 is my South East Asia, and combining his sections 12 and 13 would produce my Asian Archipelago local hierarchy. What I call South Asia is section 8 on his map. It seems that indigenous "primitive peoples" were constrained by geographic barriers and distances similar to those that affect the present-day states of much of the Third World.

Diplomatic histories of South America offer additional cross-validation of the local hierarchies. Comparison of my delineation of South America with a map of colonial South America shows that the Viceroyalty of New Granada, the Viceroyalty of Peru, and the Viceroyalty of the Rio de la Plata correspond quite closely with three of the local hierarchies (Northern Tier, Pacific Coast, and Atlantic Coast), although there was no corresponding interior Viceroyalty, or even Captaincy-General, for the Central local hierarchy of Paraguay and Bolivia.

Several major texts on South American diplomatic history (see Davis and Wilson 1975, as well as Bethell 1984–1991, esp. vols. 3 and 8) organize their subject matter into four sections consistent with my local hierarchies. More persuasively, several authors write of South American interactions as though they somehow envisioned local hierarchies. Burr (1955: 40) writes of a balance-of-power system along the Rio de la Plata (basically the Atlantic Coast local hierarchy) as well as of a balance of power between Chile and Peru (my Pacific Coast local hierarchy). In a later work Burr considers South American rivalries, all of which are located within one or another local hierarchy (1970: 101). Ortega (1984: 373) describes the War of the Pacific between Chile and Peru as arising from an inevitable rivalry, the kind of rivalry states with disparate evaluations of their status quo might generate.

Additionally, there are notable similarities between my Middle Eastern local hierarchies and Thompson's (1981) delineation of regional sub-systems based on networks of diplomatic visits among Middle Eastern states. Focusing on these actual diplomatic interactions leads him to identify sub-systems similar to those I find by focusing on the opportunity for military interaction.

In Africa, a number of the local hierarchies correspond quite closely with the geographic limits of great civilizations of ancient Africa as reported by Lester Brooks (1971). The Mali civilization at its zenith, in the period 1200–1500 AD, is nearly coterminous with my West Africa. Its successor, the Songhay (lasting until 1600 AD), also closely corresponds to my designation of a West Africa local hierarchy. The Kanem-Bornu civilization (800–1800 AD) closely resembles my Central Lowlands local hierarchy. Finally, accounts of the imperial reach of Shaka Zulu as he forged the Zulu empire, and of the larger Bantu civilization he so greatly disrupted, give the impression that Shaka and the earlier Bantu leaders dominated an area similar to what I call Southern Africa (Morris 1965). Finally, in a discussion of regional groupings in Africa, Christopher Clapham (1996: 117–118) describes regions very similar to seven of my nine African local hierarchies.

Yet another validity check is offered by comparison of my local hierarchies with a volume focusing on "regional hegemons" (Myers 1991). Six of the chapters of that volume (chapters 3–8) deal with regional leading states in the developing world. All six of the chapters discuss the strategic behaviors and responses to threats of states I identify as the local dominant powers (for all or part of the time-periods I study) of local hierarchies in the developing world.

My notion of local hierarchies is conceptually very similar to Buzan's (1991) notion of "regional security complexes." According to him, "A security complex exists where a set of security relationships stands out from the general background by virtue of its relatively strong, inward-looking character, and the relative weakness of its outward security interactions with its neighbors" (p. 193). Clearly this predecessor is extremely similar to my notion. The original contribution I make is to suggest that the ability of states to interact militarily with each other helps identify when security complexes exist. Given the similarity of our conceptualizations, it is not surprising that many of my local hierarchies bear a striking resemblance to sub-complexes within his security complexes. For example, his Horn of Africa sub-complex is the same as my Horn of Africa local hierarchy, his Eastern Mediterranean sub-complex corresponds strongly with my Arab–Israeli local hierarchy, his Maghreb is my Maghreb, etc. The functioning of his sub-complexes is complicated by occasional activity by actors able to operate in more than one, much as my local hierarchies occasionally blur into each other.

In sum, there is much evidence that the local hierarchies I identify as plausible groupings of developing states militarily relevant to each other have similarly struck other researchers, from a variety of intellectual traditions, as plausible. I have belabored the presentation of the local hierarchies because they are an important element of the project reported upon in this volume. The identification of local hierarchies is undertaken in an attempt to identify the sub-systems of the international system within which minor powers interact with each other. The identification of such local hierarchies is essential to any empirical evaluation of my multiple hierarchy model. Given the importance of local hierarchies for case selection in my analyses, it is potentially damning that there are so many places in the data collection and manipulation procedure described above where errors could creep into my dataset. I respond to this threat by being as transparent as I can about how I identify local hierarchies. I also respond by providing an alternate calculation of local hierarchy membership in chapter 6. Finally, I offer the preceding paragraphs as validation of the plausibility of the local hierarchies identified. I turn now to consideration of how I measure the important variables affecting the probability of war within these local hierarchies.

Measuring power and parity

In contrast to the concept of local hierarchies, there is widespread (if grudging) agreement about measures of power, or at least about measures of capabilities. The most widely used measure is the Correlates of War (COW) project's *composite capabilities index* introduced by Singer, Bremer, and Stuckey (1972) and described in detail by Singer (1988). This well-known indicator combines demographic, industrial, and military components of the material capabilities of states. It results in each state's share of world capabilities observed annually.

An alternate and also widely used measure of national capabilities is *gross national product* (GNP) or *gross domestic product* (GDP) (first suggested for this purpose by Organski 1958: 203; technically, Organski suggests power be measured as population multiplied by per capita gross national product, but this simplifies to GNP). Among power transition researchers GNP or GDP, often weighted by the efficiency of the government of the state in question, is the most commonly used measure of national capabilities.[19] National product is preferred by power transition researchers because of the theory's focus on domestic and demographic factors as the basis of power (recall the discussion in chapter 2).

About a decade ago an edited volume (Stoll and Ward 1989), in which all of the contributors discussed measures of power and issues raised by efforts to measure power, provided a useful commentary on the complexity of the concept of national power. A large number of measures of power were empirically compared and logically dissected. However, not surprisingly the COW and GNP/GDP measures emerged as the empirically most robust and intuitively most plausible. Also not surprisingly, at least two of the chapters in the edited volume (Kugler and Arbetman 1989a, and Merritt and Zinnes 1989) demonstrated that COW and GNP/GDP measures of power are very highly correlated.

[19] Arbetman and Kugler (1997) offer a detailed discussion of relative political efficiency, or RPE (while Organski and Kugler 1980: chapter 2 and appendix 1 offer a similar detailed discussion of the earlier concept of relative political capacity, or RPC). I have replicated most of the results from chapter 5 and the Appendix with GDP or COW power weighted by RPE, and generate reasonably similar results. The results are only "reasonably" similar because RPE is calculated on the basis of tax data. These are notoriously difficult to collect, and especially so for developing states. Consequently, when I weight power by RPE a lot of cases are lost because of missing data. I believe this change in sample size causes the variation in results between unweighted GDP or COW estimations and those weighting power with RPE.

In the empirical evaluations to follow, I employ both Correlates of War and GDP measures of power. The Correlates of War data are drawn directly from the Correlates of War project at the University of Michigan. The GDP data are primarily drawn from the Penn World Tables (Summers and Heston 1991), and are based on purchasing power parity versions of GDP. The Penn World Tables GDP data are supplemented with data from Maddison (1989) and from a variety of original sources for South American states detailed in Lemke (1993: appendix B). In the chapters to follow I place primary emphasis on the GDP-based power analyses, because I accept the argument that GDP more accurately measures power transition theory's conceptualization of power. However, in the Appendix I replicate all of the analyses from chapters 5 and 7 using the COW power indicator. That the results of this are very similar to those based on GDP is strong evidence of the robustness of the findings reported in this book.

National power by itself is not a critically important variable in the multiple hierarchy model or in traditional power transition theory. Rather, what matters is the relative power relationship between the dominant state and a would-be challenger. I measure relative power as the ratio of the weaker state's power to the stronger state's. Relative power thus can vary from nearly zero to one. In Organski and Kugler's (1980) original evaluation of power transition theory they define "power parity" as existing whenever the ratio of relative power is greater than 80 percent. Instead of this 80 percent threshold, I define any ratio greater than 70 percent as being at parity. My justification for this broadening of the range of parity values is a belief that there is more uncertainty among developing states about when they are at parity than among great powers. I think this uncertainty sufficient justification for a larger range of values being defined as power parity.

Measuring status quo evaluations

As described in chapter 2, some states are dissatisfied with the status quo because it either actively discriminates against their preferences and interests, or because they perceive they would be better off under different formal and informal institutional arrangements. Chapter 3 extends the systemic notion of dissatisfaction to the local level, and argues minor power states within local hierarchies similarly evaluate the formal and informal arrangements governing their relations with other local hierarchy members. If these formal and informal arrangements are disadvantageous, or perceived to be so, these states will be dissatisfied with their local status quo. Power transition theory and the multiple hierarchy model both identify such status quo dissatisfaction as an important variable increasing the probability of war within international hierarchies. An empirical indicator of status quo evaluations is a necessity for any empirical evaluation of the multiple hierarchy model or of power transition theory more specifically.

It is thus more than a little surprising that for most of power transition theory's history no measures of status quo evaluations were included in empirical analyses. Woosang Kim (1991, 1992, 1996) corrects this oversight with a measure of status quo evaluations based on the similarity of alliance portfolios between great powers and the internationally strongest state. The similarity of alliance portfolios between a great power and the dominant state is assumed to measure a more general similarity of foreign policy outlook. Kim argues that great powers that form alliances with states allied to the dominant state and avoid alliances with states ignored by the dominant state are likely do so because they share international preferences similar to those of the dominant state. The more a great power's alliance portfolio coincides with the alliance portfolio of the dominant state, the more it has similar preferences to the dominant state, and is thus satisfied with the international status quo.

In providing an actual measure of alliance portfolio similarity as a status quo evaluation, Kim draws on Bueno de Mesquita's (1975) earlier efforts. In that earlier work Bueno de Mesquita constructs matrices where each column or row indicates the type of alliance (defense pact, neutrality pact, entente, or no alliance) the row or column state has with every other member of the international system. If two states had identical alliance portfolios only the negatively sloping diagonal cells would contain cases. If two states had exactly opposite alliance portfolios only the positively sloping diagonal cells would contain cases. The more similar two states' alliance portfolios, the closer the negatively sloping situation is approximated. Bueno de Mesquita measures this similarity with a τ_b coefficient, equaling 1 in instances of perfect similarity in alliance portfolios and –1 in instances of perfect dissimilarity.

Kim's contribution is to calculate these τ_b alliance portfolio similarity scores for each great power with the dominant state (Bueno de Mesquita simply compares all dyads and uses the resulting τ_b scores as an indicator of similarity of foreign policy outlook rather than as a specific measure of power transition theory's status quo evaluations). In a series of papers (Kim 1991, 1992, 1996, and Kim and Morrow 1992) Kim demonstrates that the τ_b alliance portfolio similarity measure of status quo evaluations is strongly related to the probability of war within great power dyads. In fact, he routinely finds this indicator of status quo evaluations is more important than relative power calculations. Subsequently, Lemke and Reed (1996, 1998) extend the τ_b measure beyond the great powers, and use it as an indicator of status quo evaluations. Kim's power-transition-specific adaptation of Bueno de Mesquita's τ_b measure of alliance portfolio similarity has become the most widely used indicator of status quo evaluations in analyses of power transition theory.[20]

I do not employ Kim's τ_b measure (nor Signorino and Ritter's alternative S measure) in the analyses reported in subsequent chapters simply because there is so little variation in minor power alliance portfolios that τ_b (or S) does not differentiate among minor power states. For instance, in South America the standard data compilation of alliances provided by the Correlates of War project (introduced by Singer and Small 1966) lists virtually no South American alliances prior to the 1930s. Since then, all of South America (and almost all of the Western Hemisphere more generally) has been allied in a defense pact through the Organization of American States. African states are similarly almost uniformly allied in an entente via the Organization of African Unity. In the Middle East a defense pact associated with the Arab League has knitted thirteen states together for most of the time-frame I study. There are very few other alliances involving minor power states. Consequently, a τ_b measure of alliance portfolio similarity indicates all South American states, all African states, and virtually all Middle Eastern states are satisfied with their local status quos. There simply is too little variation in alliance participation behavior among minor powers to make any alliance-based measure of status quo evaluations useful.

A number of scholars convincingly demonstrate that territorial disagreements are an especially disputatious type of disagreement (Vasquez 1993; Hensel 1996; Huth 1996). My discussion in chapter 3 of the likely focus of local status quo rules strongly hints territorial issues play a major role in local hierarchy affairs (Kacowicz [1995] goes so far as to suggest territorial arrangements *are* the local status quo). Consequently, it would seem desirable to define dissatisfaction with the local status quo as being present whenever a local territorial disagreement

[20] Signorino and Ritter's (1999) reanalysis of the τ_b measure demonstrates it does not measure the similarity of two alliance portfolios; rather it measures the association of two alliance portfolios. Signorino and Ritter demonstrate how this is an important distinction, and offer an improved measure, S.

exists. Data about territorial disagreements (regardless of whether they escalate to threats or uses of force) are available in the appendix to Paul Huth's *Standing Your Ground* (Huth 1996) and as part of Paul Hensel's Issue Correlates of War project (Hensel 1998). I have used these two datasets to consider whether there is a relationship between war and territorial disagreements within local hierarchies. As hinted in previous chapters, it happens that every single instance of war in one of my local hierarchies occurred within the pre-existing context of a disagreement about territory. This is strong evidence of how important territorial disagreements are in minor power relations (and is not at all surprising given the studies cited in the opening sentence of this paragraph). But it presents the problem of perfect identification between war and territorial disagreement. Statistical models such as logistic regression will not converge if I use territorial disagreements as a variable because there are no instances of a 1 on the dependent variable (war) and a zero on this potential independent variable. Consequently, I cannot use territorial disagreements as a variable in my statistical analyses. This is unfortunate because territorial disagreements clearly matter in local hierarchies. I do not mean to suggest that territorial disagreements would be a perfect indicator of dissatisfaction with the local status quo, because I can conceive of situations in which the local status quo may not have a territorial component. Further, I prefer to use a consistent indicator of dissatisfaction for both the great and minor power levels. At a minimum, territorial disagreements are strongly related to war within local hierarchies. There are clearly important questions about why the relationship exists and of how strong it is. I hope to readdress this relationship in subsequent work.

The similarity of states' votes in the United Nations General Assembly has often been used as an indicator of a common foreign policy outlook, or of affinity more generally. Techniques for calculating the similarity of any two states' votes have been offered by Lijphart (1963), Gartzke (1998), Signorino and Ritter (1999), and Voeten (2000). Given the precedent and measures already developed, it is tempting to think the similarity of a state's UN votes with those of the dominant power of its hierarchy might be a good indicator of its satisfaction or dissatisfaction with the dominant power and thus with its relevant status quo. Unfortunately, a number of obstacles rule out the use of UN vote similarity scores for measuring status quo evaluations, especially for minor powers.

A first problem arises because UN voting has only existed since 1945. This is not a problem from an African local hierarchy (or Middle East or

Far East) perspective, but it is for my Great Power and South American local hierarchy evaluations. League of Nations voting similarity scores do not help extend the time-frame back to 1918 because the League voted by acclamation: all states voted identically, when they voted at all.

In order for UN voting patterns to be a useful indicator of affinity between states and thus of status quo evaluations, there would have to be variation in voting patterns. Put differently, if Mongolia is satisfied with China as the local dominant power but Taiwan is dissatisfied, and if UN voting patterns are a good indicator of status quo evaluations (putting aside for a moment the vexing detail that China and Taiwan have never been concurrent members of the UN), then Mongolia and Taiwan must vote differently in the General Assembly.

The unfortunate fact is that minor powers almost never vote in any differentiable way in the General Assembly. Keisuke Iida (1988) offers an analysis of voting in the General Assembly by the Group of 77 (the "Third World" group in the UN). He reports (especially in his figure 1 on p. 378) G77 members almost never vote against one another. In 1974 his defection ratio, "the likelihood that a country randomly chosen from the Group of 77 will deviate from the common position on any given resolution" (1988: 377) reached an all-time high of only 12.4 percent! It only once reaches a value half that high, and usually hovers much closer to zero. Third World states vote with astonishing similarity in the General Assembly.

This is perhaps less surprising when one recognizes the UN has always passed at least 50 percent of its resolutions without a single negative vote, and in some years has passed as many as 80 percent without a single "no" cast (Marin-Bosch 1987: table 3). When one further understands the question of Namibia "has been the subject of more resolutions than all other past decolonization issues combined" (Marin-Bosch 1987: 706) and "South Africa's policy of apartheid . . . has been the topic of . . . more General Assembly resolutions than any other single item ever to appear on its agenda" (p. 707), one sees why there is so much Third World solidarity at the UN. The votes of Third World states who hate their local status quo and of Third World states who love their local status quo do not vary because, aside from the Southern African local hierarchy, their local status quos are never at issue at the UN. Thus, there is essentially no variation in Third World voting in the United Nations.

This does not mean all Third World states see eye-to-eye on important issues. Jacobson *et al.* (1983) take the extraordinary step of actually interviewing eighty negotiators representing their states at meetings in

Europe in 1976 dealing with the New International Economic Order. The Group of 77 voted as a solid bloc on all NIEO resolutions, and thus a researcher analyzing voting records might believe they were of a single mind. Not so, according to Jacobson and his colleagues. They found substantial disagreement across Third World negotiators with respect to a variety of important developmental issues (including whether multinational corporations play a positive or negative role). Not surprisingly, they conclude "the negotiators' views are much more diverse than would appear from analyses of roll-call votes . . . The data and analyses presented here show that the LDC component of this coalition [the G77], while it might find it tactically advantageous to vote as a bloc, actually contains a wide spectrum of views" (1983: 365). Anyone skeptical that the negotiators' views might differ from their governments', should be mollified by the claim: "the answers of our respondents were strongly influenced by their official positions and responsibilities. In other words, they could hardly have been expected to give answers that would seriously contravene their governments' positions" (1983: 365). This is because the negotiators, in most cases, were the actual officials responsible for shaping their governments' positions.

Based on his comparison of UN General Assembly voting similarity variables with various other established measures of international affinity, Brian Tomlin reports: "we must conclude that . . . the validity of the voting measures has not been established" (1985: 205). However, he does allow that "voting behavior may represent a valid indicator of national orientations toward the superpower rivalry" (1985: 205 [a conclusion consistent with Voeten 2000]). Since UN voting does not vary meaningfully (or at all) across Third World states, it cannot be an indicator of status quo evaluations. It might offer a useful indicator of satisfaction with the overall status quo, but can only do so from 1945 onward.

Lacking a useable alternative, I employ Werner and Kugler's (1996) "extraordinary military buildups" indicator of status quo dissatisfaction (see Lemke and Werner 1996 for elaboration on Werner and Kugler's discussion). Extraordinary military buildups are an imperfect indicator of status quo evaluations, and I would much prefer a less imperfect alternative. Unfortunately, no such alternative is currently available. However, it is reasonable to expect dissatisfied states are disproportionately likely to undergo an extraordinary military buildup. Therefore, the lack of a satisfactory alternative and the likely confluence between such buildups and dissatisfaction with the status quo are offered as justification for my use of the buildup measure.

The conceptual connection between dissatisfaction with the status quo and military buildups is provided by the belief that military buildups often are a preparation for *potential* war. If the multiple hierarchy model is correct, dissatisfied states are especially likely to expect war as parity between them and the dominant state in their hierarchy draws near. They expect war because they know they are dissatisfied, anticipate the opportunity to demand changes to the relevant status quo, and further suspect the dominant state's resistance to these changes will lead to a war resolving the issue. Consequently, dissatisfied states should prepare for war as parity nears. Satisfied rising states, on the other hand, do not feel aggrieved with the dominant state in their hierarchy, and thus do not have much reason to expect war with the dominant power regardless of whether parity is near or not. Satisfied states are unlikely to prepare for wars they do not anticipate fighting.

Consistent with past research (Lemke and Werner 1996, and Werner and Kugler 1996), I measure military buildups by consideration of trends in the military expenditures of states (I make use of the military expenditure data reported in the Correlates of War project's composite capabilities index).[21] I identify which challengers are undergoing a military buildup by comparing the average annual percentage change in military spending for a state with the average annual percentage change for the state prior to the time-period in question. The comparison is thus between the current average percentage change and the cumulative average of all previous years. When calculating the cumulative overall average I eliminate any previous year in which the state in question was involved in a war. Whenever the average annual military expenditure increase is greater than the cumulative annual average for all previous non-war years, the state is coded as undergoing a military buildup. This military buildup is coded as dissatisfaction with the status quo, however, only if the increase is greater than any increase the dominant state in the relevant hierarchy might simultaneously show. I thus differentiate

[21] A pair of articles suggest such data are of questionable accuracy (Diehl and Crescenzi 1998; Lebovic 1998). If some states report soldiers' pensions as part of their defense budget while others do not, errors will be made when any two states' military expenditures are compared. Similarly, problems with exchange rate conversions, or of differential purchasing power, may make cross-national comparisons of military expenditures inaccurate. While crediting the veracity of these articles, I suspect the data quality problems they highlight are less troubling in my case. In computing which states are undergoing buildups, I compare a state's military expenditure in a given time period to its history of previous expenditures. In a sense, then, I standardize the errors associated with a given state's expenditure data by making a comparison with its expenditures previously, when, presumably, similar errors in data reporting were also made.

between those states simply increasing their arsenals and those doing so at extraordinary levels, levels greater even than the dominant state in their local or overall international hierarchy. Challengers expecting war should anticipate having to fight the dominant state in their hierarchy, and thus preparation for war would be directed against this state. Thus, the relevant comparison for a challenger's military buildup is to that of the dominant state. Challengers are coded as dissatisfied only if they are undergoing a military buildup and increasing their arsenals relatively faster than the dominant state. Challengers not undergoing extraordinary military buildups are coded as not dissatisfied with the status quo.

An immediate potential objection to the extraordinary military buildup indicator of status quo dissatisfaction might simply restate the conceptual connection between dissatisfaction and preparation for war alleged above. If military buildups are part of the preparation for war, then whenever military buildups are observed wars will also be observed. Simply put, this would put war on both sides of the equations estimated in chapter 5, thereby making all of my tests circular. However, this debilitating threat is operative only if "preparation for war" is always followed by war. Although it might seem likely for buildups to be followed by war, it need hardly be the case. Specifically, it could well be that preparation for war prevents war. It is possible for extraordinary military buildups to cause peace by deterrence. This is the thinking behind the adage: "if you would have peace, prepare for war." This is consistent with Andrew Kydd's (2000: 231) observation: "arms races will not cause war as the spiral model predicts. In fact the failure of status quo states to race hard enough may actually cause war by inviting attack by revisionist powers." It is also consistent with Siverson and Diehl's (1989) conclusion indicating some arms races lead to war while others lead to peace, and with Kennedy's (1984) contention of arms races as a product of political conflicts rather than a cause of war.

I am encouraged in my use of buildups as a measure of dissatisfaction by the fact that there is no consistent relationship between such military buildups and war within the existing literature. Beginning with Wallace (1979) and his immediate and strident critics (Weede 1980; Altfeld 1983; and Diehl 1983) through the most recent re-evaluations (Sample 1997), it is clear that arms buildups make militarized disputes more likely to *escalate* to war. However, the only study to investigate whether arms buildups make the initial disputes more likely to occur in the first place concludes there is no relationship between buildups and the *onset* of conflict (Diehl and Kingston 1987). Thus any claim of arms buildups causing war is not justified. The empirical studies by Wallace and his critics begin with disputes as the cases analyzed, and then estimate the influence of buildups on whether those militarized disputes escalate to war. Since the presence of a dispute necessitates militarized interaction (threats, displays, or uses of force), all of these studies select on the dependent variable of international conflict and thus may produce biased estimates of the impact of a buildup on subsequent escalation. In order to investigate whether or not buildups might cause peace by deterrence, analysts would have to include cases of non-disputes within their studies. Reed (1998) offers a cogent discussion of the problems inattention to such questions of selection can cause in statistical analyses of conflict escalation. None has followed such guidelines, and thus none can claim to have given the "if you would have peace prepare for war" argument a satisfactory hearing.[22] What is needed is a combination of Diehl and Kingston's *onset* analysis with a Wallace-like *escalation* analysis, estimated simultaneously.

In addition to the possible consequent statistical indeterminacy of the arms buildups → war question, there is a compelling theoretical argument to be made about different arms races or arms buildups leading to different outcomes. The genesis of almost all research on arms races or arms buildups is Richardson's (1960a) differential equations model. In his model, different relationships among the important defense, fatigue, and grievance terms produce very different expectations. Specifically, they determine where in his weapons plane the security lines of the arms-racing states lie. If they lie such that each state's security line passes through the axis representing its own arms levels, all arms buildups will tend toward a stable equilibrium where the security lines intersect. What this means is that the arms increases (or decreases) of each state will move both states closer to their security lines, until ultimately the states find themselves at the intersection of their security lines. The security lines represent the amount of weapons each state feels it requires given the arsenal of the other. A situation in which both states are on their security lines would be a situation in which each state feels secure with their arsenals. I suggest this is a situation in which they are likely to be at peace. If both states started with arsenals below this equilibrium point, both would increase their arsenals (engage in military buildups)

[22] It is also relevant that none of these studies includes minor powers; all are studies only of the influence of buildups on the probability that great powers will escalate their preexisting disputes to war.

until the equilibrium was reached. They would be engaged in arms buildups in which they come to feel more secure.[23] In contrast, if each state's security line passes through the axis representing the other state's arsenal, arms races will tend to make arsenals increase toward infinity. In the process the two states will increase their arsenals out of a feeling of insecurity generated by the other's arsenal, but in so doing they will cumulatively move farther from their security lines. Taking steps to react to the other will make both feel less secure. It seems reasonable to suggest that such a situation would be especially likely to end in war.

The different scenarios within Richardson's model lead to very different expectations about war and peace. In the first, the states feel secure and eventually stop increasing their arsenals; in the second, they feel less and less secure and consequently never stop increasing their arsenals. The implication is that the question of whether arms buildups make war more or less likely by increasing or decreasing security, depends very much on within which scenario the arms race or buildup occurs. Past studies have not considered the context within which the arms buildups occur, and thus cannot distinguish between arms buildups leading to war and those leading to peace.

Although arms buildups make disputes more prone to escalate (the studies from Wallace to Sample make this clear), this is not the same thing as saying two states totally without disputes but engaged in a buildup are going to go to war (Diehl and Kingston's [1987] results suggest they are not). So, it is far from established that preparation for war and occurrence of war are the same thing. There are empirical and theoretical reasons to expect some arms buildups would lead to war while others would not. By looking at arms buildups within the context of changing power relations between dominant states and challengers, I am adding in some of the context of relations which is generally omitted. Consequently, I have not introduced war on both sides of the equation. The tests offered are not circular.[24] That fully a third of the wars in my dataset occurred in the absence of buildups is further evidence war and buildups do not perfectly covary.

[23] A similar outcome is offered by Intriligator and Brito's (1984) arms race model. In their nuclearized version of the arms race, if two states increase their arsenals beyond the point of mutual assured destruction, peace by deterrence follows.

[24] That said, if a study including cases of non-disputes, or if a study employing a selection model such as introduced by Reed (1998), were undertaken and found arms buildups do increase the probability of war, my use of arms buildups as a measure of dissatisfaction would be inappropriate. In order to be completely persuasive, however, this study would have to include minor power interactions as well as cases of non-disputes.

Nevertheless, I do not think military buildups are an ideal measure of status quo dissatisfaction. If nothing else, I am unwilling to claim the absence of a buildup necessarily indicates satisfaction with the status quo. I also am unwilling to claim that buildups as a measure of dissatisfaction are especially persuasive in situations where the challenger is far inferior to the dominant state. In such situations the weak challenger may be undertaking an extraordinary military buildup in reaction to a domestic insurgency or in an attempt to stimulate its domestic economy. Similarly, even near parity it could be that an arms buildup is caused by a domestic threat. Consequently, a satisfied state could engage in an arms buildup even at or near parity. Ideally I would like a measure of status quo evaluations that would predict which states will undertake military buildups. Unfortunately, an alternative causally prior to preparation for war does not currently exist, and thus I measure dissatisfaction with buildups by default. I express caution in using buildups as an indicator of dissatisfaction, but I do not mean in so doing to suggest I have no confidence that buildups indicate dissatisfaction. I suspect they generally do. I stand by the results in the next chapters. I simply mean to indicate my awareness that buildups are a less-than-perfect indicator of the theoretically relevant concept of status quo evaluations, and readers may want to discount my findings accordingly.

Conclusions

In this chapter I have introduced, explained, and justified the operational choices I make in my identification of local hierarchies and in my measurement of power parity and status quo evaluations. The result is an appropriate set of local hierarchies and useful measures of the theoretically important independent variables central to the multiple hierarchy model.

That said, I am aware readers may not agree with the sagacity of all of the many implicit assumptions and operational decisions I make. Readers may disagree about the appropriateness of my set of local hierarchies. I find the list satisfactory in terms of both intuitive recognition and cross-validation with other literatures. However, others might disagree about the ability to interact militarily being as important as I claim. They might accept the importance of the ability to interact militarily but reject the claim that my application of the loss-of-strength gradient captures the concept. They might accept the application of the loss-of-strength gradient conceptually, but be unconvinced the formula is correct. Readers might accept the formula, but be concerned about the transit ranges I specify based on military histories and explorer accounts. Finally, readers might accept all of the assumptions and coding decisions, yet still worry the data are of questionable reliability. I have tried to allay as many of these concerns as possible by offering a lot of information about my rationale for making the assumptions and coming to the coding decisions. I also offered some additional validity checks on the end product. At a minimum I hope I have provided sufficient information for any interested reader to replicate my efforts. I am convinced the renewed focus on regional concerns and regionalism, described in the previous chapter, is a promising renewal. However, without some agreement about what constitutes a region, I think the Renaissance of regional considerations will revert to a Dark Age of regional neglect. For this reason I believe efforts such as mine to offer reasonably clear empirical definitions of regions are worthy undertakings. I hope my regional classifications will be of use to researchers exploring questions other than those suggested by the multiple hierarchy model.

I suspect more readers will object to the military buildups measure of status quo evaluations than to the measures of power parity. In an effort to allay concerns about the status quo evaluations measure, I provided a rather detailed justification for why I believe it does not make the empirical evaluations in subsequent chapters circular. The buildups are conceptualized as preparation for war. I argue dissatisfied states are likely to prepare for war as parity nears. If preparations for war always or usually lead to war, then there will be a bias in favor of finding that status quo dissatisfaction so measured is associated with war. My reading of the empirical and theoretical literatures on arms races and arms buildups suggests that although buildups may make disputes escalate, there is no evidence arms buildups make the dispute occur in the first place. At the same time, there is no evidence arms buildups lead to peace either. The question remains open, and it seems plausible some arms races lead to war while others lead to peace. Thus the use of military buildups to measure status quo dissatisfaction is not ruled out *a priori*. The alliance similarity and UN voting similarity measures of status quo evaluations are not useful for my analyses because there is so little variation in minor power alliance portfolios and UN voting patterns. All, or almost all, minor powers would be identified as satisfied if I used those measures.

A common reaction when reading any empirical analysis of international relations is to object to the measurement of specific variables and to the rules for case selection. I know readers of this book will raise such objections to my measures and case selection rules. The tendency to do so is common because most of the theoretically important concepts in international relations research do not lend themselves to obvious measurement. Consequently, there is a lot of disagreement about measurement issues. Most of this disagreement is productive; over time we develop better measures. The measures I use are imperfect, I know they are imperfect, but I use them because there are no superior alternatives. I look forward to the productive outcome of disagreement about my measures and coding rules. Such a productive outcome will increase confidence in the relationships the multiple hierarchy model hypothesizes exist. I provide the first evaluation of those relationships in the next chapter.

5 Empirical investigations

This chapter begins the presentation of tests of the multiple hierarchy model's main hypothesis. In general what I am testing is whether the multiple hierarchy model's expectation of power parity and dissatisfaction with the status quo making war more likely is true in minor power regions as well as among the great powers. Specifically, I evaluate the hypothesis that power parity and status quo dissatisfaction increase the probability of wars involving the dominant power in international power hierarchies, be they global or local. Doing so leads to additional empirical analyses.

Units of analysis and the dependent variable

In order to test my hypothesis, I study dyadic combinations within global and local power hierarchies. I analyze whether power parity and status quo dissatisfaction tend to be present when wars are fought, and whether they tend to be absent when peace prevails.

As mentioned in the previous paragraph, the analysis is of dyads, or pairs of states. Unlike most international conflict analyses, however, I do not study all dyads nor do I observe the dyads in my studies annually. My case selection procedure is thus somewhat different from standard analyses. It differs because my theoretical structure, the multiple hierarchy model, necessitates it.

Rather than observing all dyads annually, I observe dyads of the dominant power with each contender within its power hierarchy over decade-long intervals. The multiple hierarchy model hypothesizes that when a dissatisfied challenger achieves parity with the dominant power in its hierarchy, the probability of war within the hierarchy increases. Thus, the hypothesis is about wars involving the dominant power and a primary contender within a given hierarchy. Consequently the only dyads relevant to evaluation of this hypothesis are those involving the dominant power. A few past studies (Organski and Kugler 1980: ch. 1; Houweling and Siccama 1988; Kim 1989) analyze all great power dyads whether they include the dominant power or not. I do not think power transition theory nor my multiple hierarchy model provide expectations about when two great powers, neither of which is the dominant power, will or will not wage war against each other.[1] Nor do I think traditional power transition theory or the multiple hierarchy model tell us what such wars might be about. Wars among non-dominant great powers certainly do occur (for example, great powers Russia and Japan went to war in 1904–1905 with over 200,000 battle fatalities). But power transition theory cannot tell us much about them. There is a great deal of domain restriction within power transition theory and the multiple hierarchy model, but it is not *arbitrary* domain restriction. Rather, it is domain restriction based on the theory. Remaining true to this *theoretical* domain restriction allows more accurate evaluation of the theory's hypothesis, and provides a clear benchmark for what would constitute better theory; namely, a theory accounting for relations involving the dominant powers and also additional relations in other dyads. Consequently, I only consider dyads in which one of the states is the dominant power of a local or the global international power hierarchy.

I observe these dyads over decade-long intervals. The standard duration of an observation in international conflict analyses is one year. In contrast, the standard duration of an observation in power transition research has been two decades (see Organski and Kugler 1980: ch. 1; Houweling and Siccama 1988; and de Soysa, Oneal, and Park 1997). In their initial empirical analysis of power transition theory, Organski and Kugler (1980: 48) ask: "Should one anticipate war or peace a year, ten years, or twenty years before or after the point when two countries become equal?" And then answer themselves: "We thought that a period of roughly twenty years . . . would be sufficient time" (1980: 48). The twenty-year duration of an observation is thus chosen because it is unclear when achieving parity will result in war. If parity is achieved in 1900 and the dissatisfied challenger decides it now has the opportunity for war but needs some diplomatic excuse to initiate the war (perhaps to influence potential war-joiners), there could be a delay before the

[1] However, Kim and Morrow (1992) offer an alternate power-transition-like formal model of power overtakings and war in all dyads. For an informal presentation, see Morrow (1996).

achievement of parity is acted upon via war. Consequently there needs to be some flexibility built into what is an observation so that a "true" hypothesis is not rejected.[2]

That said, however, one must be careful about allowing too generous a time-interval for an observation. Wars are infrequent events to be sure, but they are far from being as rare as we might like. Too long an interval for an observation might predispose analysis to uncover covariation between rough equality (or dissatisfaction) and war. As John Vasquez writes (1996: 37–38): "While some time lag is reasonable, a twenty-year lag is a very long time and raises the possibility that any association between a power transition and war could be coincidental." Siverson and Miller (1996: 64–65) agree: "twenty years is an arbitrary selection. There is nothing obviously wrong with it . . . At the same time, there is nothing to prevent investigators from re-testing the same relationships on periods of, say, fifteen, twenty-five, or thirty years to explore the robustness of the results."

I agree: twenty-year lags may be too generous a period within which to allow the independent variables to manifest themselves in war. However, annual observations require us to assume the effects of the independent variables are felt instantaneously. This seems too strict an assumption given our ignorance of decision processes and the crudity of our data. Consequently, I split the difference between "too generous" and "too strict," and observe dyads involving dominant powers for ten-year periods. A case, in my analyses, is thus a dyad involving a dominant power and a challenger observed over a decade. Such decade-long observations are curtailed in the event of war. Consequently, a great power dyad observation beginning in 1910 would end in 1914, rather than persisting until 1919. In this way I can ensure war does not precede my observation of parity or dissatisfaction. I aggregate each independent variable, control variable and dependent variable over the decade of each observation.[3]

The dependent variable in my analyses is a dichotomous indicator of the occurrence (1) or avoidance (0) of interstate war as defined by the

[2] This is similar to the question of what is parity or what is an overtaking, described in chapter 2. Leaders of countries may not have access to empirical datasets of national capabilities and thus might not be aware a power transition occurs in exactly 1913 (or whenever it actually occurs). Consequently, we should anticipate only a general relationship between parity and war and be concerned about periods of approximate equality rather than exact equality. Similarly, there may be some time-lag between the onset of parity and its manifestation in war.

[3] Wayman (1996) also studies decade-long dyadic observations.

Correlates of War (COW) project (Small and Singer 1982, updated by Singer 1991). Instances of militarized conflict between states in which 1,000 or more battle fatalities occur are wars according to the COW definition. When a COW war occurs and pits the members of one of my dyads against each other, the dependent variable takes on the value of 1. Otherwise, the dependent variable is coded 0. Wars persisting from one decade to the next are recorded only for the decade in which they started, since the hypothesis of the multiple hierarchy model concerns only the onset of war, not its duration. There is one instance in which more than one COW war occurred within a dyad within a decade, specifically the 1960s observation of Egypt–Israel in which both the Six Day War (1967) and the War of Attrition (1969) occurred. This is the only observation for which the dependent variable is arguably something other than 0 or 1, and I default to what appears the most appropriate category and code the observation as a 1.[4]

Theoretical and statistical issues in pooling observations

In order to evaluate the empirical validity of the multiple hierarchy model I have to aggregate regional analyses into a global whole. If the multiple hierarchy model is accurate, such aggregation is appropriate. Whether the aggregation is appropriate, however, must be determined by consideration of the data rather than by my preference that the multiple hierarchy model be found accurate. There are important theoretical issues at stake in the simple act of aggregation. However, there are wider epistemological issues at stake too: specifically whether the causes of war are truly global phenomena or whether they differ across parts of the world. These theoretical and epistemological issues are discussed in chapter 1, so I only briefly review them here.

A common caricature contrasts area specialists (who implicitly or explicitly assume there is something different about the area they study which makes it intrinsically interesting or otherwise justifies its isolated

[4] Since my cases are dyads involving the dominant powers, the wars involving such dyads are: the War of the Pacific, the Chaco War, the Iran–Iraq War, the Yom Kippur War, the Six Day War, the 1982 Israeli–Syrian War in Lebanon, the Korean War, India and Pakistan's 1965 and 1971 wars, the Vietnamese–Cambodian War of 1975–1980, the Vietnam War, the Ugandan–Tanzanian War of 1978–1979, the Somali–Ethiopian War of 1978–1979, the eastern and western fronts of World War I and World War II, the Franco-Prussian War, and the British–Russian and French–Russian warring dyads in the Crimean War.

analysis) with social scientists (who seek to uncover general patterns of political behavior free of regional context). The former supposedly would say the globe is not the sum of its regional parts, while the latter would allegedly reach the opposite conclusion.

Aggregating regional analyses into a global whole requires us to assume the caricatured political scientists are correct while the caricatured area specialists are wrong. This is exactly the assumption made by the vast majority of quantitative international conflict researchers, most of whom employ a case selection procedure of all-dyads in their analyses. They assume agglomerating dyads from every region is appropriate.

I treat this question of aggregation as a hypothesis rather than as an assumption. The multiple hierarchy model includes no region-specific, cultural, or other contextual variables as components of the story it tells about how international systems function. The model implicitly assumes global aggregation is appropriate. Nevertheless, I begin my analyses with the question of whether such aggregation is technically appropriate. Thus, I ask a statistical question: is pooling of observations from different regions the correct statistical procedure? Pooling refers to the aggregation of disparate cross-sections of observations into a unified analysis. Answering the question is thus a reasonably simple statistical reaction to my assumption that global aggregation is appropriate. Again, the answer to this simple statistical question has very important theoretical and epistemological ramifications.

An example of a statistical circumstance in which pooling would not be appropriate would be a situation in which the relationship between the independent and dependent variables is negative in one cross-section of observations but positive in the other(s). If the relationship between parity and war is negative in Africa and the Middle East, but positive in South America, the Far East, and among the Great Powers, the net effect of aggregating these regional analyses would likely yield a finding of no relationship between parity and war (since the positive relationships would cancel out the negative ones). In such a situation, pooling the regional analyses would mask parity's relationship to war, and would specifically mask the fact that this relationship varies across different regional contexts. Any analysis that pools cross-sections of data necessitates an assumption of consistent effects of the independent variables across each cross-section (for detail, see Gujarati 1995: 522–525; while for an accessible introduction to the potential statistical problems of pooling, see Stimson 1985). Thus, the first statistical question is whether I *can* pool the five regions into one unified analysis.

The procedure by which one determines whether pooling is appropriate within logistic regression estimation (the technique used throughout this book) involves comparison of the log likelihoods for regional and global (pooled) models. In this "likelihood ratio test," if the sum of the log likelihoods for separate regional analyses is not statistically significantly different from that calculated for the global/pooled analysis (multiplying these log likelihoods by –2), then pooling is appropriate. The difference between the sum of the regional log likelihoods and the log likelihood for the global model is distributed as a χ^2 statistic, where the degrees of freedom are the number of parameters estimated in the separate regional analyses less the number of parameters estimated in the pooled model. In order to address whether pooling is appropriate, I estimate regional and global versions of a model where the dependent variable is "war onset" while "power parity," "dissatisfaction with the status quo," and an interaction term multiplying parity by dissatisfaction are the independent variables. I then compare the log likelihood estimated in the global model with the sum of the corresponding log likelihoods in the five separate regional models. The difference in log likelihoods between the global and regional models is quite small. For the version of the model reported in table 5.1, the difference is just over 14. With twelve degrees of freedom this value is very far from statistically significant. I am thus confident that pooling regional analyses is statistically appropriate. However, even though I report only pooled analyses hereafter, I do not assume pooling means that the relationship between the covariates is identical across the regions, and do not make any "global" conclusions other than that there does appear to be a positive relationship between parity, dissatisfaction, and war in all of the regions studied.

A clear implication of this likelihood ratio test is that if I analyze the multiple hierarchy model, I uncover relationships across the five regions *similar enough* to be treated as parts of the same general global pattern. This is important good news for the multiple hierarchy model and support for the prevailing tendency to pool observations in international politics research.

Another consideration: controlling for time

An additional statistical issue that must be addressed before discussion and interpretation of results concerns the impact (or potential impact) of time on my analyses. Above I have described how my data represent local and global hierarchy cross-sections of the world. In addition to being cross-sectional in this specific form, my data are also time-series of the dyads over the course of their relations within their specific hierarchies. Most international relations analyses of cross-sectional time-series with a binary dependent variable ignore the fact that adjustments must be made for the possibility that observations of the same units at different points in time may not be independent. It seems impossible to argue, for instance, that British–Russian relations in the 1890s are completely independent of British–Russian relations in decades prior to the 1890s. And yet, exactly this sort of assumption is implied by not controlling for the possibility of temporal dependence of observations. Causes of the dependent variable omitted from the analysis will make the error terms for a given cross-section exhibit correlation over time. This will tend to dampen the standard errors for other covariates included in the model, thereby over-stating the confidence we have that the covariates are statistically significant. Further, if any of the variables included in the model are correlated with time itself, i.e., if there is a trend in one or another of the variables, the estimated coefficient for that variable will be inconsistent.

Beck, Katz, and Tucker (1998) offer a simple correction for such potential problems in cross-sectional time-series analyses of binary dependent variables. They demonstrate the inclusion of a series of time-interval dummy variables indicating the number of observations since the cross-section was first observed, or since the dependent variable last took on a value of 1 for that cross-section, explicitly models the effects of time on the dependent variable. Inclusion of such a string of time-interval dummy variables produces accurate standard errors and consistent coefficients. In all of the analyses below I include a series of dummy variables indicating the number of decades the dyad in question has been observed, or the number of observations for the dyad since the last instance in which a war occurred between them. In order to save space, none of the time variables are reported in the tables; none of them are significant.

Empirical results

A first analysis

Table 5.1 presents the first set of empirical results directly evaluating the multiple hierarchy model's hypothesis that parity and dissatisfaction with the status quo increase the probability of war in dyads involving

Table 5.1. *Logistic regression estimates*

Dependent variable is War Onset	
Covariate	Coefficient (Probability)
Constant	−4.337***
Parity	2.735*** (0.0082)
Dissatisfaction	2.552*** (0.0107)
Parity* Dissatisfaction	−1.929* (0.0788)
Observations: 289; Model χ^2: 22.759*; correct predictions: overall: 94.46%, wars: 0%, non-wars: 100%	

Notes: Twelve time-interval dummy variables to control for duration dependence are included but not reported in order to preserve space.

$^{*}p < 0.10$ $^{**}p < 0.05$ $^{***}p < 0.01$

the dominant states within the global power hierarchy and local hierarchies. The model estimated in table 5.1 is a unified, or pooled, model aggregating cases among the Great Powers, and from African, Far Eastern, Middle Eastern, and South American local hierarchies. A set of twelve temporal dummy variables is included to correct for the possible problems of time dependence.

I focus on GDP-based models in my discussions throughout this and the next two chapters because I believe GDP is a more accurate measure of power as conceptualized by power transition theory, and thus GDP-based models are more theoretically appropriate. However, as perusal of the Appendix will indicate, the model is supported regardless of whether power is measured by GDP or COW's composite capabilities index. The multiple hierarchy model is supported by the analysis in table 5.1 because the joint presence of parity and dissatisfaction greatly increases the probability of war within the dyads analyzed. The negative sign of the interaction term in table 5.1 should not be interpreted as refuting the hypothesis of the multiple hierarchy model. In order for the interaction of parity and dissatisfaction to be non-zero, it is mathematically necessary that both the parity and dissatisfaction individual variables be non-zero as well. Consequently, when parity and dissatisfaction are observed to be jointly present the coefficient of −1.929 for the multiplicative term is observed, but at the same time the statistically significant coefficients of +2.735 and +2.552 must also be observed for the individual terms of parity and dissatisfaction respectively. These positive individual effects combined with the negative interactive term *jointly* lead to an expected *increase* in the probability of war when parity and dissatisfaction are both present – exactly as anticipated by the multiple hierarchy model.[5] The negative coefficient on the interaction term *does not* mean the joint presence of these variables decreases the probability of war, but rather the multiplicative effect is smaller than the additive combination of the individual effects. The overall effect (multiplicative and additive) of the joint presence of parity and dissatisfaction is to increase the predicted probability of war.[6]

Table 5.2 presents the substantive impact of variation in parity and dissatisfaction on the conditional probability of war based on the results estimated in table 5.1. When neither parity nor dissatisfaction is observed, the pooled estimated probability of war for all of the dyads in the analysis is just over 1 percent. When parity and dissatisfaction are jointly present, the conditional probability of war is much higher, over 27 percent. This large change in the conditional probability of war suggests the correct signs on the variables in the model reported in table 5.1 are substantively as well as statistically significant. Combined, tables 5.1

[5] This discussion of the interaction term ignores the constant. Obviously even when the variables for parity and dissatisfaction take on values of 1 so that we get +2.735 and +2.552 but also the −1.929 value, we also get the −4.337 value of the constant. This "sums" to a negative number, but this does not mean the probability of war is negative or lower than when parity and dissatisfaction are absent. Logistic regression coefficients can only be interpreted when we exponentiate the entire function. Thus, the calculation when parity and dissatisfaction are present is $e^{(-4.337+2.735+2.552-1.929)}$ which simplifies to $e^{-0.979}$. This equals 0.376 (e being 2.71828 . . .). In order to calculate what the probability of war given these values is, we reapply the logistic functional form, and consider 0.376/1.376 which is 0.273 or 27.3%. When neither parity nor dissatisfaction is present, the calculations are simplified since we multiply all the estimates except the constant by 0. We thus consider only $e^{-4.337}$ which equals 0.0131, leading to a probability of 1.3%. So, even though the overall sum of coefficients and the constant may be less than zero, given the exponential nature of the calculations this simply means the outcome will be less than one. Given the dependent variable is the *probability* of war, a fraction is a perfectly understandable value.

[6] Significance levels for all of the variables included in table 5.1 are one-tailed because of the use of directional hypotheses. The multiple hierarchy model clearly makes directional hypotheses about the theoretically important parity and status quo evaluation variables. Those dissatisfied with one-tailed tests can determine what the probabilities of the coefficients being statistically significantly different from zero are in table 5.1 by multiplying the reported probabilities by two.

Table 5.2. *Substantive effects of Parity and Dissatisfaction for model reported in table 5.1*

Neither Parity nor Dissatisfaction	1.3%
Parity, no Dissatisfaction	16.7%
Dissatisfaction, no Parity	14.3%
Parity and Dissatisfaction	27.3%

and 5.2 provide strong global support for the multiple hierarchy model's hypothesis about war onset.

Persistent cross-regional variation

The results presented in table 5.1 are for a pooled model. Such pooling is appropriate statistically in my analysis of the multiple hierarchy model. But the appropriateness of pooling does not mean the relationship between the covariates is identical across the different regional contexts. In fact, there is reason to suspect that in spite of the statistical appropriateness of pooling the regional analyses, the relationships of parity and dissatisfaction with war should *not* be identical across regions. In chapter 1 I summarized persuasive arguments about international interactions in the developing world "looking" different from those of the developed world (Ayoob 1995; Holsti 1996; Neuman 1998). If nothing else, we might expect the relationship between parity, dissatisfaction, and war to vary somewhat across regions owing to region-specific data limitations (as will be substantiated by anyone who has looked closely at data for the Third World). Consequently, it seems very reasonable to allow for the possibility that the impact of parity and dissatisfaction with the status quo on the probability of war *will* vary across regions in spite of the result of the likelihood ratio tests reported in the previous section. I allow for the possibility of cross-regional variation by including a series of region-specific dichotomous, or dummy, variables in my statistical models.[7] I admit there is, as yet, no theoretical justification for doing so, and there is specifically no justification based on the multiple hierarchy model of power transition theory. However, as the reader will see, the inclusion of these region-specific dummy variables is not without precedent, and provides the ability to calculate region-specific

[7] "Dummy variable" refers to a dichotomous indicator constructed from an originally qualitative variable. Hardy (1993) offers an exhaustive discussion.

substantive significance of the covariates. I am thus able to respond to claims that the Third World is "different" from the First by estimating exactly how much different a given Third World region is in terms of the statistical effect of parity and dissatisfaction on the probability of war. I thus can use the region-specific dummy variables to provide evidence about these asserted differences.

But first, whether or not the inclusion of the region-specific dummy variables is a good idea statistically must be determined by the same sort of likelihood ratio tests used above to ascertain whether pooling is appropriate. Here the comparison is between the log likelihoods of global/unified/pooled models with and without the regional dummy variables. If the log likelihoods of global models with the regional dummy variables are statistically significantly different from the log likelihoods of models without them, then their inclusion is statistically justified. In order to assess the statistical appropriateness of including the regional variables, I ran models in which the dependent variable was war and the independent variables were parity, dissatisfaction, and an interaction term multiplying parity and dissatisfaction. I vary whether or not regional dummies are included in these models. I use four regional dummy variables, one for the Middle East, one for the Far East, one for Africa, and one for South America. Great Power dyads are thus the index category as no dummy specific to the Great Powers is included. The difference in log likelihoods between the models with and without regional dummy variables is just over 8. With four degrees of freedom this value is statistically significant at the $p \leq 0.05$ level. Adding regional dummy variables to my analyses is statistically appropriate and improves the overall fit of the model. A clear implication of this likelihood ratio test is that there is important information gained by including region-specific dummy variables in models evaluating the multiple hierarchy model. The regional parts of the global analysis are similar, but not uniform. There is something different about the minor power regions which distinguishes them from the Great Powers. As a result, in all the statistical models to follow, I include the four regional dummy variables.

Some readers may wonder why I do not include a dummy variable specific to each of my local hierarchies. Donald Green, Soo Yeon Kim, and David Yoon (2001) argue exactly that such "fixed effects" modeling is a major omission of most quantitative research in world politics. They demonstrate how inclusion of dyad-specific control variables substantially revises the results of a number of prominent published studies.

Table 5.3. *Logistic regression estimates with regional variables*

Dependent variable is War Onset	
Covariate	Coefficient (Probability)
Constant	−3.04**
Parity	2.003* (0.0575)
Dissatisfaction	2.395** (0.0177)
Parity* Dissatisfaction	−1.810* (0.1020)
Africa	−2.031** (0.0231)
Far East	−0.753 (0.2424)
Middle East	−0.293 (0.3685)
South America	−1.980* (0.0588)
Observations: 289; model χ^2: 30.735**; correct predictions: overall: 94.81%, wars: 6.25%, non-wars: 100%	

See notes to table 5.1.

Sensitive to such concerns, I have estimated a version of the model reported in table 5.3 with such local hierarchy-specific dummies rather than regional dummies.[8] None of the local hierarchy dummies in that analysis is anywhere near statistically significant, although the overall model is, and the coefficients for the parity and dissatisfaction variables are virtually unchanged from those reported in table 5.3. At a minimum, the results reported in this book are not affected by controlling for fixed effects, as advocated by Green, Kim, and Yoon. This non-result is not surprising theoretically. The multiple hierarchy model makes no hypothesis about variation across local hierarchies (quite the reverse,

[8] In this analysis, dummy variables were included only for those local hierarchies that experienced both peace and war. This significantly reduces the local hierarchy dummies included because seven of nine African local hierarchies, two of four South American local hierarchies, one of three Middle Eastern local hierarchies, and four of seven Far Eastern local hierarchies experienced no war during the time I study.

since it hypothesizes they function as parallels). In contrast, the critical work of Ayoob, Neuman, and Holsti, summarized repeatedly in this book, suggests larger *regional* variations.

The addition of region-specific dummy variables in table 5.3 does not change the previous finding of support for the multiple hierarchy model. Even in the presence of these new variables, both parity and dissatisfaction increase the probability of war. Again, the multiplicative term is negative, but the overall interactive effect, including the additive as well as multiplicative variables, is positive and strongly so. Perhaps most surprising are the statistically significant Africa and South America coefficients (all region-specific dummies have the anticipated negative sign).[9]

Table 5.4 reports the substantive impact of variation in parity and dissatisfaction on the probability of war within each of the five regions. Here the value of the region-specific dummy variables is dramatically clear. Having such variables in the models amounts to the logistic regression equivalent of a change of intercept parameter for ordinary least squares regression. Statistically, "switching on" the Africa dummy variable, for example, allows me to determine what the impacts of parity and dissatisfaction are across the nine African local hierarchies as opposed to within the local hierarchies of some other region or among the Great Powers. The region-specific dummy variables act like switches which allow me to calculate the substantive strength of the relationship between parity, dissatisfaction, and war within each region individually. When the four region-specific dummy variables are all "switched off," the results are specific to the Great Powers.

Clearly situations in which there is neither parity nor dissatisfaction are, according to the model estimated in table 5.3, very unlikely to coincide with wars involving the dominant power of local hierarchies or the dominant power of the overall international system. The estimated

[9] As was the case in table 5.1, all of the theoretically relevant variables are reported with one-tailed significance levels because of the use of directional hypotheses. In addition, I also make directional hypotheses about the regional control variables because I have reason to believe they should all be negative. There have been a rather large number of studies establishing how much more war-prone great powers are than minor powers (see, *inter alia*, Bremer 1980; Gochman and Maoz 1984; Jones, Bremer, and Singer 1996). Since all of my regional dummy variables represent minor power regions, it is reasonable to expect them to be negative compared to the indexed Great Power "region." Past research on the war-proneness of great powers is thus a precedent establishing a strong prior expectation of a negative estimated coefficient for each regional dummy variable. Moreover, in chapter 7 I attempt to specify variables to capture what makes the minor power regions less war-prone; in effect I attempt to specify variables which will make the regional dummy variables insignificant. One-tailed significance is easier to establish than two-tailed, so the one-tailed significance levels used here make my task harder in chapter 7.

Table 5.4. *Substantive effects of Parity and Dissatisfaction for model reported in table 5.3*

	Great Powers	Middle East	Far East	S. America	Africa
Neither Parity nor Dissatisfaction	4.6	4.6	4.6	0.7	0.6
Parity, no Dissatisfaction	26.3	26.3	26.3	4.7	4.5
Dissatisfaction, no Parity	34.6	34.6	34.6	6.8	6.5
Parity and Dissatisfaction	39.0	39.0	39.0	8.1	7.8

Cell entries are the estimated conditional probability of war (expressed as a percentage) given the conditions specified in each row in the region designated in each column.

conditional probability of war in the absence of parity and dissatisfaction ranges from less than 1 percent in Africa and South America to between 4 and 5 percent in the rest of the world. However, when parity and dissatisfaction are present, the same estimated conditional probabilities of war rise dramatically. In Africa and South America the probability of war increases more than tenfold (although admittedly a tenfold increase above a base probability of less than 1 percent is far from staggering), while in the other three regions the probability of war rises from less than 5 percent at the base to almost 40 percent.[10]

Taken together, tables 5.1 through 5.4 suggest that parity and dissatisfaction increase the estimated probability of war in the aggregate and in all five regions studied. This supports the multiple hierarchy model's hypothesis about the incidence of war within international systems. The results reported in the tables also suggest that how much parity and dissatisfaction affect the probability of war varies considerably around the world. While parity and dissatisfaction make war more likely in all five regions, the impact of these variables in the minor power regions, in

[10] One unanticipated outcome is the reasonably large independent effects of parity and dissatisfaction. The multiple hierarchy model anticipates parity and dissatisfaction are conducive to war when jointly present. Thus, though not directly contradictory to my model (since their joint presence is clearly more dangerous than the presence of either in the absence of the other), they are a surprise. Any explanation I might offer for them would be *ad hoc*, so I leave this to future investigation.

Africa and South America especially, is much smaller than among the Great Powers. Clearly power parity and dissatisfaction with the status quo do not make war as likely in Africa as they do in Europe. Thus, whereas the multiple hierarchy model *is* supported by these analyses, a new empirical puzzle is presented by considering how substantively important the covariates are within each region.

A digression about proper-noun control variables

To recap: the presence of statistically significant region-specific variables allows me to diagnose and calculate cross-regional variation in the substantive importance of the theoretically interesting variables of parity and dissatisfaction. However, the region-specific dummy variables are not theoretical concepts by any stretch of the imagination. Rather, they are *proper nouns*. Proper nouns make very poor variables for those interested in theory because they have no ready theoretical interpretation. Being in Africa, for instance, cannot *cause* dyads to vary in their war-fighting behavior compared to dyads elsewhere. There must be something else, some other factor simply more or less prevalent in Africa (such as the level of development, political capacities of the governments, etc.) causing African dyads to be different. It is this something else one would prefer to specify as a variable.

Proper-noun variables like "Africa" are of obvious statistical importance (they improve the fit of the model), but are of no immediate theoretical importance. Consequently, in spite of the interesting puzzle of cross-regional variation they allow me to discover, readers may find their inclusion in the analyses theoretically objectionable. Although sympathetic to such objections, I nevertheless include the proper-noun variables because I think the finding of such large cross-regional variation in the importance of parity and dissatisfaction is very likely to produce theoretical elaboration in the future. Further, the dummies are important statistically, as demonstrated by the likelihood ratio tests above. Finally, there are interesting precedents for inclusion of proper-noun variables in research on American politics, comparative politics, and economics.

The statistical importance of the region-specific dummy variables is that they improve the overall fit of the model to the data on war occurrence. Discussing the meaning of such variables, James Stimson (1985: 923) writes: "the estimated dummy coefficients are not explanation, but rather summary measures of our ignorance about the causes of between-unit differences, what Maddala (1971) called 'specific ignorance' as opposed to the general ignorance represented by the error term."

Stimson is referring to pooling time-series cross-sections of American politics data, in which his "units" are regions of the United States. The statistically significant regional dummies in table 5.3 are summary measures indicating something is different about Africa or South America compared to the other regions, but what that something is, is unknown. I am ignorant as to why some minor power regions differ from the Great Powers (I write "some" because in the analysis reported in table 5.3 the Far East and Middle East do not differ from the Great Powers), but I nevertheless "know," based on the statistically significant coefficients for Africa and South America, they do differ. The term "specific ignorance" nicely captures the state of my knowledge about the sources of cross-regional variation in parity and dissatisfaction's impact on war.

In American politics research such as Stimson describes, the use of proper-noun variables to represent similar specific ignorance is widespread. In presidency research it is common to include a dummy variable for specific presidential administrations to capture how "Nixon," for example, varies from other modern presidents (see Brace and Hinckley 1992 for an excellent example; and see Green, Palmquist, and Schickler 1998 [esp. p. 889] versus Erikson, Mackuen, and Stimson 1998 [esp. pp. 902–904] for a debate about the use of such proper-noun presidency control variables). In American politics voting studies and state-level public policy analyses, it is common to find a dummy variable for the South, often justified by some reference to V. O. Key's *Southern Politics in State and Nation* (1949). Since Key's time, at least, researchers in American politics have known there is "something different" about the South (party structure, racial characteristics, political culture), but often, even after controlling for such conceptual constructs, the South remains statistically significantly different.[11]

[11] For example, Timpone (1998) recently reports a statistically significant "South" variable in his analysis of turnout, in spite of the inclusion of seven demographic and five social "connectedness" variables which, one would think, would tend to account for how the South differs. Burden and Kimball (1998) similarly report a distinction between Southerners and others in ticket-splitting. In addition to the South's ubiquitous presence in such analyses, other regions may be distinct too. Joel Lieske (1993) identifies ten distinct regional sub-cultures and suggests empirical researchers in American politics might benefit from specifying their specific ignorance of more regions than simply the South.

Perhaps the most interesting precedent specific to my regional dummy variables is offered by some of Robert Barro's (1991) research on economic growth. Barro finds that in addition to theoretically appealing conceptual variables such as debt ratios, investment in human capital, and past economic performance, dummy variables for Africa and Latin America are statistically significant in virtually all of the models he runs.[12]

The point of this digression discussing the use of proper-noun dummy variables in other areas of social scientific research is to suggest a wide precedent for including regional dummies even though there is no prior theoretical justification for their inclusion. Moreover, I argue they should be included because their very inclusion uncovers a statistical puzzle of cross-regional variation in the substantive importance of theoretically interesting variables. But, this cross-regional variation will be productive only if it stimulates future theoretical elaboration.[13]

I do not mention these studies to ridicule a-theoretical inclusion of the South by American politics researchers. On the contrary, I think they are right to include variables improving the fit of their models. I also applaud their efforts to specify variables to account theoretically for why the South (or other regions) might differ from the national norm. I mention these studies to describe how "specific ignorance" variables are employed in sub-fields of political science other than international politics research. A rather fun exercise undertaken in preparation for writing this section involved perusing recent issues of *American Political Science Review* in search of proper-noun variables and discussion thereof in the text. I was very surprised by how common the practice is. Often there are interesting discussions of what the proper nouns may be capturing. In comparative politics research Kaufman and Zuckermann (1998) report a statistically significant variable called "Mexico City" in their analysis of Mexican attitudes toward economic reform. Clarke, Stewart, and Whiteley (1998) report a statistically significant "Mad Cow" variable in their analysis of Labour support in Britain. Apparently international politics researchers are alone in *not* admitting specific ignorance in their statistical models (although, for an exception in which international politics researchers do include proper-noun variables, see Kugler *et al.* 1997).

[12] In a similar vein to the exercise I undertake in chapter 7 to account for Africa's statistical significance, Barro (1991: 435) writes: "A common view is that countries in Africa or Latin America have poorer growth performance than other countries. Of course, if the nature of being in Africa or Latin America is already held constant by the other explanatory variables, continent dummies would be insignificant in equations for growth, fertility, and investment. Thus, the finding of significant coefficients on these dummies indicates that some regularities are missing from the model." Given that Africa and South America are the dummy variables for which consistently statistically significant coefficients are reported in this book, I may well be missing what this prominent economist is missing. I find it very comfortable to be specifically ignorant in such good company.

[13] Przeworski and Teune (1970: 8) write: "The goal of comparative research is to substitute names of variables for the names of social systems, such as Ghana, the United States, Africa, or Asia." In chapter 7 I substitute variables representing concepts such as level of development and political instability in an effort to replace the proper names Africa, Far East, Middle East, and South America.

A second analysis: adding additional control variables

The results presented thus far ignore a lot of empirical literature identifying important correlates of war.[14] At a minimum, these variables should be included to see if the relationships reported above might be sensitive to consideration of these known (or at least strongly suspected) correlates of war. Consequently, I now turn to a second analysis of the multiple hierarchy model. This second stage differs from the first by assessing the impact of power parity and status quo dissatisfaction while controlling for the potentially mitigating effects of alliances, joint democracy, and how militarized dyad members are.

Before discussing the results of this second-stage analysis, some explanation and justification of the control variables is in order. The first control variable indicates whether there is any form of *alliance* within the dyad in question during the decade under observation. I employ Correlates of War alliance data (described in detail in Singer and Small 1966 and Small and Singer 1969, and subsequently updated by the Correlates of War project), coding this variable as 1 whenever the dyad members are simultaneously signatories of bilateral or multilateral ententes, neutrality pacts, or defense pacts. Otherwise this variable is coded 0.[15] James Morrow's (1991) capability-aggregation model suggests alliances signify coinciding security interests and are an aggregation of capabilities against a common threat. If alliances are actions in recognition of common security interests, they should be associated with the avoidance of war between allies. In contrast, Bueno de Mesquita (1981: ch. 5) reports allies suffer an *increased* risk of finding themselves at war with one another compared to non-allies.[16] Specifically, Bueno de Mesquita (1981: 160–161) reports: "wars between allies are about three times more

[14] In fact, I am unaware of any past evaluation of power transition theory's war hypothesis or of the multiple hierarchy model in which control variables were included in the analysis. As a frequent recent contributor to the power transition literature, this is something of a guilty confession. My inclusion of control variables here is intended as more than mere atonement; I believe including them represents added value by this volume to the power transition research program.

[15] I also ran the analysis in table 5.5 with an alliance variable equal to 1 only if the dyad members were joint signatories of a defense pact. The results do not change noticeably with this alternate specification.

[16] Stuart Bremer (1992: 328) also reports allies are disproportionately likely to experience war compared to non-allies. Depending on how one aggregates types of alliances, Bremer reports that allies are from 4.5 to 5.6 times *more* likely to fight each other than are non-allies.

likely than one would expect from the distribution of bilateral military agreements . . . In fact, if we focus only on Europe . . . we find that allies fight with each other almost five times more often than expected by chance." Bueno de Mesquita accounts for this finding by suggesting allies are disproportionately likely to interact with each other, and consequentially might be more likely to discover they have serious disagreements. Given that the argument and the findings lead to contradictory expectations about whether allies will be more or less likely to fight each other, I do not make any directional hypotheses about the role of alliances.[17]

Perhaps the strongest "known" correlates of war and peace in international conflict studies are the pacifying effects of joint democracy (excellent recent summaries are offered by Chan 1997 and Maoz 1998), the bellicose potential of contiguity (compellingly demonstrated by Bremer 1992), and the inherent danger posed when two states disagree about the control of some physical territory (Vasquez 1993; Huth 1996). Of these three "prime suspects" only *joint democracy* is included here. The reason for the omission of the other two variables is the same in both cases; neither varies much, or with respect to war onset, in my dataset. Specifically, almost all of my minor power dyadic observations are directly contiguous by a land or river border because of the way I identify cases for my analyses. Since contiguity is so similar to my case selection procedure, it is statistically inappropriate to include it as a control variable. Similarly, as already discussed in chapters 3–4, the existence of a territorial disagreement (as reported by Huth 1996 and/or by Hensel 1998) is observed in every instance in my dataset in which minor powers fought wars. The territorial disagreement data available from Huth or Hensel do not systematically record such disagreements for great powers prior to 1919. Consequently, I am unable to include this variable for all of my cases. Since, for the cases I can include, the observations

[17] It seems quite possible that including an alliance control variable could substantially weaken the effect of status quo evaluations on the probability of war. If some state is satisfied with the status quo, it would seem likely to be allied with the dominant power in its hierarchy. Dissatisfied states would, in contrast, be unlikely to ally with the dominant power. As a result of these two tendencies, alliances might strongly correlate with status quo evaluations. This possibility has occurred to Woosang Kim (1991, 1992, 1996), who measures status quo evaluations via comparison of states' portfolios of alliances to the dominant power's portfolio. If Kim is right, the simple alliance variable included here is not as strongly related to status quo evaluations as one might think. I do not use the more complicated alliance portfolio version of status quo evaluations in my analyses, for reasons detailed in chapter 4.

of a 1 on my dependent variable are simultaneously observations of a 1 on this potential control variable, statistical evaluation including it is impossible.[18]

Again, the only one of these three strongest known correlates of war included is joint democracy. Both Chan (1997) and Maoz (1998) summarize a vast amount of literature seemingly conclusively demonstrating that jointly democratic dyads are disproportionately unlikely to go to war with each other. I anticipate joint democracy will decrease the likelihood of war within local and global hierarchies, and thus offer a directional hypothesis anticipating a negative coefficient. Further, the inclusion of a joint democracy measure might diminish the impact of my status quo evaluation variable specifically because the dominant powers of the global system, over the past two hundred years, have been democracies. Since the dominant power creates a status quo that is the externalization of what has proven successful in its domestic governance, other democracies should be disproportionately likely to be satisfied with the status quo of a democratic dominant power. Thus, a variable for joint democracy might correlate very highly with status quo evaluations in the global hierarchy. I measure joint democracy with Tucker's (1998) formula, which not only indicates a dyad's joint democracy, but also gauges how similarly democratic its members are. It measures what Maoz and Russett (1993) intended with their "jointreg" variable.[19]

[18] Again, as described in chapter 4, this strong overlap between territorial disagreements and war suggests such disagreements with the local dominant power *are* dissatisfaction with the local status quo. This seems very plausible to me, and might suggest additional ways to conceptualize local dissatisfaction more intuitively, or perhaps more concretely than I do. (I should mention that Hensel, Huth, and Vasquez have repeatedly made such suggestions to me about what it might mean to be dissatisfied with a local status quo.)

[19] The specific procedure I use begins with Polity III's "institutionalized democracy" score (see Jaggers and Gurr 1995 for a description of Polity III, and Gleditsch and Ward 1997 for an evaluation). This score assumes only whole-number values between 0 and 10. The first transformation I make is to add 1 to each state's democracy score to avoid having to take the square root of zero in step three. I then have values ranging from 1 to 11. The second step multiplies the democracy scores of both dyad members. This produces a value ranging from 1 to 121. The third transformation takes the square root of the multiplied adjusted democracy scores. This results in a joint democracy score for the dyad that can assume any value between 1 and 11. I then aggregate this value for the dyad over the decade in question. The problem with Maoz and Russett's "jointreg" variable (as described in Oneal and Russett 1997), is that it increases and decreases non-monotonically as a dyad member's democracy score increases, holding the other dyadic member's democracy score constant. Multiplying the modified democracy values and taking the square root overcomes this problem. The more democratic, and the more similar, two states' democracy scores are, the higher the value with Tucker's formula.

Finally, I also include a pair of variables indicating the *militarization* levels of the two states in the dyad. This variable, introduced in Bremer (1992), is the ratio of a state's share of military (number of troops and military expenditures) components to its share of demographic (total and urban population) components of the Correlates of War capabilities measure. I include the militarization level of each dyadic member, averaged over the decade under observation. States with a ratio above 1 are militarized, and are believed to be predisposed to settling disputes militarily. I anticipate militarized dominant powers will tend to deter war while militarized challengers will tend to provoke it. Consequently, I offer opposite directional hypotheses anticipating a negative coefficient for the dominant power's militarization but a positive coefficient for challenger's militarization. The primary justification for inclusion of these variables as controls here is that there might be a relationship between militarized states and my buildup measure of status quo dissatisfaction. Specifically, given the nature of the buildup measure, some states may be designated as "dissatisfied" simply because they tend always to have a large, and increasingly larger, military establishment. The preexistence of a large military establishment may be due to a cultural predisposition supporting martial values, the existence of a long-term domestic insurgency, etc. None of these potential other sources of a large military is conceptually the same thing as dissatisfaction with the local or global international status quo, and thus inclusion of a militarization variable for each dyad member could diminish the estimated coefficient for dissatisfaction. Of course, a state could be both militarized and dissatisfied, or could be dissatisfied for the same reason it is militarized. In either case militarization would inappropriately dampen dissatisfaction's effect. As a result, including militarization variables introduces a conservative bias against my dissatisfaction variable.

Table 5.5 reports a model re-estimating the effects of parity and dissatisfaction on the probability of war in pooled models with region-specific dummies, temporal dummies controlling for duration dependence, and four control variables suggested by the existing literature on the causes of war. The four new control variables potentially could diminish the importance of status quo evaluations, but this is not the case. The results reported in table 5.5 indicate that both power parity and status quo dissatisfaction increase the probability of war. The interactive term is not statistically significant at traditional levels in the model reported in table 5.5 (although it does not miss by too much), but nevertheless

Table 5.5. *Logistic regression estimates with regional and control variables*

Dependent variable is War Onset	
Covariate	Coefficient (Probability)
Constant	−2.488*
Parity	2.184** (0.0455)
Dissatisfaction	2.252** (0.0256)
Parity* Dissatisfaction	−1.508 (0.1517)
Alliance	−0.688 (0.3672)
Joint Democracy	−0.092 (0.2999)
Dominant Power's Militarization	−0.211 (0.2758)
Challenger's Militarization	0.203* (0.0787)
Africa	−1.809* (0.0806)
Far East	−0.731 (0.2821)
Middle East	−0.761 (0.2337)
South America	−1.850* (0.0819)
Observations: 287; Model χ^2: 35.319**; correct predictions: overall: 95.12%, wars: 18.75%, non-wars: 99.63%	

See notes to table 5.1.

the joint presence of parity and dissatisfaction is positive, and rather substantial (as demonstrated in table 5.6 which reports the substantive impact of changes in parity and status quo dissatisfaction).[20] Of the control variables, only challenger's militarization is statistically

[20] Readers may be interested to know that the inclusion of the challenger's militarization variable causes the standard error on the multiplicative interactive term to increase such

Table 5.6. *Substantive effects of Parity and Dissatisfaction for model reported in table 5.5*

	Great Powers	Middle East	Far East	S. America	Africa
Neither Parity nor Dissatisfaction	9.8	14.8	9.5	1.4	1.4
Parity, no Dissatisfaction	49.1	60.7	48.2	11.3	11.4
Dissatisfaction, no Parity	50.8	62.3	49.9	12.0	12.1
Parity and Dissatisfaction	67.0	76.5	66.2	21.1	21.3

Cell entries are the estimated conditional probability of war (expressed as a percentage) given the conditions specified in each row in the region designated in each column. Control variables are set at their regional means.

significant, and it has the anticipated positive sign. Dominant power's militarization has the correct sign but is not significant. The insignificant joint democracy coefficient might surprise some, but it is consistent with past analyses combining status quo evaluations and various measures of joint democracy (Lemke and Reed 1996; Clark and Hart 1998).

Table 5.6 reports substantive effects of power parity and status quo dissatisfaction based on the estimates in table 5.5.[21] As with the first-stage analysis, these tables suggest very large impacts of parity and dissatisfaction on the probability of war within all regions. The substantive effects are greater at this second stage than in the first for two reasons. First, the dampening effect of the multiplicative interaction term (the negative sign of which, again, indicates only that the multiplicative combination is smaller than the additive sum) is diminished by the introduction of the additional control variables. The second reason is that

that the coefficient is not statistically significant. If challenger's militarization is dropped from the model, the multiplicative term is statistically significant. I have no explanation for why this variable should have this effect.

[21] In all of the substantive effect calculations reported in this book I include regional means (or modes) for control variables whenever the p-value for their coefficients is smaller than 0.20. Such values are not statistically significant in the standard sense, but given the possible inefficiency introduced by my reasonably small sample size, I thought it better to err on the side of cautious inclusion.

the challenger's militarization variable (held constant at regional averages in these calculations) is positive. Including it in these calculations simply raises the estimated probability of war for all dyads.

In the absence of parity and dissatisfaction, the estimated probability of war ranges from an African and South American low of just over 1 percent, to a Middle Eastern high of almost 15 percent. Comparing situations in which both power parity and dissatisfaction with the status quo are present with these baselines, we see substantial increases in the estimated probability of war. Great Powers are almost seven times more likely to engage in war given parity and dissatisfaction. Similar increases are observed for Far Eastern and Middle Eastern local hierarchy dyads. In South America and Africa the increases are more than tenfold (again, however, a tenfold increase over a baseline probability of around 1 percent is far from overwhelming).

The expectations of the multiple hierarchy model are strongly supported by this second-stage analysis. Power parity and dissatisfaction with the status quo greatly increase the estimated probability of war within all of the regions studied, even after controlling for the possibly mitigating effects of alliances, joint democracy, and militarization levels. All of the models estimated in the first and second stages support the war-onset hypothesis of the multiple hierarchy model. Whether one considers competitions like those between Uganda and Tanzania in the 1970s or between Germany and Britain at the beginning of the twentieth century, parity and dissatisfaction seem to increase the likelihood such competition will result in war.

This is strong support for the multiple hierarchy model's expectation about when wars are more likely. However, the reader must bear in mind that this expectation about when wars will be more likely only applies to dyads which include the local or global dominant power. Above I referred to this restricted applicability as *theoretical domain restriction*, and this is an accurate description. Wars have occurred outside of the set of dyads comprising the multiple hierarchy model's theoretical domain. Neither traditional power transition theory nor the multiple hierarchy model can say anything about these wars. Earlier in this chapter I referred to the Russo-Japanese War as a war between great powers, neither of which was the systemic dominant power. As such, the Russo-Japanese War was an event my model does not anticipate. This is not to say the model suggests the Russo-Japanese War should not have occurred. Rather, it is an event beyond the theoretical domain of the model. Other wars among non-dominant great powers, such as the 1866 Seven Weeks War and the 1939 Nomohan War between Japan and the Soviet Union, are similarly beyond the theory's purview. In the minor power regions, wars external to the theoretical expectations have also occurred. In 1962 China and India went to war along their Himalayan border. China and Vietnam went to war in 1979 and again in the mid 1980s. None of these wars are anticipated by the multiple hierarchy model because the states fighting them are not identified as members of the same local hierarchy.[22]

I mention these wars that are beyond my model's theoretical purview as a caution against my otherwise unrestrained tendency to trumpet the empirical validity of the multiple hierarchy model of power transition theory. The model does a very good job accounting for international relations within the circumscribed set of dyads comprising its theoretical domain. But readers should bear in mind there are dyads beyond this theory-restricted domain, and a theory accounting for both the behavior of the multiple hierarchy model's dyads and that of additional dyads would be a superior theory. Readers might also keep in mind that in the next chapter I extend the theory's domain and include dyads like China–Vietnam.

Conflict prior to the time-frame of my analysis

In addition to wars and relations beyond the theoretical domain of the multiple hierarchy model, there have also been wars and relations between states relevant to the theory but prior to the time-frame included in the preceding analyses. The specific periods I analyze are dictated by data limitations or by the fact that the states in the minor power local hierarchies were not sovereign entities until relatively recently. An exception is offered by Sino-Japanese relations in the East Asian local hierarchy of the Far East prior to World War II. China and Japan have interacted for many centuries, and have waged war repeatedly in the modern era (in 1894–1895, 1931–1933, and 1937–1945). Have these wars coincided with the presence of power parity and dissatisfaction with the status quo?

[22] I calculate that at the times of these wars, China could reach Hanoi, but Vietnam could not reach Beijing. China could almost reach New Delhi. Given this, it is not surprising that the wars occurred far from China's core territory, that all three were initiated by China, and that fatality levels were reasonably low in all three events. However, the occurrence of these three wars demonstrates these states did interact militarily. This contradicts what their relations should be given my conceptual definition of local hierarchies.

This is a difficult question to answer because persistent upheaval and turmoil in China as the Manchu dynasty disintegrated make data either scarce or unreliable (or both) for China prior to the Communist takeover in 1949 (at which point other problems of data reliability and availability arise). Nevertheless, I make an effort to determine whether Sino-Japanese relations prior to World War II are consistent with the multiple hierarchy model's expectations by considering what limited information is available in extant datasets and from historical accounts.

Angus Maddison (1989) offers historically reconstructed estimates of gross domestic product in constant prices. Included in his series are estimates for both China and Japan back to 1900. As perusal of his estimates makes abundantly clear, China's GDP was consistently much larger than Japan's throughout the period 1900–1939. In fact, China's GDP is estimated to have been from two to four times as large as Japan's in this period.

The immediate conclusion is Japan was not as powerful as China at any point during this time-period, and consequently none of their wars were fought at parity. However, this conclusion is, perhaps, a superficial one. If one consults any account of Chinese history for the period in question (such as that offered by Langer 1948), it becomes clear how much turmoil plagued China in the latter half of the nineteenth and the first half of the twentieth century. In the 1860s the Taiping Rebellion eventually concluded, but not before laying waste much of the country and resulting in an estimated 20 million deaths. In 1900 the Boxer Rebellion resulted in far fewer deaths, but generated foreign interventions and the near total disruption of civil administration for the ensuing few years. In 1911 the Chinese Revolution led to the selection of Sun Yat Sen as president, but his presidency ended within a few months as he resigned in favor of General Yuan Shih-k'ai. In 1912 the last Manchu emperor, Pu Yi, abdicated. The ensuing Chinese Republic proved untenable, and was rapidly undermined by local military leaders who ignored it. From 1920 to 1926 a civil war among the various local military officials further devastated the nation. In 1927 the Kuomintang and the Chinese Communist Party began their long struggle against each other (a depressing but gripping account of Chinese political disintegration at the end of the Manchu dynasty is offered by Jansen 1975: ch. 2).

This overly brief summary of the low-points of Chinese history during this period is presented in order to suggest that estimates of Chinese GDP at the beginning of the century and the likely amount of resources available to the central Chinese government are vastly different quantities. In contrast, in the same period, Jansen (1975: 62) informs us that at no point was "the government of Japan . . . unable to collect its taxes or meet its obligations." It seems likely, based on Chinese disintegration and Japanese stability, that the GDP reported for Japan might well represent the resources available to the Japanese government, but that the GDP reported for China is a gross over-statement of the resources available to China's government(s).

The question then becomes how much of an over-statement is China's GDP? The question reintroduces the concept of relative political capacity (discussed in chapter 4), traditionally used in power transition analyses to gauge the efficiency of governments (Organski and Kugler 1980: appendix 1; Arbetman and Kugler 1997). I suspect Japan's RPC was very high during this period, while China's was very low.

Unfortunately my suspicion about Chinese RPC can be neither confirmed nor refuted because in order to calculate the RPC of a government, data on tax revenues and on the relative size of important sectors of the economy are required. Such data do not exist for China during this period. Not surprisingly, such data do exist for Japan. Kugler and Domke (1986: 51) report that in response to the demands of fighting the Russians in 1904–1905, the Japanese government extracted so much in taxes from its population that its RPC statistic was 4.4. RPC is a ratio of *actual* tax extraction to *expected* tax extraction, where the "expected" is calculated by comparison with as many other countries as possible in terms of level of development, which sectors of the economy are prominent, etc. Thus, the Japanese extracted over four times as many resources from their population and economy as they might be expected to have done based on the extractive capacity of similarly endowed states at that time. This is very impressive indeed. The Japanese government was clearly a very capable one.

There is one source of data about the revenue available to both the Japanese and Chinese governments for much of the period of interest here. Arthur Banks (1971) reports "national government revenue" of the central government in current US dollars as well as revenue per capita.[23] Government revenue may come from a variety of sources (taxes, loans,

[23] Banks (1971: ix–xxiii) himself cautions users about the reliability of some of his data. In discussing his national revenue data he writes: "Revenue and expenditure data, particularly when expressed in US dollar equivalents, are peculiarly susceptible to both random and systematic error" (p. xviii). Banks also indicates which data points are "real" observations and which are linear interpolations or extrapolations, so that researchers will know where to be especially cautious in using his data. For the period 1874 through 1913 Banks reports two actual observations (1883 and 1913). The rest of the years are interpolations

tribute, etc.) and is not the same thing as the tax revenue central to RPC. Since a large revenue could be symptomatic of government weakness, as would be the case if much of the government's revenue came in the form of loans, one should be careful in using such data as an indicator of governmental strength. At a minimum though, the revenue of the government, from whatever source, is an indication of the resources available to that government, if only for that year.

The Chinese government did not enjoy vast resources, judging by its revenue and especially by its revenue per capita. Banks reports the Chinese government enjoying, in 1900, a revenue of $233 million. This represents $0.59 per capita. In contrast, the Japanese government had revenues of $174 million, but this represents $3.88 per head of population. Given a much smaller demographic base and economy with which to work, the Japanese government collected almost as much revenue in aggregate as the Chinese government, and substantially more relatively.

An indicator, albeit a crude one, of the capacity of the Japanese government compared to the Chinese government can be constructed by dividing Japan's national government revenue per capita figure by China's. This gives us a ratio indicating how much revenue Japan collected, given its demographic potential, compared to China. If we weight Maddison's estimate of Japan's GDP with this ratio, we produce figures suggesting that in the early part of the twentieth century, Japan and China were approximately equal in power. This situation persisted through the early 1920s, beyond which point Japan pulled clearly ahead (although the two states were again approximately equal in the early to mid 1930s).[24] If we adjust the power relationship between China and Japan in order to account for Chinese political disintegration, it looks as though the two states were equal in power when they fought their war in the 1890s (extrapolating the trends back just a few years), but that Japan was clearly superior by the time the two states fought their wars in the 1930s. This is mixed support of the multiple hierarchy model's expectations.

What about dissatisfaction with the status quo? Was Japan undergoing an extraordinary military expenditure increase prior to the wars? Again, the empirical record for China is very incomplete and estimates

or extrapolations. Given how chaotic Chinese history was during this time, linear extrapolations must be treated as suspect. As a consequence of this, I encourage readers to treat my discussion of Chinese power trends with a healthy dose of skepticism.

[24] Actual figures available from the author.

prior to the 1894 war are unavailable. However, the COW project does report military expenditure data for China and Japan consistently after 1896, and this data, with the procedure detailed in chapter 4, indicates the Japanese were not undergoing a buildup relative to China in the late 1890s, but were thereafter. According to this measure the Japanese were dissatisfied from the early 1900s through World War II. This suggests the wars in the 1930s were fought under a situation of status quo dissatisfaction, as anticipated by the multiple hierarchy model.

In the foregoing pages I have attempted a pseudo-empirical analysis of Chinese and Japanese power trends and status quo evaluations in order to determine whether pre-1950 relations within this East Asian local hierarchy were consistent with my model's expectations. The answer is one of mixed support. I cannot determine whether the Japanese were dissatisfied prior to the 1894–1895 Sino-Japanese War (they were not dissatisfied after the war, which is consistent with the fact that they were the victors), but it does seem that China and Japan may have been at parity at that time. When the wars occurred between China and Japan in the 1930s, the Japanese were dissatisfied, according to the buildup measure, but they were clearly more powerful than the Chinese. Support for multiple hierarchy model expectations is thus mixed.

Historical accounts of Sino-Japanese relations prior to World War II also offer mixed support for my expectations. Several contemporary statements by Japanese opinion leaders suggest the 1894–1895 Sino-Japanese War was viewed in Tokyo as a struggle over the status quo in East Asia. Until the 1890s East Asia was totally dominated by China (Jansen 1975: ch. 1), and Korea was economically little more than a tribute-paying Chinese enclave. The Japanese had wanted greater access to Korean resources and consumers for some time. Matters came to a head when the leader of the pro-Japanese faction within Korean politics was assassinated in China, and when the Chinese returned his assassin in triumph to Seoul. The Japanese dispatched troops to Korea in July 1894, sunk a Chinese troopship on July 24, and declared war on August 1.

Contemporary newspaper editorials in Tokyo described the Sino-Japanese War as one in which "We intend only to develop world civilization and to defeat those who obstruct it . . . this is not a war between people and people and country and country, but a kind of religious war" (quoted in Jansen 1975: 47). That the Japanese were dissatisfied with the East Asian status quo is strongly suggested by claims Japan could not compete under the Chinese-dominated system, and that things would be very different once Japan beat China: "Japan's victory shall mean free government, free religion, free education, and free commerce for 600,000,000 souls that live on this side of the globe" (again, quoted in Jansen 1975: 47).

The Sino-Japanese War of the 1890s appears to have been a conflict between actors with widely different views about international politics in East Asia. The long-standing status quo in East Asia was one in which China dominated all interactions. Language, culture, trade, and diplomacy all flowed through the Chinese capital, and usually involved both tangible and intangible tribute paid to the Chinese. This status quo went unchallenged until Western incursions into the region, beginning in earnest with the Opium War in the 1840s, allowed the possibility of questioning Chinese dominance. Increasing interaction with the West necessitated a change in East Asian politics, but the Chinese and Japanese elites disagreed strongly over what this change meant. In China, the elite denied any reform was necessary. In Japan, the elite was convinced modernization, although within an Asian framework, was necessary. Consequently, the Japanese and Chinese held quite different views about the status quo in their local hierarchy. Jansen (1975: 69) writes: "the 1880s witnessed a vigorous polemic against the backward-looking societies and governments of Korea and China, as well as enthusiastic and romantic views of the role a modernized and democratic Japan might play in Asia." Swift victory in the Sino-Japanese War "proved" to the Japanese (and to many of the Chinese counter-elite too) that their reaction to changed reality was superior to Chinese retrenchment.

Such historical presentations, and certainly the contemporary quotes cited above, are consistent with multiple hierarchy expectations that wars are fought within local hierarchies in order to change the patterns of inter-state interactions within them. It seems possible to argue the 1890s saw the culmination of a rise of Japanese power coupled with a decline of Chinese power, which provided the Japanese with a window of opportunity to beat the Chinese and change relations, specifically economic relations, in East Asia.

It is harder, based on the diplomatic histories I have consulted, to make similar arguments about the conflicts between China and Japan culminating in their wars in the 1930s. Brecher and Wilkenfeld (1997: 150–157) describe Japanese decision-making in the 1930s as extremely disjointed. They claim the Emperor, the civilian government, the general staff in Tokyo, the Kwantung Army headquarters in Manchukuo, and local field commanders all made foreign policy decisions affecting Sino-Japanese relations, and these various decision-making groups frequently contradicted each other.

A somewhat more unified view of Japanese revisionist goals in the 1930s (and one certainly more consistent with the multiple hierarchy model) is offered by Beasley (1987, esp. ch. 13), who recounts how the Great Depression's effects in Asia led the Japanese to begin thinking of "the concept of a New Order (*shin-chitsujo*). The expression was first applied to Japan, Taiwan, Korea, North China, and Manchukuo" (1987: 199). Ignoring ethnic chauvinist overtones, this New Order was to be one of economic cooperation and integration. The Japanese would offer the industrial engine transforming raw materials from these other states into finished goods all the peoples of East Asia could share. The idea was a Japanese-dominated East Asian separatist reaction to the losses in trade suffered since 1929.

A multiple hierarchy model interpretation of the Japanese New Order might suggest the Japanese were dissatisfied with the lack of coordination between states in East Asia, were specifically dissatisfied with the economic consequences of this lack of coordination, and sought to redraw the rules of interaction within East Asia in order to correct these flaws. Beasley (1987: 202) goes on to describe how this New Order developed in Japanese thinking to produce the Greater East Asian Co-Prosperity Sphere: "From the point of view of ministers in Tokyo, none of this was meant to bring about territorial expansion. They still thought in terms of informal empire, that is, of securing an increase in Japan's privileges through pressure exerted on Asian governments, including that of China." If Brecher and Wilkenfeld's contention of disjointed centers of Japanese decision-making is accurate, it might well be that the military elite had a different point of view about what the Co-Prosperity Sphere entailed. At a minimum, it appears clear (based on Morley 1983) that the Chinese were opposed to a Japanese-dominated sphere of economic cooperation. Consequently, war broke out.[25]

[25] Nish (1977: 37) and Beasley (1987: 198) suggest that in both the 1890s and 1930s, the impact of European or American influence on the foreign policies of China and Japan with respect to each other was nonexistent or negligible. Nish suggests this was true because the non-Asian great powers themselves were divided about whether Chinese or Japanese supremacy was more desirable in East Asia in the 1890s. Beasley suggests the non-Asian great powers did not concern themselves in Sino-Japanese affairs (and infamously did not do so when China specifically asked the League of Nations for help in resisting Japanese aggression) in the 1930s because they were so concerned with domestic economic affairs and with military threats closer to home.

This is an admittedly limited and perhaps unrepresentative survey of diplomatic histories of Sino-Japanese relations prior to World War II. Nevertheless, there are some intriguing pieces of evidence of these relations conforming with what the multiple hierarchy model would suggest relations within an East Asian local hierarchy should have been. It seems likely the 1894 Sino-Japanese War was one pitting a dissatisfied Japan against the complacent traditional local dominant power, China. It is less obvious that the wars of the 1930s were consistent with patterns anticipated by the multiple hierarchy model, but a case can be made that the Greater East Asian Co-Prosperity Sphere was an alternate local status quo preferred by a dissatisfied Japan. Claims that there was no unified Japanese position on foreign policy, the absence of a unified Chinese position, and the great importance of non-East Asian forces in creating Japanese dissatisfaction (the Great Depression was not East Asian in origin, after all), must all temper any claim that the 1930s in East Asia conform to the model's expectation. Thus, the diplomatic histories offer mixed support for the multiple hierarchy model.

Conclusions

In this chapter I evaluated the multiple hierarchy model, and specifically analyzed the hypothesis linking power parity and dissatisfaction with the status quo to a greater likelihood of war in the global and local hierarchies. In so doing I investigated the prior hypothesis that pooling disparate evaluations of regions into a global whole is statistically appropriate. I found it is. I then determined that in spite of the general similarity across regions which makes pooling statistically appropriate, there are nevertheless important cross-regional differences which make it statistically appropriate to include region-specific control variables.

Having established what the statistical model employed to test my hypothesis should look like, I then turned to the actual analysis of the hypothesis. I first presented straightforward models using GDP-based measures of power (replications with COW-based measures are offered in the Appendix). I found power parity and dissatisfaction with the status quo increase the likelihood of war. I then found this hypothesis-confirming result persists even when controlling for a set of control variables which plausibly could confound the relationship between my theoretically important variables and war. I conclude that this is strong support for the empirical validity of the multiple hierarchy model, at least for the five regions and the time-periods analyzed here.

In order to evaluate how well the multiple hierarchy model's expectations conform with empirical reality beyond the dyadic relationships evaluated in the global statistical analysis, I conducted a pseudo-empirical case study of Sino-Japanese relations prior to World War II. I traced, as best I could given the quality of available data, relative power relationships and Japanese status quo evaluations over the 1900–1939 period. Doing so suggests the Chinese and Japanese were roughly equal in power for the first half of this period, but Japan was stronger for the second half. I also discovered Japan was undergoing an extraordinary military buildup after 1900, and consequently the wars fought in the 1930s were ones in which status quo dissatisfaction was present. I also consulted the accounts of Sino-Japanese relations provided by historians to determine if those relations were consistent with my model's expectations. I am reasonably convinced that in the early part of the period (and importantly in the Sino-Japanese War of 1894–1895) those relations were consistent with the multiple hierarchy model's expectations. The latter half less clearly fits theoretical expectations, but it is possible to depict Japanese behavior as that of a dissatisfied actor with an alternate view of what the local status quo should be, and subsequently acting to institute this alternate status quo.

The combination of the general analysis of all the regions and the detailed analysis of Sino-Japanese relations prior to World War II suggests substantial support for the multiple hierarchy model. All models are simplifications of reality, but the multiple hierarchy model focuses on sufficiently important variables that it accords quite well with reality as demonstrated in this chapter. The various analyses reported here clearly justify continued evaluation of the multiple hierarchy model.

As described at length above, I include a set of region-specific dummy variables in the statistical analyses of the main hypothesis. These variables should be included, if only on statistical grounds, because they improve the fit of the statistical model. However, their inclusion has important and, I think, fascinating implications. Their inclusion allows me to calculate the importance of power parity and status quo evaluations for the probability of war for each region individually. Consequently, I can determine power parity and status quo dissatisfaction make war very likely among the Great Powers, quite likely in the Middle and Far East, but only marginally likely in South America and Africa. There is a diminishing importance, substantively, of parity and dissatisfaction as focus shifts from the Great Powers to Africa. Parity and dissatisfaction *do* increase the probability of war in all five regions, but they do so at much lower rates of increase in some regions.

The coefficient for the Africa dummy variable in tables 5.3 and 5.5 is generally always the largest, and certainly the most consistently significant, of the regional dummy variables. That it is negative means that Africa is, according to this analysis, the most peaceful region studied. Thus, another way of rephrasing the question of why there is cross-regional variation in the substantive importance of parity and dissatisfaction on the probability of war is to ask why Africa is so peaceful? Is there an "African Peace"? I take up such questions in chapter 7.

Before doing so, I undertake one more diagnostic consideration. As described in chapter 3, the multiple hierarchy model assumes the local hierarchies function as parallels to the overall global hierarchy provided the great powers do not interfere. Clearly some great powers can interfere in some local hierarchies. In chapter 6 I replicate and extend the analyses presented here, but do so allowing directly for great power participation in local hierarchies.

6 Further investigations I: great power interference?

Perhaps the most obvious criticism of the results reported in chapter 5 is they are based on analyses of a dataset which includes neither cases nor variables representing great power interference in minor power interactions. This may be especially egregious in some situations. For instance, it is hard to think of the outbreak of various Arab–Israeli wars without consideration of American and Soviet activity in providing weapons, intelligence, etc. At the same time, it is not hard to imagine that Israel and Egypt were at parity, one of them dissatisfied with the local status quo, and both itching to go to war with the other in, say, 1965. However, escalation in Vietnam might have drawn American strategic attention away from the Middle East, and thus the Americans might have pressured the Israelis into avoiding war at that point in time.

In these hypothetical cases the actions of external great powers affect whether minor powers wage war. In the first case superpower activity makes war more likely, while in the second it makes it less likely. In both cases the activity of one or both superpowers might have been an important causal factor in whether war occurred. In none of the analyses in chapter 5 is such activity represented in any way. Consequently, if external great power activity is systematically related to the occurrence of minor power war, the analyses in chapter 5 are potentially contaminated by omitted variable bias. Omitting variables does not mean I believe they have no effect. But it does force me to assume, when interpreting my results in the previous chapter, that parity, dissatisfaction, the regional variables, and the four control variables are completely statistically independent of the activity of powerful external actors. The less accurate this assumption, the more reason to question chapter 5's results.

However, it would be rash to reject the conclusions of that chapter out of hand. Rather, I suggest confidence in my empirical claims would be bolstered were I to show the inclusion of great power activity does not meaningfully change my results. If I am able to replicate chapter 5's analyses with great power activity included yet estimate similar results, then we know great power interference does not negate the strong support chapter 5 seems to show for the multiple hierarchy model. I undertake exactly this sort of replication here. I then extend the analyses by including the extent of possible great power interference as a fifth control variable. Doing so leads to estimates consistent with my claim that the multiple hierarchy model enjoys empirical support, but also consistent with an argument recognizing great power activity as an important independent factor in the onset of minor power war.

Including great power interference in local hierarchies

Two alternatives occur to me as possible techniques for including great power activity in my analysis of war and peace in local hierarchies. I might include a set of independent variables indicating whether various types of great power interference occurred. This would essentially control for great power activity in the analysis of the variables central to my argument. A problem with this technique arises because I am unconvinced systematic data on great power interference can be obtained. Some interference is overt and easily observed. Some is not. Moreover, I suspect the data quality varies dramatically from great power to great power (some being better able, or more motivated, to hide their interference) as well as from region to region (with, for instance, Middle Eastern coverage being better than African coverage). I do not see how this technique could overcome the omitted variable problem. Rather, I suspect it would simply introduce profoundly non-random missing data problems.

Happily an alternative exists, consistent with the basic conceptualization driving the identification of local hierarchies in the first place. Recall from chapter 4 that local hierarchies are constructed based on the ability of states to interact militarily with each other. In extending this thinking to great power interference, I suggest a satisfactory way to overcome the non-random missing data problems discussed above is to calculate which great powers can overcome the tyranny of distance and transport military resources into the various local hierarchies. When I discover Britain is able to transport more than 50 percent of its power to Dakar, for example, I conclude Britain can interfere in West Africa. If I then include Britain as a contender in the West Africa local hierarchy and treat it like any other local contender, I am, at least partially, representing Britain's ability to interfere in West African local relations. Undertaking similar calculations for all great powers for all local hierarchies, allows me to determine with which local hierarchies each great power might be able to interfere. I propose *including* great powers in various local hierarchies based on their ability to interact militarily with them.

This requires me to relax the mutual reachability assumption central to identification of local hierarchies as described in chapter 4. Since I do not propose relaxing the mutual reachability assumption for identification of minor power local hierarchy members, I am suggesting assigning great powers differently to local hierarchies than I do minor powers. Generally I believe consistent coding is good. However, I do not think my revised and inconsistent coding here is especially troublesome, because I am interested in great power ability to interfere in local hierarchies, not in minor power ability to interfere in the global hierarchy. American participation in the Vietnam War had enormous consequences for the Southeast Asian local hierarchy (essentially prolonging the war for ten years), but it never threatened the global power hierarchy. There was never any possibility North Vietnamese soldiers would fight on American soil, or even against American military bases elsewhere in Asia. What I am suggesting is mutual reachability identifies minor power contenders within local hierarchies for reasons argued in chapter 4, but one-way reachability identifies which great powers are contenders in which local hierarchies and only in those local hierarchies.

The result of this revised case construction technique (the nuts and bolts of which are described in the next section) is a reasonably large number of additional cases included in my analyses. All of the cases included in the analyses in chapter 5 are included in the revised version of the dataset investigated in this chapter. But added to these existing cases are decade-long observations of dyads composed of a great power and a local dominant power. This adds a set of cases highlighting great power interference, if it occurs, by treating great powers as local hierarchy members.

Defining great power membership in local hierarchies

The first step in assigning great powers as members of local hierarchies is identifying which states are great powers. I default to the well-worn set identified by a historians' consensus for the Correlates of War project: United States (from 1898), Great Britain (from 1816), France (from 1816), Prussia/Germany (1816–1945), Austria-Hungary (1816–1918), Italy (1860–1943), Russia/Soviet Union (from 1816), China (from 1950) and Japan (1895–1945). For these states I consulted Gardiner's (1979, 1983) compendia of the world's navies. I define states with navies featuring at least ten ships of 10,000 tons as sufficiently large enough for global reach. In chapter 4 I identified a navy of at least ten ships of 1,000 tons as large enough for regional maritime troop transit. The greater demands of trans-oceanic movement of military forces suggest the need for a larger navy than is required to move troops along a coastline. Perusal of Gardiner's entries for various states produced a reasonably valid list with global reach capabilities.[1] The list of great powers with sufficiently large navies includes: the United States (from 1901), Great Britain (from 1888), France (from 1891), Germany (1900–1920), Italy (1890–1920), Russia/Soviet Union (1894–1945, and from 1953), and Japan (1900–1904, and 1913–1945). The Austro-Hungarian Empire and China never had navies with at least ten ships of 10,000 tons during the period I study.[2]

Having identified which great powers are able to move by sea, I also need to determine which great powers can move by land. This entails consideration of the transportation infrastructure between the Soviet Union and the Middle and Far East, and between China and her Far Eastern neighbors. My consultation with the various atlases and compendia described for roads and railways in chapter 4 suggests that by the 1950s (the time-period in which Far Eastern local hierarchy analyses begin), the Soviets had so many railroads and paved roads they could

[1] Readers unfamiliar with the size of naval vessels might perceive a ship of 10,000 tons as gargantuan. This size is actually quite modest by modern standards. The aircraft carrier USS *Ronald W. Reagan* is over 100,000 tons. India has had several vessels in its navy since independence at well over 10,000 tons. The figure is not gargantuan. Many navies have several ships this large, but it is very rare for a navy to include at least ten ships of this size.

[2] Perhaps I should include airlift capabilities. Although I agree this could offer an improvement, I do not include them because of complications. One would want to know how the troops would be landed. If they are dropped, how are they supplied? If the planes land, how do we know that a "friendly" airfield is available? Should I use naval transport until World War II and airlift capacity thereafter? If I use both simultaneously, how do I trade off between them, i.e., what is the air–sea "exchange rate"? Finally, states with big navies often also have large airlift capacity. Thus, consideration of airlift capacity might needlessly complicate data collection for little, if any, gain. Of course, these are untested assertions. Were someone to include airlift capacity, their results might differ from and/or be more valid than mine.

move forces at Bueno de Mesquita's (1981) 500 miles per day, at least to their own borders. These sources suggest China has not been so well equipped in transportation infrastructure. As a result I default to my chapter 4 Asian 100 miles per day transit range, but the infrastructure is especially poor through the Himalayas, and consequently I assume 50 miles per day for Chinese transit there.

Having determined what the transportation capabilities of the great powers are, I next need to know what distances must be overcome in transporting troops from home to each local hierarchy. I use the capital city of the local dominant power as the end point of such potential troop transits, and the great power's capital as the starting point. I employ the technique described in chapter 4 to calculate, using ExpertMaps, the most likely route that would be taken. For minor powers with inland capitals, I calculate straight line coast-to-capital distances and use the miles-per-day figures described for land travel in the region-specific descriptions given in chapter 4. The power figures degraded are shares of global hierarchy power (i.e., the shares of GDP among great powers listed above), with only the degraded "remainder" used to indicate each great power's power in any local hierarchy in which it can interfere.

Employing this technique I calculate the United States is an actor in all South American local hierarchies from 1901 (although only from 1920 in the Central local hierarchy), Britain can reach the Northern Tier local hierarchy from 1888, France can do so from 1960, and the Soviet Union can do so in the period 1940–45 and from 1953. Additionally, the Soviet Union can reach the Atlantic Coast local hierarchy of South America from 1960.

Turning to the Middle East, I calculate the United States can interfere within all three local hierarchies over the entire 1960–1990 period, Britain and France can interfere in the Arab–Israeli local hierarchy for all three decades, and the Soviet Union can interfere in both the Arab–Israeli and Northern Rim local hierarchies of the Middle East by sea and land, respectively. In the Far East, China is able, by land, to interfere in the Southeast Asian, Burma–Thailand, and Korean Peninsula local hierarchies.[3] Similarly, I calculate the Soviet Union is able to interfere,

[3] My calculations suggest China expends slightly over 50 percent of its power resources in transit to New Delhi and/or Islamabad; consequently I do not include China in either the South Asia or Afghanistan–Pakistan local hierarchies. I understand my measures are somewhat imprecise and overly rigid adherence to my 50 percent power loss cut-off might be objectionable. However, my sense is I am already over-generous in my estimation of transit ranges and thus feel the 50 percent cut-off should be adhered to here. The fact

by land, in the East Asia and Korean Peninsula local hierarchies. Finally, the United States is able to exert influence in all seven Far Eastern local hierarchies for the entire period. Readers may be surprised Britain and France are not calculated as able to interfere in Far Eastern local hierarchies. This seems to fly in the face of the fact they had colonies in this region as World War II ended. I suggest to skeptics that the tyranny of distance, in a world where the superpowers were replacing them as the main international interferers, offers a rather simple explanation for why they ultimately acquiesced in decolonization.

Only the United States is able to interfere with all nine local hierarchies in Africa (although the calculations indicate substantial power loss in movement from Washington DC to the Central Lowlands and Central Highlands local hierarchies). Great Britain, France, and the Soviet Union are all able to interfere in the Maghreb, West Africa, and Gulf of Guinea local hierarchies from 1960.

One last calculation must be described. Vasquez (1996: 41–42) argues persuasively about American exclusion from the great power hierarchy until after World War II as one of the most objectionable coding decisions within power transition research. Consequently, I took advantage of the opportunity of calculating all of these distance and power projection figures to determine if the United States could "reach" Britain (as "local" dominant power of the global hierarchy) prior to 1945. Not surprisingly, I calculate that the United States can reach Britain from 1901, but in so doing, especially into the 1920s, some 40 percent of US power share is "spent" in transit. Thus the United States that "reaches" the other great powers in the first half of the twentieth century is a much weakened US. Britain remains the strongest state, and is thus the legitimately dominant power, so long as the global hierarchy is Eurocentric. In the empirical analyses to follow, a set of US–UK dyads is included in which the United States effectively "interferes" in the global hierarchy.

Replication with great powers as actors in local hierarchies

This section offers straightforward replications of the analyses reported in chapter 5. In each of the tables to follow, I run the same model as in

India and China have gone to war only partially undercuts my confidence in doing so. Their 1962 conflict was of limited duration, low casualties, and has not been repeated. I think this is because the transit ranges are simply too costly to allow them to bring their militaries fully to bear on each other.

Table 6.1. *Logistic regression estimates*

Dependent variable is War Onset	
Covariate	Coefficient (Probability)
Constant	−4.996***
Parity	3.372*** (0.0015)
Dissatisfaction	2.760*** (0.0058)
Parity* Dissatisfaction	−2.271** (0.0458)
Observations: 449; model χ^2: 30.085***; correct predictions: overall: 96.44%, wars: 0%, non-wars: 100%	

Notes: Twelve time-interval dummy variables to control for duration dependence are included but not reported in order to preserve space.

*$p < 0.10$ **$p < 0.05$ ***$p < 0.01$

the corresponding analysis reported in the previous chapter. The only difference is that the set of cases is somewhat larger (about 150 additional cases), since the dataset now includes dyads having external great powers as actors within local hierarchies.

Table 6.1 reports the results when I regress the probability of war within local hierarchies against parity and dissatisfaction. In this first analysis I estimate results substantively very similar to those reported in table 5.1. There I found positive and statistically significant coefficients for parity and dissatisfaction, and a smaller but negative coefficient for the multiplicative interaction term. Here I find larger coefficients, and the overall equation has a larger impact on the likelihood function than was the case in the previous analysis. Substantively, the results are identical. The joint presence of parity and dissatisfaction with the status quo has a substantial impact in increasing the probability of war. Including great powers as local hierarchy actors introduces no change in this supportive finding.

Table 6.2 reports the substantive effects of changes in parity and dissatisfaction on the estimated probability of war. In chapter 5 the joint presence of parity and dissatisfaction increased the risk of war from

Table 6.2. *Substantive effects of Parity and Dissatisfaction for model reported in table 6.1*

Neither Parity nor Dissatisfaction	0.7%
Parity, no Dissatisfaction	16.5%
Dissatisfaction, no Parity	9.7%
Parity and Dissatisfaction	24.4%

1.3 to 27.3 percent. Here it increases the risk a very similar amount, from 0.7 to 24.4 percent. The only difference is that in these estimations parity has a larger individual effect than does dissatisfaction. The opposite was true in chapter 5.

Next I introduce region-specific dummy variables to see if, even when I introduce great powers as local hierarchy actors, there are still cross-regional differences in the probability of war. As in the previous chapter, I find when I add four region-specific dummy variables to the mix, parity and dissatisfaction still have a large positive impact on the probability of war. The coefficients reported in table 6.3 all have the same sign as the parallel coefficient estimates in table 5.3, and every variable that was significant there is so here as well. Importantly, the African and South American dummy variables are both statistically significant and negative.

Table 6.4 parallels table 5.4 in offering the region-specific impacts of changes in parity and dissatisfaction on the probability of war. As in chapter 5, the impact of moving from neither parity nor dissatisfaction to their joint presence increases the estimated probability of war approximately tenfold across all four regions and for the Great Powers. Again, the absolute increases in Africa and South America are tiny compared to those elsewhere. The only difference is that in table 5.4 the probability of war remained lower in Africa than in South America, while in table 6.4 the probabilities are essentially identical for these two least war-prone regions.

Finally, I turn to consideration of control variables. Table 6.5 parallels table 5.5, again save for the fact that table 6.5 reports analyses on an enlarged set of cases. Aside from a few minor differences, the results are again extremely similar. All coefficients have identical signs across the two analyses. Parity and dissatisfaction increase the probability of war. In this estimation the multiplicative interaction term is statistically

Table 6.3. *Logistic regression estimates with regional variables*

Dependent variable is War Onset	
Covariate	Coefficient (Probability)
Constant	−3.654***
Parity	2.576** (0.0199)
Dissatisfaction	2.736*** (0.0067)
Parity* Dissatisfaction	−2.213* (0.0570)
Africa	−2.123** (0.0186)
Far East	−1.210 (0.1226)
Middle East	−0.310 (0.3609)
South America	−2.239** (0.0355)
Observations: 449; model χ^2: 39.219*** correct predictions: overall: 96.66%, wars: 6.25%, non-wars: 100%	

See notes to table 6.1.

significant whereas it just failed to satisfy conventional levels of significance in the analysis reported in table 5.5. Similarly, challenger's militarization was statistically significant in table 5.5, but just misses the $p < 0.10$ level in table 6.5. In table 5.5 only the Africa and South America region-specific variables were statistically significant, whereas in table 6.5 the coefficient for Far East is almost statistically significant at the $p < 0.10$ level. Turning to table 6.6 we see the region-specific substantive effects of changes in parity and dissatisfaction have similar patterns across the two analyses, although the absolute size of the effects are slightly smaller throughout table 6.6 than they were in table 5.6 (and are much smaller for the Far East in table 6.6 than was the case in table 5.6).

It is hard to imagine more similar results than obtained in this replication exercise. It is impossible to argue that failure to include the great

Table 6.4. *Substantive effects of Parity and Dissatisfaction for model reported in table 6.3*

	Great Powers	Middle East	Far East	S. America	Africa
Neither Parity nor Dissatisfaction	2.5	2.5	2.5	0.28	0.3
Parity, no Dissatisfaction	25.5	25.5	25.5	3.6	3.8
Dissatisfaction, no Parity	28.0	28.0	28.0	4.1	4.1
Parity and Dissatisfaction	36.5	36.5	36.5	5.8	5.8

Cell entries are the estimated conditional probability of war (expressed as a percentage) given the conditions specified in each row in the region designated in each column.

powers as actors in local hierarchies compromises the conclusions offered in chapter 5. The multiple hierarchy model was robustly supported there and is bolstered substantially here.

A second consideration of great power interference

Skeptics might complain these replications are a relatively easy test to pass. In the second section of this chapter I outlined two possible techniques for incorporating great power interference into my analysis of parity and dissatisfaction's effects in minor power local hierarchies. Including control variables to represent specific types of great power interference is very appealing conceptually, but introduces seemingly insurmountable problems of data availability and quality. Despairing of obtaining such data I opt for the alternative. I include great powers as actors in local hierarchies provided they can "reach" those local hierarchies. This allows me to include great power interference in my analysis for the new cases. But it is questionable whether or not doing so affects estimates for the cases initially in the dataset. Essentially what I may have done in the replications thus far is to have introduced a set of cases which, at worst, could have "watered down" the relationships I observed in chapter 5.

Table 6.5. *Logistic regression estimates with regional and control variables*

Dependent variable is War Onset	
Covariate	Coefficient (Probability)
Constant	−2.839*
Parity	2.621** (0.0206)
Dissatisfaction	2.595*** (0.010)
Parity* Dissatisfaction	−1.982* (0.0817)
Alliance	−0.543 (0.4448)
Joint Democracy	−0.113 (0.2350)
Dominant Power's Militarization	−0.245 (0.4780)
Challenger's Militarization	0.151 (0.1219)
Africa	−2.347** (0.0315)
Far East	−1.481* (0.1025)
Middle East	−0.700 (0.2458)
South America	−2.238** (0.0445)
Observations: 446; model χ^2: 42.905***; correct predictions: overall: 96.86%, wars: 12.5%, non-wars: 100%	

See notes to table 6.1.

Happily, the calculations associated with determining which great powers to include in which local hierarchies can be useful in another way. Specifically, knowing which great powers can interfere within which local hierarchies provides information about the extent to which each local hierarchy suffers from *potential* great power interference. To the extent potential and actual great power interference covary (one would think they must), a measure of potential great power interference

Table 6.6. *Substantive effects of Parity and Dissatisfaction for model reported in table 6.5*

	Great powers	Middle East	Far East	S. America	Africa
Neither Parity nor Dissatisfaction	6.9	8.8	1.7	0.7	0.6
Parity, no Dissatisfaction	50.4	56.9	19.0	8.8	8.4
Dissatisfaction, no Parity	49.8	56.3	18.6	8.6	8.2
Parity and Dissatisfaction	65.3	70.9	30.2	15.1	14.5

Cell entries are the estimated conditional probability of war (expressed as a percentage) given the conditions specified in each row in the region designated in each column. Control variables are set at their regional means.

might be used as a proxy to indicate the types of great power interference for which I cannot obtain reliable data.

What I can do is return to the original dataset and cases used in all of the analyses reported in chapter 5, and include a new control variable representing the ability of great powers to interfere in local hierarchies. If great power interference covaries with potential for great power interference, and if great power interference is an important cause of minor power wars, then such a proxy control variable will generate a statistically significant coefficient when war is the dependent variable. Further, if great power interference is correlated with any of the other independent variables included in my analyses, inclusion of great power interference in a statistical model will change the estimates for those other independent variables.

In table 6.7 I estimate the same model as employed in table 5.5. I have the same 287 cases as in that analysis. The independent variables included in table 5.5 are all included in table 6.7. The only difference is that the analysis reported in table 6.7 includes "great power interference," a dichotomous variable equal to 1 if two or more external great powers are able to interfere within the local hierarchy in question.[4] The data for this variable are available as a consequence

[4] I have no argument to make justifying why I code this variable as equaling 1 when two or more external great powers are able to interfere in a hierarchy. I specify the

Table 6.7. *Logistic regression estimates with great power interference*

Dependent variable is War Onset	
Covariate	Coefficient (Probability)
Constant	−2.028
Parity	2.539** (0.0335)
Dissatisfaction	2.664** (0.0137)
Parity* Dissatisfaction	−1.818 (0.1197)
Alliance	−0.479 (0.5290)
Joint Democracy	−0.211 (0.1334)
Dominant Power's Militarization	−0.537* (0.0949)
Challenger's Militarization	0.249** (0.0475)
Great Power Interference	−2.824** (0.0319)
Africa	−1.856* (0.0809)
Far East	0.011 (0.4966)
Middle East	1.498 (0.1755)
South America	−2.005* (0.0680)
Observations: 287; model χ^2: 40.494** correct predictions: overall: 95.12%, wars: 18.75%, non-wars: 99.63%	

See notes to table 6.1.

variable this way for convenience. I have rerun the analysis reported in table 6.7 with great power interference as a variable ranging from 0 to 4 to indicate the number of external great powers able to interfere in a hierarchy. I have also specified great power interference as equal to 1 when one or more external great powers is able to interfere. I have also specified it as a series of dummy variables indicating whether one, two, three, or four great powers are able to interfere. In all of those alternate analyses great power interference is not statistically significant, and some combination of the regional and/or control variables demonstrates enormous change in coefficient values and of having undertaken the reachability calculations to see which great powers might be included in which local hierarchies. This variable has a large *negative* effect on the probability of war within hierarchies. Its coefficient is not only large, but also highly statistically significant. A likelihood ratio test comparing this analysis with the one reported in table 5.5 produces a χ^2 statistic of 5.175 which, with one degree of freedom, is statistically significant at well beyond the $p < 0.05$ level. Great power interference is thus an important covariate, noticeably improving the fit of the model to the data. Its inclusion is warranted on statistical grounds, and very appealing for anyone concerned that great power interference affects the probability of war among minor powers.

The especially interesting result from the multiple hierarchy model perspective is that parity and dissatisfaction are still important causes of war in hierarchies, even controlling for great power interference. The size of coefficients for the parity and dissatisfaction variables are slightly larger in table 6.7 than they were in table 5.5, and the multiplicative interaction term is closer to statistical significance on its own than was the case previously. The four other control variables show a few changes, with joint democracy almost attaining statistical significance for the first time, and dominant power's militarization now being statistically significant. Also of interest, especially as we move to the next chapter, is the fact that the Africa and South America dummy variables are still statistically significant (they are very nearly unchanged from what they were in table 5.5, suggesting there is no multicollinearity between potential great power interference and these two regional variables). The main report is that controlling for great power interference does not diminish

especially standard errors. In all of these alternate analyses the change in the likelihood ratio from what it was for table 5.5 is large enough to be statistically significant, indicating that even though there are fewer statistically significant variables than reported in table 5.5, the overall model is a better fit to the data. These improvements in statistical fit via insignificant variables suggest to me the alternate specifications of great power interference introduce substantial multicollinearity with respect to some of the other variables. I could investigate some of this multicollinearity further but do not do so for two reasons. First, in all of the alternate analyses the parity and dissatisfaction variables are statistically significant with very nearly unchanged coefficients and standard errors. Thus, the multicollinearity does not affect the theoretically important relationships which the replications and extensions in this chapter are designed to probe. Secondly, I think it would be inefficient to probe correlations and partial correlations, trying to tease out a relationship, when I have no theory of great power interference to guide me. Thus, I report the analysis as I do in table 6.7 because what is important is recognition that great power interference *does* matter (hence the statistically significant impact on the likelihood function), but it does not change my findings about parity and dissatisfaction.

parity and dissatisfaction's impact on the probability of war in hierarchies. Chapter 5's results are robust.

Conclusions

I began this chapter by admitting that the omission of great power interference undermines confidence in the results offered in the previous chapter. I described two possible techniques I might employ to control for great power interference and thus bolster confidence in my results. The first technique was dismissed because of the subsidiary data problems it introduces. The second technique, requiring calculation of which great powers could "reach" which local hierarchies and then re-creating my dataset to include cases with great powers as local hierarchy actors, was adopted instead. The process of undertaking the second technique suggested a way to control for *potential* great power interference within the original dataset analyzed in the previous chapter. Since potential and actual great power interference are likely strongly related to each other, this strikes me as a satisfactory way to get at the first technique. I thus undertake two types of analyses to determine if my chapter 5 results are compromised by great power interference.

I find my results are not compromised by great power interference. Whether I correct for the omission of great power interference by introducing additional cases or an additional control variable, I persistently find parity and dissatisfaction are important correlates of war in hierarchies around the world. My results appear robust; confidence in them appears justified.

Throughout the dozen or so empirical analyses undertaken in this and the previous chapter, the dummy variables specific to Africa and South America have consistently been statistically significant, despite the various control variables which might have accounted for some of the characteristics that cause these regions to vary systematically. As persistently as I find support for the multiple hierarchy model's expectations about parity and dissatisfaction, I find evidence of cross-regional variation in how well the multiple hierarchy model fits the different regions. This cross-regional variation is the subject of the next chapter.

7 Further investigations II: an African (interstate) Peace?

In the analyses reported in the previous chapter, the Africa and South America dummy variables are always statistically significant. The statistical interpretation is Africa and South America are persistently different from the other regions in terms of war-fighting. I "know" these regions vary from other regions, but I have no idea why. I am *specifically ignorant* about the sources of cross-regional variation.

A consequence of estimating statistically significant region-specific coefficients is I can switch the regional dummies on and off and calculate how large an effect parity and dissatisfaction have on the probability of war within each specific region. When I do this I find a diminishing impact, substantively, of parity and dissatisfaction as I move from analysis of the Great Powers, through analysis of the Far East and Middle East, to analysis of South America and Africa. The diminishing impact and negative sign of the region-specific coefficients suggests an increasing pacificity. Regardless of whether parity and dissatisfaction are present, war is less likely in some regions than others. Since Africa's coefficient is the most negative, and since the corresponding substantive effect of parity and dissatisfaction on the probability of war is the smallest, we might conclude from this that Africa is the most peaceful region.

The notion of an African Peace is not intuitively appealing. News coverage of atrocities in Rwanda, of seemingly constant strife in the Horn of Africa, and within Congo/Zaire in the late 1990s, presents an image of a Hobbesian world, of the "war of all against all" (see Kaplan 1994, and *Economist* 2000a, 2000b). Nevertheless, the results presented in chapters 5 and 6 suggest that the cross-regional variation highlights a greater propensity for *interstate* peace in Africa. Since this is so counterintuitive and seems unlikely, I investigate the possibility of an African Peace as part of a larger question of why the region-specific dummy variables in chapter 5 are statistically significant. If I can account for the cross-regional variation, I might be able to understand why my results suggest an African Peace. In the process I speculate at length on why data-driven scholarly conclusions are so at odds with popular perceptions of Africa.[1]

The term "African Peace" is meant to refer only to *inter*state relations in Africa. I am attempting to extend a theory of great power relations to help understand and anticipate interactions among minor power states. I am well aware there may not be much interaction among underdeveloped states to either understand or anticipate in the first place.[2] However, I do not see this likely lack of interactions as negating the value of my theoretical extension of power transition theory. Rather, I think the continued investigation of theoretical anomalies like an African Peace might lead us to understand why there are fewer interactions among underdeveloped states and how this systematic difference should be built into general efforts to understand world politics.

In this chapter I explain why the existence of an African Peace is paradoxical from the standpoint of international politics conflict research, and offer a detailed discussion of whether there really is an African

[1] Readers may wonder why I restrict myself to discussion of an African rather than an African *and* South American Peace, since both dummy variables for these regions are persistently significant. The reason is South America more convincingly fits the pattern of state development and interstate conflict sketched out in the remainder of this chapter (although see Centeno 1997 for a dissenting view). South American states frequently fought wars in the nineteenth century, and seemed to do so to decide where their borders would be, who could control mineral resources, who would have access to important waterways, etc. Those issues have been resolved and South America's states are much more established than are Africa's. Further, power relationships in South America are more stable than in Africa, and not surprisingly war has become rare. Consequently, I think that South America's coefficient is not too hard to understand. Africa's, in contrast, seems much at odds with expectations and thus more controversially illuminates the pattern of state development and conflict developed here. What follows is a critique of standard practice in world politics empirical research; Africa simply better makes my case. This does not mean I think South America fails to do so.

[2] As Kalevi Holsti (1998: 106–107) writes:

> The problem of interstate war . . . is not the critical problem facing most Third World and post-Socialist states. It is there in some areas at some times – particularly in the Middle East – but it is not a ubiquitous phenomenon as was war in the eighteenth, nineteenth, and first half of the twentieth centuries in the European and Cold War contexts. If this generalization is essentially correct, then International Relations Theory as it has developed over the past 250 years may be of limited relevance in helping to explain the crucial issues facing contemporary Third World and post-Socialist states.

I suspect this is true to an extent, but would add that one should make all possible efforts to learn the limits of one's existing theory before undertaking efforts to elaborate (or further elaborate) it.

Peace (even if only statistically). After that, I offer three possible explanations for the broader issue of cross-regional variation represented by the statistically significant region-specific dummy variables. I first consider whether the cross-regional variation might be coincidental. I then turn to a preliminary effort to build a theoretical explanation for cross-regional variation by reconsidering the African Peace. This loosely theoretical explanation represents an attempt to account for the significance of the proper noun region-specific variables with variables representing theoretical concepts. Finally, I take up the possibility that region-specific measurement error produces the statistically significant regional coefficients. Each of these possible sources of the puzzling cross-regional variation is treated separately, but there is always the possibility that two or more of them operate simultaneously.

An African Peace?

Anyone familiar with international conflict research has heard of the "democratic peace." Few or none, however, have heard of or written about an African Peace. I suspect some might respond that no one has written about an African Peace because the concept is absurd. Regardless of how absurd it might sound, the statistical results reported in chapter 5 suggest Africa is the least war-prone of the five regions studied. Either Africa really is especially peaceful, or there is something about how we collect data or otherwise analyze interstate conflict that fails to capture conflict dynamics equally well in all parts of the globe. It seems worthwhile to consider in depth whether there is an African Peace. In getting to that question, however, I first summarize what previous research on the causes of war and peace suggests about how war-prone Africa *should* be.

Consistent with popular expectations, existing research on the causes of war and conditions of peace suggests the likelihood of war in Africa is especially *high*. Known or suspected correlates of war are widespread, while known or suspected correlates of peace tend to be absent. One relevant argument about the causes of war is offered by Starr and Most (1976, 1978), who contend that the number of borders a state has should correlate with the frequency with which it engages in interstate conflict (an expectation first advanced and evaluated by Richardson 1960b). Starr and Most suggest that, as points of interaction, borders offer an opportunity for war between neighbors. Further, if neighboring territories have intrinsic value, borders can also provide willingness for war (see Diehl 1991 for another discussion of borders as both opportunity and willingness for war). For these reasons, Starr and Most expect, and find, a correlation between the number of borders a state has and the frequency with which it engages in wars.

Currently the average African state has 3.92 directly contiguous land borders. The average number of directly contiguous land borders characterizing non-African members of the interstate system (as defined by the Correlates of War project) is 2.89.[3] There are a larger average number of interaction opportunities on the continent of Africa than in the rest of the world. If one omits the six island states ringing Africa, the average number of such direct borders increases to 4.43. If one omits island states from the larger Correlates of War dataset, the average number of direct borders is 3.73. Again, African states have more borders than do other states, on average. Since many or most of Africa's borders are a legacy of imperialism and are of questionable legitimacy, the potential for these interaction opportunities to represent willingness for war increases. The raw number of border/interaction points should lead one to expect frequent war.

In addition to borders, another characteristic of the African map suggests frequent interstate wars might be anticipated there. Recent research on the role of ethnicity in interstate conflict suggests ethnic differences are an especially difficult issue to resolve peacefully (Carment 1993; Carment and James 1997, 1998). A glance at the distribution of ethnic groups across Africa shows a crazy-quilt pattern (Ray 1998: 115). With the possible exception of Somalia, true nation-states are absent in Africa. This is relevant because Davis and Moore (1997) report that when an ethnic group is a minority at risk in one state but a dominant ethnic group in a neighboring state, the potential for interstate conflict increases dramatically. This is reminiscent of interactions between South Africa and the frontline states prior to the 1990s.

A large body of literature dealing with incentives for leaders to use external conflict to divert attention from domestic problems suggests a third argument anticipating frequent war in Africa. Many African governments are plagued by problems of domestic instability occasioned by a variety of economic, ethnic, and political factors. The diversionary theory of war (summarized by Levy 1989) suggests some domestically challenged leaders will use war to divert attention from domestic troubles, or to punish external scapegoats for domestic problems. Similarly, Michael Haas (1973) argues the processes of development make states war-like

[3] Author's calculations.

because the changes engendered by development upset societal norms and institutions. The resulting upheaval causes wars via civil strife. In earlier work, Haas (1968) reminds us that arguments historically advanced by the likes of Comte and Spencer suggest non-industrial states could use war as a means for growth. Agriculture-based states need new land in order to grow more crops and become more powerful. They favor war for conquest. Given that many African states have governments plagued by domestic instability, have non-industrial economies, and are arguably attempting to undergo development, the potential for diversionary wars must be high.

A cautionary note is introduced by the possibility there is so much domestic instability in some African states that even if their leaders would like to divert, they cannot. However, the inability of State A to act on its diversionary incentives against State B might provide an incentive for B to attack weak and disorganized A. If there are any outstanding claims by B against A, A's weakness might prompt B to take advantage. In short, domestic instability in A could provide incentives for war started by either A or B.[4]

Zeev Maoz (1989) writes about the occasion of national independence as a special kind of instability that can make war more likely. He demonstrates how new states which emerge suddenly (in contrast to states achieving independence gradually) are prone to experience much more international conflict than states on average, although this propensity diminishes as the state ages. Many writers remark on the speed with which former colonies became independent African states (see Clapham 1996: part I). Based on Maoz's empirical analysis, it would have been understandable if the sudden emergence in the early 1960s of dozens of new states in Africa occurred violently. Specifically, it would have been consistent with Maoz's research if there had been a large number of disputes and wars in Africa tapering off over time since 1960. Thus, patterns associating international conflict with the sudden emergence of new polities would lead us to expect many wars and disputes in Africa.

Numerous articles and books remind us democracies either do not fight each other, or else fight each other much less frequently than do

[4] This argument is attenuated by a lack of clear evidence supporting the diversionary theory. Additionally, evidence by Morgan and Bickers (1992) suggests only troubles originating in the leader's core constituency are related to diversionary behavior. More recently, Smith (1996b), as well as Leeds and Davis (1997), complain that diversionary studies ignore strategic interactions. Domestic discontent is usually transparent. If neighboring states wish to avoid conflict, their leaders will be especially likely to accommodate, or at least not provoke, leaders of states suffering from domestic crises.

non-democracies or mixed dyads (for comprehensive recent summaries, see Chan 1997 and Maoz 1998). The democratic peace suggests regions with many democracies should be especially peaceful. A perusal of the Polity III dataset (Jaggers and Gurr 1996) demonstrates quite clearly that Africa is not overly endowed with democracies. The average institutionalized democracy score for the entire world between 1960 and 1994 is 3.53. For Africa over the same period the average score is only 1.45. While it is true there are democracies in Africa (Botswana, for example, has scored a perfect 10 on this scale since independence in 1966), there are few of them. What is more, the average democracy score for the continent is quite low, both relatively and absolutely. Based on the democratic peace literature we should *not* expect war in Africa to be prevented by the presence of many liberal regimes.

In addition to joint democracy as a pacifying condition, some have argued that the enormous costs that could be inflicted by nuclear weapons deter conflict (Waltz 1981; Mearsheimer 1990). When both adversaries have large nuclear arsenals the pacifying effect is supposedly enhanced (Intriligator and Brito 1984). No such pacifying effect exists for Africa. The only known or suspected possessor of nuclear weapons in Africa was South Africa under the apartheid regime, but even in this case the suspected arsenal was believed to have been tiny. Therefore, this presumed correlate of peace cannot operate at all in Africa, I would argue. Expected costs of conflict are unlikely to prevent war in Africa either. Although some African leaders have initiated large weapons increases, generally the military establishments of the continent are underdeveloped. Evidence of this is provided by calculating Bremer's (1992) "militarization ratio" (discussed and employed as a control variable in chapter 5) for Africa and comparing it to the average value in the rest of the world. The average militarization ratio value for the entire world for the years 1960 to 1993 is 0.92. The average value for Africa for these same years is 0.35. African military establishments are smaller, relative to demographic potential, than military establishments around the world. Given that African states are poorer too, this is not surprising. But what is consequential is the fact these underdeveloped military establishments are unlikely to be able to inflict large costs on other states. One of the most consistent deductions from game-theoretic treatments of war is high expected costs make war less likely (e.g., Powell 1999). Since the expected costs of war in Africa are generally quite low, owing to underdeveloped military establishments, we might expect war to be relatively frequent.

This admittedly unsystematic literature survey highlights many theoretical and empirical arguments anticipating frequent interstate conflict in Africa. Unfortunately for Africans, the conditions associated with war are virtually uniformly present, while those associated with peace are virtually uniformly absent. These extant literatures suggest war should be common in Africa, or should at least be no less common in Africa than elsewhere.

Scholarly arguments, when naïvely applied to generate expectations regarding war in Africa, anticipate that war will be relatively frequent. What is the empirical reality? There have been only two events in post-colonial African history qualifying as interstate wars according to the standard definition provided by the Correlates of War project.[5] Over the fall and winter of 1977–1978 Somali and Ethiopian armed forces clashed for control of the Ogaden territory, resulting in 6,000 battle deaths. In the fall of 1978 Idi Amin ordered the Ugandan army to invade north-western Tanzania. The Tanzanians fought back successfully, ultimately reconquering their territory and driving Amin from power. Three thousand battle deaths resulted (Singer 1991: 63). Aside from these two events, the armed forces of African states have not been reported to have engaged each other in any conflict resulting in more than 1,000 battle deaths.

An immediate objection is that Africa has had much more interstate violence than the observation of two wars since independence suggests. Starr and Most (1983, 1985) argue Africa is an especially good place to study conflict diffusion because during the period they study "the region became a major locus of international conflict" (1983: 99). James, Brecher, and Hoffman (1988) begin their article with the observation that international crises in Africa are frequent. Similarly, Agyeman-Duah and Ojo study interstate conflict in West Africa specifically because "Over the past decade and a half West Africa has been rife with interstate conflicts" (1991: 299). None of these authors are wrong. However, their definitions of interstate conflict differ from the one employed in this book.[6] Starr and

[5] Although, pending updates of the Correlates of War project, it seems quite likely renewed clashes between Eritrea and Ethiopia have been sufficiently deadly to qualify their ongoing violence as an interstate war. This would be a third *interstate* war in African post-colonial history. Also, Ray (2001) argues that the Democratic Republic of the Congo's civil war in the late 1990s may have been an interstate war.

[6] It is interesting to note, as an example of the lack of scholarly consensus about what international conflict is, that West Africa is "rife with interstate conflict" according to Agyeman-Duah and Ojo, but is a "zone of peace" according to Kacowicz (1998: ch. 4).

Most employ Kende's (1971, 1978) "local wars" dataset. Kende's operational definition for local wars includes not only *intra*state conflict, but can also include conflicts in which there are zero fatalities. James, Brecher, and Hoffman employ the International Crisis Behavior dataset, which can include as crises, events perceived by a single actor, as well as events in which no fatality occurs. Finally, Agyeman-Duah and Ojo employ a definition so broad that diplomatic criticism qualifies as interstate conflict. These may all be useful definitions of interstate conflict, but they can differ sharply from what we might think of as interstate wars. Of course, if African interstate conflict is as rife as these authors suggest, it still remains to be explained why only two instances escalated to the point where more than 1,000 soldiers lost their lives. It seems very odd, especially given the arguments summarized above, that African states frequently engage in a variety of interstate conflicts, yet generally avoid only those interstate conflicts the Correlates of War project defines as war.

Maybe, however, two wars is not fewer than we would expect based on a comparison with observed frequencies of war around the world. War is itself a rare event. Most African countries have only existed as independent states since 1960 or so (more recently for some). Given there have been so few years of independent existence, maybe the "surprisingly few" observations of war in Africa are not so surprisingly few after all.

Table 7.1 reports the expected frequencies of a variety of aspects of interstate war Africa could be expected to have experienced based on the worldwide occurrence of war. It also reports what has actually been observed for Africa. The values in the top half of the table include the expected frequencies for Africa based on global war experience 1816–1993 (the temporal limits of the Correlates of War project's interstate conflict datasets). The bottom half reports the expected frequencies for Africa based on global war experience 1960–1993, arguably a more appropriate period since it is the one in which post-colonial Africa has existed as an independent region. The first column reports observed frequencies of various indicators of war in Africa, the second reports the expected value, and the third reports a summary statistic indicating the degree of statistical significance between observed and expected.

Calculation of these values is relatively straightforward. The values for dyad-years of war (row 3 of table 7.1a), for example, are calculated as follows. First, the global frequency of dyad-years of war relative to

Table 7.1. *Expected and observed frequencies of wars*

a. *Based on world experience 1816–1993*

	Observed	Expected	Z-score
# of interstate wars	2	10	−2.589**
Nation-years of war	10	53	−6.087***
Dyad-years of war	6	63	−4.747***

b. *Based on world experience 1960–1993*

	Observed	Expected	Z-score
# of interstate wars	2	6	−1.667*
Nation-years of war	10	31	−3.833***
Dyad-years of war	6	11	−4.430***

Note: Z-scores are based on the formula presented in Bremer (1992: 327); negative values indicate that the observed value is lower than the expected.

*$p < 0.05$ **$p < 0.01$ ***$p < 0.001$.

dyad-years of existence is calculated. This gives:

(dyad-years of war, globally)/(dyad-years, globally)
or 883/532, 426 = 0.0017.

This is the observed number of dyad-years of war per dyad-year of existence globally and historically. This value is multiplied by the number of African dyad-years (36,805) to arrive at an expected frequency of war in Africa if Africa were representative of global and historical war propensity. The value arrived at is 0.0017*36,805 = 62.569. If African dyads are as likely to experience war years as dyads throughout the entire international system have been, there should have been approximately 63 dyad-years of war in Africa. That there have been only 6 suggests Africa is not representative of the rest of the international system's annual dyadic war propensity. Whether we compare Africa's number of wars, nation-years of war, or dyad-years of war with those for the historical or contemporary international system, we find Africa is substantially less war-prone (generally three to five times less) than the wider international system.[7]

[7] The rows in table 7.1 that do not calculate dyad-years use nation-years as the basis of comparison. Thus, the value of ten expected wars in Africa based on the historical

Table 7.2. *Expected and observed frequencies of militarized interstate disputes*

a. *Based on world experience 1816–1993*			
	Observed	Expected	Z-score
# of MIDs	172	274	−6.875***
Nation-years of MIDs	481	909	−22.064***

b. *Based on world experience 1960–1993*			
	Observed	Expected	Z-score
# of MIDs	172	301	−8.33***
Nation-years of MIDs	481	919	−22.568***

See notes to table 7.1.

Table 7.2 provides a similar presentation of expected and observed frequencies of "militarized interstate disputes" (MIDs) in Africa. According to Correlates of War coding rules (Jones, Bremer, and Singer 1996), a MID occurs whenever one state threatens, displays, or uses government-sanctioned force against another. This is clearly a lower threshold of interstate conflict, yet again we see Africa is less conflictual than would be expected based on the system-wide probabilities of such disputes. Whether we consider the number of disputes or how many years nations are involved in disputes, Africa appears to be only about half as disputatious as it "should be," based on system-wide experience.

Tables 7.1 and 7.2 indicate that the observed frequencies of interstate conflict in Africa are substantially lower than the frequencies we might expect based on the experience of the international system more broadly. Given that every row of the two tables reports that the observed frequency is substantively and statistically significantly lower than the expected frequency, it is safe to conclude that Africa is unexpectedly

system-wide experience is derived as follows: (number of wars, globally)/(nation-years, globally) = 75/11,495 = 0.00652 wars per nation-year of existence historically and globally. This is multiplied by the number of African nation-years: 0.00652*1551 = 10.11252, which I round to 10. If Africa were representative of the number of wars per nation-year the rest of the system has evidenced, there would have been about ten wars in Africa. This assumes that each nation-year provides an opportunity for an independent war, a questionable expectation perhaps. Although potentially flawed, this procedure does allow standardized comparisons of observed and expected frequencies of wars (and disputes).

peaceful in terms of what empirical interstate conflict researchers define as interstate relations. This is the case with both wars and disputes.[8] Given that the theoretical and empirical arguments reviewed above lead us to expect a greater than average propensity to engage in interstate conflict, this African Peace is especially surprising.[9] The African Peace is interesting specifically as an example of the larger cross-regional variation in war propensity reported in chapter 5. It clearly seems important to try to understand why this general cross-regional variation, and its specific and dramatic African Peace manifestation, exists. What "causes" the regional differences?

Cross-regional variation is coincidental

A first reaction might be that the region-specific coefficients are statistically significant simply by coincidence. It could be the case that, given

[8] Surprisingly, Africa may have a Civil War Peace as well. Henderson and Singer (2000) estimate what makes civil war (defined as sustained armed conflict within one state and resulting in at least 1,000 battle fatalities per year) more likely. They do so for African, East Asian, and Middle Eastern states. They include dummy variables indicating East Asia and the Middle East, leaving Africa as the referent category. In many of their analyses these two region-specific dummies are positive and statistically significant. This means that in these two regions civil wars are more likely than in Africa. Henderson and Singer's results do not mean there is a relative lack of domestic militarized violence within Africa, but rather indicate that this domestic militarized violence either does not escalate to the 1,000 fatalities per year level, or otherwise goes unreported.

[9] There is additional evidence of an African Peace. Consideration of average fatality levels in *inter*state wars (according to Small and Singer 1982; updated by Singer 1991) suggests that when Africans do go to war with each other, they kill far fewer soldiers than does the rest of the world. The average combat fatality level in African wars is 4,500 dead. The average in the wider international system is 441,414. Since averages can be skewed by extreme cases, and since there are a number of extreme cases historically (World War II accounts for nearly half of the total battle fatalities for the entire 1816–1993 period), it might be more interesting to consider the average excluding the six wars in which over one million soldiers were killed. This smaller, less skewed, set of wars produces an average of 35,088 battle fatalities. A second additional piece of evidence about an African Peace is offered by a replication of results about escalation published by Bill Reed (2000). Bill was kind enough to replicate some of the results from that article, introducing a control variable equal to 1 whenever the dyad under observation comprises two African states (the article in question employs the Oneal and Russett [1997] relevant dyads dataset for the years 1950–1985). The other covariates are alliance, joint satisfaction, joint democracy, development and interdependence. For the entire dataset with 20,990 observations, when the dependent variable is war onset the coefficient for the variable African dyad is negative and statistically significant at $p = 0.039$. When the dataset is restricted to only those dyads experiencing a dispute and the dependent variable is whether the dispute escalates to war or not, the coefficient for the variable African dyad becomes even more negative and is now statistically significant at the $p < 0.001$ level. I encourage any interested readers to replicate their war analyses controlling for African dyad. I predict they will persistently estimate a statistically significant negative coefficient for this variable.

as small a dataset as I employ here (only around 300 observations in the analyses in chapter 5 and later in this chapter), some outlier observations could have a disproportionately large impact on the estimated relationships between variables. Thus, including a few of these disproportionately weighty cases in an aggregated sub-set of cases might make the whole sub-set appear to be substantively "different" when in reality it is only the few cases coincidentally included that produce the result. If this were the case, there really would be something coincidental about the statistical significance of aggregating observations into sub-sets of the specific sizes of my regions. It could be that any similar aggregation, whether we called the sub-set "Africa" or organized it along some other potentially arbitrary line such as "states represented on the PGA tour," would include a few of these weighty observations and also attain statistical significance.

This possibility can be evaluated by determining whether some totally arbitrary aggregation of cases into random regions, for instance, would also produce statistically significant estimates. If a randomly assigned "regional" classification of the cases into five sub-sets also produced significant differences between the sub-sets, we might reasonably conclude there is nothing different about Africa *per se*, but rather there is something different introduced by looking individually at a given 25.1 percent of the cases. That a "random-regions" analysis will be conclusive seems a long shot, but it is reasonably easy to perform, and worth trying.

In order to determine whether randomly designated regions exhibit similar properties to my geographically designated regions, I first determine what proportion of my cases fall into each regional sub-set. I next construct a column of random numbers in my dataset. I then sort my cases along ascending values of the random number column, and designate the first *x* percent "Random Region 1" (so that *x* percent corresponds with the actual percentage of my dataset that is South American), and continue on through four more random regions (each equivalent in size to my Middle East, Far East, African and Great Power sub-sets). I then rerun the models from tables 5.3 and 5.5 of chapter 5 replacing the Africa, Far East, Middle East and South America region-specific dummy variables with the random-region dummy variables. Not surprisingly, the estimates for the parity and dissatisfaction variables (as well as for the alliance, joint democracy and militarization control variables) are virtually unchanged and none of the random-region dummy variables are statistically significant.

This is a very modest evaluation of whether I can reproduce the statistically significant results for aggregated sub-sets of my observations by constructing random regional aggregations.[10] Nevertheless, I believe it safe to conclude that, even given the rudimentary nature of this exercise, there is something about the regions as designated by their true geographic determinants that is not reproducible with a random-region specification. It seems unlikely the region-specific dummy variables are statistically significant only by coincidence.

"Theory"-driven explanation for cross-regional variation

I know the cross-regional variation exists because the statistically and substantively significant region-specific variables improve the overall fit of the empirical model to the data on war. As mentioned repeatedly, this knowledge is really specific ignorance, since I do not know what causes the cross-regional variation. An ideal solution to my problem of ignorance would be the identification of a variable, or set of variables, representing theoretical concepts, the inclusion of which would make the region-specific dummy variables statistically or substantively insignificant (or both). I would then have an explanation for why the regions vary, and would no longer be ignorant (specifically or otherwise).

In this section I offer a pre-theoretical (or loosely theoretical) explanation for why the cross-regional variation should exist. I describe a set of variables I expect will make the regional variables insignificant. I then present an empirical analysis evaluating whether my expectation is correct. To foreshadow that outcome: I am partially correct in my expectation.

In chapter 5 I discussed Robert Barro's (1991) work on economic development. I mentioned that Barro also estimates statistically significant coefficients for region-specific dummy variables. Since that initial study, Barro has succeeded in specifying a set of alternate variables, suggested

[10] Mathematically, this exercise should not be able to produce statistically significant random-region coefficients. Since the cases assigned to each random region are randomly assigned, they should tend to be normally distributed around the sample means. Thus the hypothesis test that a given random-region coefficient is statistically significant compares observations in that random region to the mean observation, and divides by the standard error. The difference between the random-region observations and mean observations should be zero on average, so all random-region designations should tend to be statistically insignificant. The random-region results are not reproduced in the text, but curious readers may request them directly.

by neo-classical growth theory, which make the region-specific variables in his analyses insignificant. He reports (1997: ch. 1, esp. pp. 30–32) that inclusion of an inflation rate variable makes his Latin America dummy variable statistically insignificant, the inclusion of a governmental consumption variable makes his sub-Saharan Africa variable insignificant, and the inclusion of a male schooling, rule of law, or democracy variable makes his East Asia variable insignificant. In a similar way, I am attempting here to specify interpretable concepts that will make my region-specific dummy variables insignificant too.

In order to do so, I offer a loosely theoretical story about why the conflict propensity and impact of parity and dissatisfaction should vary from region to region. In so doing I am strongly influenced by the authors discussed at length in chapter 1 (specifically Ayoob 1995, Holsti 1996, and the contributors to Neuman 1998). These authors suggest that in much of the Third World, and specifically in Africa, the degree of political centralization is vastly lower than in the rest of the world. In the Third World, endemic poverty, lack of human capital, lack of infrastructure, and resulting domestic unrest mean very often the threats governments face are domestic rather than international. Consequently, when a governing regime in the Third World contemplates its strategic future, it does not think about conflict with other states, but rather with some of its own citizens / subjects. In the underdeveloped countries, military forces serve different purposes than in the developed or developing worlds. Further, the conditions listed above may mean Third World leaders cannot use force outside of their borders even if they have a desire to do so (presumably they would have this desire when they observe the existence of parity between themselves and the local dominant power and feel dissatisfaction with the local status quo).

Consider a scenario involving the president of a hypothetical African republic. Call it Ishmaelia.[11] The Ishmaelian president might observe Ishmaelia is at parity with its neighbor, Azania. He might believe Azania's economic hegemony and treatment of Ishmaelian nationals are unacceptable. He might perceive Ishmaelian dissatisfaction with

[11] Readers unfamiliar with this fictional African country are referred to Evelyn Waugh's 1930s' novel *Scoop*. It tells the story of an inexperienced journalist sent to East Africa to cover a civil war in Ishmaelia. The fictional republic is useful for my purposes because it prevents me from making any blatantly incorrect statements in my hypothetical examples, and is of interest to political scientists because Waugh wrote that its constitution was written by a committee of political science professors who, perhaps anticipating Arend Lijphardt, saddled Ishmaelia with the single transferable vote. Its neighbor, Azania, is the fictional African country in Waugh's *Black Mischief*.

Azania's governance of the local status quo. For all these reasons he might very well like to go to war with Azania in order to change the local status quo. However, were he to initiate this war, he would have to send Ishmaelia's army into Azania's territory. If he did that, the private militia of an opposition tribe might storm into the capital, assassinate him, and thereby take over the political system. Moreover, sending the Ishmaelian army away would perhaps anger army leaders. Having been ordered away, they might instead storm into the presidential palace, kill the President, and thereby take over the political system. Consequently, all the pieces might be in place (parity between Ishmaelia and Azania, and Ishmaelian dissatisfaction with the Azanian local status quo), but the president of Ishmaelia cannot choose war because it is not a good policy option given his larger political context. Part of political development is political stability. Political stability allows the leader to dispatch troops. Political *in*stability might prevent this.

A second hypothetical situation again imagines the situation confronting an Ishmaelian president. He perceives Ishmaelian dissatisfaction with the local status quo, and would like to do something about it. He would be willing to go to war with Azania, but only if the chances of victory are even or better. In short, having read all about the multiple hierarchy model, the president would be willing to fight if parity obtains. How might he know what the relative power relationship between Ishmaelia and Azania is? He might ask the leader of Ishmaelian Intelligence, or perhaps the chairman of the Ishmaelian Joint Chiefs for a strategic assessment. These sources might even provide him with their estimates of the situation. Should the president trust the estimates? What if one or both of the individuals consulted are of questionable loyalty to the current president? Alternatively, maybe they are loyal, but how good are their sources? Are the communication, intelligence, analysis, etc. facilities of their respective agencies adequately funded to answer the strategic question satisfactorily? If not, it could be perilous for the president to act on their recommendation. If Ishmaelia is as politically and economically underdeveloped, and as fragmented ethnically, as the average African state, then the president would be a fool to put too much trust in such advice. In short, he would have a lot of trouble knowing when the (theoretically correct) time is ripe for war with Azania.

These hypothetical examples are intended to elucidate a loosely theoretical argument that the foreign policy options available to the leaders of profoundly underdeveloped states may not be comparable to the options available to leaders of developed states confronted with the same foreign policy stimulus.[12] Power transition theory (and most other theories about when states go to war) represents the onset of war as a conscious policy choice. For the leaders of developed states, this is not a difficult scenario to imagine. It could well be, however, that in the less developed parts of the Third World, leaders do not have sufficiently centralized control over the resources necessary to foreign military action (either because of general poverty, or because of concerns about what the local opposition will do while the troops are away) for the "choice" of going to war to be an option as it is in the developed world. War in the developed world occurs because the challenger and the dominant power decide to fight each other. War in the underdeveloped world may sometimes occur for this reason, may occasionally occur for different reasons altogether, and, most importantly, may *fail to occur in spite of the existence of the conditions associated with war*. The general consequence of these scenarios is that the relationship between any specific "cause" of war and the actual occurrence of war will be weaker in the underdeveloped world than in the developed world. The specific consequence for the multiple hierarchy model is that parity and dissatisfaction will have less impact in regions where governments have less control over resources or have fewer resources to begin with.[13]

I attempt to determine whether such considerations might account for the cross-regional variation by specifying a pair of variables designed to represent this "lack of control," or "lack of resources" facing the leaders of underdeveloped states. The first of these variables is intended to represent political instability. It indicates the number of nonconstitutional changes of government occurring in either dyad member during the decade in question. "Coups" is thus the number of such

[12] The point is more eloquently put by Holsti (1996: 116): "Weak states face a fundamental difficulty that is rarely resolved satisfactorily. While giving the appearance of authoritarian power, the reach of the state is severely limited by local centers of resistance, by bureaucratic inertia and corruption, and by social fragmentation along religious, ethnic, tribal, factional and cultural lines."

[13] My thinking in this chapter is heavily influenced by Robert Jackson's work on quasi-states. Since he is more eloquent than me, consider the following from Jackson and Rosberg (1982: 8): "In proportion to their territories and populations, African governments typically have a smaller stock of finances, personnel, and material than Asian or Western governments, and their staffs are less experienced and reliable. As a result, the concept of governmental administration as a policy instrument bears less relation to reality." And from Jackson's solo work (1990: 177): "Economic underdevelopment and technological backwardness do not mean that quasi-statesmen have any less right to make decisions than other statesmen. It means that they have far fewer means and resources with which to implement and enforce their decisions and consequently must face harder choices as to what they will concentrate their scarce resources and energies on."

domestic political events according to the Polity II dataset.[14] I suspect leaders of states prone to coups face different considerations when deliberating about using force abroad. At a minimum, I suspect the number of coups occurring within a dyad within a given decade is a reasonable indicator of political instability within that dyad.

The second variable, "underdevelopment," is intended to represent lack of resources. It is a dichotomous variable equal to 1 if both dyad members are underdeveloped according to the United Nations Conference on Trade and Development. UNCTAD (various years) defines states as underdeveloped if their per capita GDP (in 1990 values) is below $700. States with GDP per capita this low are profoundly underdeveloped. The leaders of such states would clearly have far fewer resources upon which to draw when reacting to foreign policy stimuli. Given that such poverty is likely to be concentrated in certain parts of the Third World, it seems quite possible such a variable could account for the cross-regional variation.[15]

If my loosely theoretical account is accurate, then I should include variables designed to represent those factors which arguably deny leaders the luxury of free choice about when to wage war. Doing so should improve the fit of the statistical models to the data on war onsets (i.e., the model χ^2 should become larger and/or the variables coups and

[14] A description of this variable within the Polity II dataset is provided by Gurr, Jaggers, and Moore (1989: 49). One problem is that this dataset lists only successful coups. The concept of political instability suggests a variable also including unsuccessful attempted coups would be better. Luttwak (1969) and Thompson (1973b) provide data on failed as well as successful coups. I have constructed an alternate coups variable combining the unsuccessful Luttwak and Thompson coup attempts with the successful Polity II coups, but do not employ it in the model reported in table 7.3 because the data on unsuccessful coups are available for only a very limited span of years. Another version of the model reported in table 7.3, estimated with the alternate coups variable is not much different from those with the Polity II coups variable except for the fact that whereas the Polity II coups variable is nearly statistically significant in table 7.3, the alternate coups variable does not come close to attaining statistical significance.

[15] I estimated the model reported in table 7.3 with a variety of alternate measures of economic development and/or underdevelopment. One was simply GDP per capita averaged across both states and over the decade observed. Another was the GDP per capita of the poorer dyad member. A third was the GDP per capita of the richer dyad member. A final version was the development variable suggested by Bremer (1992) based on COW power components. This is the ratio of a state's share of economic components (iron/steel production and fuel consumption) to its share of demographic components. It is thus equivalent to Bremer's militarization variable, used throughout my analyses. One big advantage of Bremer's development index is that the data required to calculate it are much more available than are GDP per capita data; consequently, fewer cases are lost. However, none of these alternate development/underdevelopment variables attained statistical significance (in contrast to the UNCTAD-based variable), although otherwise the models were generally quite similar to that reported in table 7.3.

underdevelopment should be statistically significant), and also should eliminate or at least attenuate the cross-regional variation.

Finally, I include a third control variable not related to the loosely theoretical story advanced above. Some research (Werner and Lemke 1997; Gowa 1999; Werner 2000) suggests that in addition to a democratic peace, there appears to be an autocratic peace. Autocracies tend to be more peaceful with each other than are dyads composed of mixed regime types. This finding does not contradict the democratic peace, since it does not deny democracies are pacific in their relations with each other. Democratic-peace researchers themselves either report observing an autocratic peace, or otherwise hint at its existence (Maoz and Abdolali 1989; Oneal and Russett 1997). However, it may be of specific interest here because so many African states are non-democracies. In order to ascertain whether the African Peace is a sub-set of a larger peace among autocracies, I include a "joint autocracy" variable in the model estimated in table 7.3. This is calculated exactly like the joint democracy variable described in chapter 5, except that it uses Polity III's autocracy index rather than its democracy index.[16] If the African Peace, and larger cross-regional variation, are the result of an autocratic peace throughout the regions of my analyses, inclusion of joint autocracy will eliminate or attenuate the region-specific coefficients.

Including these three variables in a statistical model of war onset represents my effort to erase the statistical significance of the region-specific variables. Location within a specific region cannot "cause" dyads to vary in their war-fighting behavior compared to dyads elsewhere. There must be something else, something systematically more prevalent in Africa, causing African dyads to be different. The claim here is that political instability and economic underdevelopment, and possibly the prevalence of similarly autocratic regimes, makes dyads in Africa (and other regions) vary from global norms.

What I am trying to do by including these variables is demonstrate that the relationship between region-specific variables and war onset reported in chapter 5 is spurious. However, it is logically impossible to demonstrate that the region → war-onset relationships are spurious.

[16] Readers suspicious the joint democracy and joint autocracy variables are highly correlated with each other will not be surprised to learn the correlation between them is –0.8. I have run the model reported in table 7.3 alternately omitting either joint democracy or joint autocracy, with virtually no change in the reported results. There is high collinearity between these two variables, but it does not seem to affect the important estimates of coefficients for the region-specific dummy variables (nor for parity and dissatisfaction).

Table 7.3. *Logistic regression estimates with additional control variables*

Dependent variable is War Onset	
Covariate	Coefficient (Probability)
Constant	−3.912*
Parity	1.949* (0.0653)
Dissatisfaction	2.828** (0.0111)
Parity*Dissatisfaction	−1.887* (0.1000)
Alliance	−0.634 (0.4567)
Joint Democracy	0.0189 (0.4732)
Dominant Power's Militarization	−0.087 (0.3920)
Challenger's Militarization	0.020* (0.0990)
Joint Autocracy	0.095 (0.3398)
Coups	0.496 (0.1244)
Underdevelopment	2.514* (0.0588)
Africa	−3.088** (0.0203)
Far East	−1.077 (0.1970)
Middle East	−1.224 (0.1526)
South America	−3.441** (0.0209)
Observations: 279; model χ^2: 40.652**; correct predictions: overall: 94.98%, wars: 18.75%, non-wars: 99.62%	

Notes: Twelve time-interval dummy variables to control for duration dependence are included but not reported in order to preserve space.

*$p < 0.10$. **$p < 0.05$. ***$p < 0.01$.

The definition of a spurious relationship is that some alternate variable causes both of the related variables to occur. An hypothetical relationship between going to a good school and securing a high-quality job after graduation would be spurious if it were demonstrated that being lucky enough to have wealthy parents leads to both enrollment in prestigious schools and later success in life. In my situation, it is logically impossible that the variables coups or underdevelopment could *cause* dyads to be African. It cannot be the case that the region → war-onset relationships are technically spurious.

So, the purpose of including these new variables is that they represent the theoretically interesting "something" that might be systematically prevalent in Africa (and other regions), that causes dyads in those regions to vary in their war behavior. The Africa coefficient in chapter 5 is negative and large in an absolute sense. The interpretation of this coefficient is that African dyads are less war-prone than non-African dyads. If at the same time, African dyads are disproportionately likely to be composed of underdeveloped states, then underdevelopment and Africa should covary. If this happens, either the estimated coefficient for Africa will become statistically insignificant, or smaller (and thus substantively less significant), or taking into account underdevelopment when calculating probabilities of war will reduce the difference between African dyads and those in other regions (also changing the substantive significance of the African effect).

The new version of the model, including variables intended to wipe out the African Peace and the larger phenomenon of cross-regional variation, is reported in table 7.3. The inclusion of these new control variables does improve the fit of the statistical models to the data on war onsets. The model χ^2 statistic in table 7.3 is larger than the corresponding value in table 5.5 (but the difference between them is just over 5 and, with three degrees of freedom, not statistically significant). By itself, underdevelopment is statistically nearly significant at the $p < 0.05$ level, while coups is nearly significant at the $p < 0.10$ level. Joint autocracy not only has an unanticipated positive sign, but also never attains statistical significance.

Both the coups and underdevelopment variables have positive estimated coefficients. Although I have not advanced any directional hypotheses about these variables, this seems inconsistent with the Ishmaelia–Azania account presented (although it is consistent with Haas's [1968, 1973] arguments summarized earlier in this chapter). Readers will note that all of the estimated coefficients for the

Table 7.4. *Substantive effects of Parity and Dissatisfaction for model reported in table 7.3*

	Great Powers	Middle East	Far East	S. America	Africa
Neither Parity nor Dissatisfaction	3.0	1.7	3.4	0.2	0.2
Parity, no Dissatisfaction	17.9	10.7	19.7	1.4	1.4
Dissatisfaction, no Parity	34.6	22.5	37.4	3.3	3.3
Parity and Dissatisfaction	35.8	23.4	38.6	3.5	3.5

Cell entries are the estimated conditional probability of war (expressed as a percentage) given the conditions specified in each row in the region designated in each column. Control variables are set at their regional means.

region-specific dummy variables are larger (in an absolute sense) than the corresponding estimates reported in table 5.5. It is clear that the inclusion of the new control variables has not erased either the African Peace or the larger cross-regional variation. However, the positive coefficients for the new variables somewhat balance the now larger negative coefficients for the region-specific dummies because the minor power regions tend to have high values on the new variables while the Great Powers tend to have fewer coups and are not underdeveloped.

Table 7.4 reports the substantive effects, or estimated conditional probabilities of war across the five regions, holding all of the other reasonably statistically significant covariates constant at the average corresponding to each specific region.[17] These estimated effects demonstrate that the diminishing impact of parity and dissatisfaction on the probability of war as we move from consideration of the Great Powers through the other regions to Africa persists even with the addition of the new variables. However, these estimated effects also suggest the *differences* in the impact of parity and dissatisfaction on the probability of war across

[17] The use of these region-specific average values accounts for the differences across Great Power, Middle East, and Far East dyads' estimated conditional probabilities even though the Middle East and Far East variables are not statistically significant in the model. "Reasonably" statistically significant in this table corresponds to p values smaller than 0.20.

regions are smaller, in an absolute sense, than the corresponding differences when not controlling for coups and underdevelopment (as in table 5.6). Also, the four non-Great Power regions are more similar to each other in this set of analyses than they are in chapter 5.

It seems quite clear that controlling for political instability and underdevelopment does not erase either the African Peace or the larger phenomenon of cross-regional variation. However, the inclusion of these two variables does seem to diminish *how different* the various regions are from each other in terms of the substantive effects of parity and dissatisfaction on the probability of war. Even though two of the region-specific dummy variable coefficients are still statistically significant, they are less substantively significant. More impressive evidence of this lessening of the region-specific dummy variables' substantive significance is provided by considering the estimated conditional probability of war in a hypothetical African dyad marked by underdevelopment and three coups in a decade, and comparing these new estimated conditional probabilities to those calculated for the Great Powers. This scenario differs from that reported in table 7.4 in which regional *average* values on these variables were included. Even though Africa has the highest average value on underdevelopment, this average is less than 1. Also, even though Africa has nearly the highest average value on coups, that average is far below the 3 employed here (recall these are "successful" coups only). Thus, the change from regional average values to a value of 1 on underdevelopment and 3 on coups is a rather substantial change. It is not, however, an unreasonable change. In fact, these values are frequently observed within West African dyads. Making these changes and recalculating the substantive effects of varying the presence of parity and dissatisfaction produces the new estimated conditional probabilities of war reported in table 7.5. Clearly, employing these higher, but not unreasonably high, values of these important additional variables makes the African Peace *substantively* disappear. In table 7.5 the effects of parity and dissatisfaction actually become *smaller* for Great Power than for underdeveloped and unstable African dyads.

Thus, while there is still cross-regional variation, the amount of cross-regional variation seems smaller when taking into account the number of successful coups and whether or not the members of a dyad satisfy UNCTAD's definition of underdevelopment. This suggests to me that further efforts to erase the cross-regional variation, hopefully with more appealing, less crude indicators of instability and lack of resources, are

Table 7.5. *Substantive effects of Parity and Dissatisfaction for hypothetical African dyad with Coups = 3 and Underdevelopment = 1*

	Great Powers	African dyads
Neither Parity, nor Dissatisfaction	3.0	5.1
Parity, no Dissatisfaction	17.9	27.3
Dissatisfaction, no Parity	34.6	47.7
Parity and Dissatisfaction	35.8	49.0

Cell entries are the estimated conditional probability of war (expressed as a percentage) given the conditions specified in each row in the region designated in each column.

justified.[18] Nevertheless, the persistently statistically significant region-specific coefficients seem unambiguous evidence that the regions do differ from each other.[19] The reason why remains an important topic for continued research. The recalculated effects in table 7.5 are presented as evidence that analyses such as those undertaken in this section offer a promising avenue along which specific ignorance may be transformed into knowledge.

Cross-regional variation is due to region-specific measurement error

A third possible cause of the cross-regional variation may be that data quality issues cause me mistakenly to discover variation in how much

[18] Przeworski and Teune (1970: 13) anticipate situations such as mine: "The problem is that the same language may not be applicable across all systems but may have to be adjusted to specific systems. This is the central problem of comparative measurement: to incorporate into measurement statements the *context* within which observations are made." (Emphasis added)

[19] It need hardly be mentioned, except in a self-serving note, that the new model estimated in this chapter strongly continues to support the main hypothesis of the multiple hierarchy model. Even the introduction of new statistically significant control variables does not change the fact that parity and dissatisfaction with the status quo strongly increase the probability of war.

parity and dissatisfaction with the status quo affect the probability of war around the globe. If, to mention the most likely scenario, a large number of disputes and wars occur in Africa but go unnoticed in the West, I would necessarily observe an African Peace because there would be systematic measurement error on the dependent variable. How likely is this scenario?

Perhaps quite likely. Maier (1991) writes about a number of supposedly unimpeachable data sources with potentially enormously consequential biases in their reporting. American census data are among the best in the world, but Maier (pp. 11–13) recounts how even the Census Bureau admits it misses a non-negligible proportion of the US population. Moreover, this small proportion is not evenly distributed around the country. The missing Americans are disproportionately likely to be minorities, inner-city residents, homeless persons, etc. There is thus substantial bias in who is omitted from the census.[20] Maier reports similar non-random omissions from data collections on AIDS cases (p. 57), crime (p. 80), and informal-sector economic activity (p. 101). In all these examples it is the poorer, harder-to-measure segments of the population which are underreported. In international relations, the corresponding underreported groups would be the least developed countries.[21]

If the pathologies of data collection highlighted by Maier also beset international conflict datasets, then wars and disputes should be systematically underreported for the most underdeveloped region: Africa. There are a number of reasons African interstate conflict might be underreported. First, it could be that Western scholars and news organizations are not as interested in Africa as in other regions of the world. Consequently, there will be fewer people gathering data on Africa and thus a higher probability that interstate conflict (specifically in the less-intense dispute categories) will go unnoticed. Second, it could be that scholars and reporters actually do transmit lots of information about

[20] This example was suggested to me by a colleague from graduate school who worked on the 1990 Census in rural Arkansas. Although she faithfully visited the non-respondents on her list, she occasionally felt uncomfortable doing so, and perceived that other, less conscientious, census-takers might strategically miss an occasional residence.

[21] These data concerns should be considered in addition to two other rather major sources of data quality problems potentially systematically mis-measuring political activity in less developed countries: non-comparability (for instance, difficulties attendant upon converting national currency units to a single, meaningful standard) and motivated bias (for instance, CIA over-estimation of military expenditures by communist states during the Cold War – see Maier 1991: 170–172 specifically).

interstate conflict in Africa, but the information is not "received." If a militarized dispute between Chad and the Central African Republic occurs on the same day the United States launches cruise missiles against some Balkan state, how much coverage would the *New York Times* devote to the dispute in Africa? Precious little, one suspects. Similarly, imagine the scenario of an African specialist meticulously documenting the interstate nature of Zaire's various insurgencies. Surely these data would be fascinating, but publication and thus retention of them are uncertain. Consequently, the "fact" that Rwanda may have been an actor in the 1967 insurrection by mercenaries in eastern Congo (Kinshasa) would be lost.[22]

I am not insinuating that the various conflict datasets compiled over the years *are* inaccurate. I am simply speculating about the *possibility* that data are missing, and that those data are not randomly missing. I decided to submit the Correlates of War project's militarized interstate dispute (MID) dataset's coverage of Africa in 1967 to a simple reliability probe. I assess the reliability of the MID dataset's coverage of Africa because this is the region that, if the above concerns are valid, should be most inaccurate. I choose the year 1967 because I presume Southeast Asia dominated international news coverage then, and because the very dramatic Nigerian Civil War began in the summer of 1967. Consequently, it seems likely that any attention Africa received would have been restricted to the Gulf of Guinea local hierarchy, leaving coverage of the rest of Africa wanting. I consulted a variety of sources (Facts on File 1967; Keesing's 1967; *New York Times* 1968; Cook and Killingray 1983), all of which are authoritative chronologies of political events.

The sources I consulted all paint the same picture of conflict in Africa for 1967. There were violent ongoing independence struggles throughout Portuguese Africa (in Mozambique, Portuguese Guinea, and Angola), there was a violent insurrection in the eastern part

[22] There might also be motivated bias, whether conscious or not, in reports from the Third World. Evelyn Waugh's memoir of travel in late colonial East Africa is rather dramatic evidence. As he traveled from one colonial villa to another in 1959, repeated articles in *The Times* (reaching him after some delay) reported protests in which natives were stoning cars in Rhodesia. Upon reaching Rhodesia he wrote: "There is a current explanation of the reports that European cars are being stoned. The responsible Ministry in Rhodesia is said to have instituted an investigation into traffic. Since the native observers are not handy with paper and pencil, they were instructed to put a stone into a basket for every vehicle that passed them. A journalist finding a man at the side of the road with a basket of stones asked what they were for and received the answer: 'For cars'." (1960: 110) One wonders how many similarly easily misled reporters have filled the events datasets so popular among Western social scientists?

of Congo/Zaire, the Nigerian Civil War began during the summer months,[23] the Eritrean secessionist struggle continued, and civil war in Sudan and Chad was also ongoing. Some of these conflicts spilled across borders and involved neighboring African states, but little of this conflict expansion occurred in 1967 specifically.

Instead, interstate conflict in Africa in 1967 was restricted to just a few instances. In late May, Somalia dispatched troops to the Ethiopian border to offset an Ethiopian buildup in the area. This qualifies as a display-of-force dispute. Guinea and the Ivory Coast engaged in a potentially nasty round of ship seizures, diplomatic hostage-taking, etc., which qualifies as a use-of-force dispute. Kenya and Somalia escalated their simmering border conflict via Kenyan threats of dire consequences should the Somalis fail to curb raids into Kenyan territory. Kenya made good on these threats with pitched battles against Somali forces later in the year. This too is a use-of-force dispute. Finally, Rhodesia warned Zambia that if it did not take steps to deny Zambian territory to Rhodesian rebel forces, Rhodesia would hold Zambia militarily accountable. This would seem to qualify as a threat-to-use-force dispute. All of these "disputes" were reported in all four of the sources I consulted. Additionally, Keesing's reports a use of force between Sudan and Ethiopia in February 1967. If one is willing to accept the Sudan–Ethiopia use-of-force dispute based only on Keesing's report, there were five militarized interstate disputes between African states in 1967.

What of the COW militarized interstate dispute dataset? There is close concordance between my (admittedly potentially incomplete) consultation of sources and the disputes reported by COW. The Somali–Ethiopian and Somali–Kenyan disputes are linked in the COW dataset within MID #1378. The Guinea–Ivory Coast stand-off is faithfully represented as MID #1352. Keesing's Sudanese–Ethiopian imbroglio finds itself in the COW dataset as MID #1422. Additionally, the COW dataset includes disputes between various African states and Portugal in 1967 (MIDs #1332, 1392, and 3271), all related to the

[23] Readers may object that the Biafran/Nigerian Civil War was a domestic conflict only in hindsight. Had Biafra prevailed and won its independence, this struggle very likely would have been recorded as an interstate war. Gabon's, Ivory Coast's, Tanzania's, and Zambia's recognition of Biafra suggests at least four African states viewed the struggle as an international one. My perusal of the sources listed above uncovers no militarized *inter*state interactions in 1967 specifically, while the four states recognizing Biafra did not do so until 1968. Given the coding rules employed by the Correlates of War project, this conflict does not qualify as an interstate war. As discussed below, however, maybe those coding rules are not optimal for the very underdeveloped.

independence struggles mentioned above. The only "dispute" I identified which is not included in the COW dataset is the Rhodesian–Zambian threat to use force. Given I find evidence of this interstate threat in all of my sources, I am unsure why it is not included in the COW dataset. I initially thought Rhodesia did not, perhaps, satisfy the COW interstate system membership criteria in 1967, but find Small and Singer's (1982: 49) list of interstate system members includes Rhodesia from 1966 on.

In general, the COW list of interstate conflicts in Africa for 1967 is very consistent with my list of such conflicts. Perusal of Correlates of War project publications describing the conflict dataset suggests we should not be surprised my analysis identifies the MID dataset as reliable. The collectors of the MID dataset went to enormous pains to ensure they did not omit any interstate conflicts. Gochman and Maoz (1984: 589–590) recount how the initial MID compilation was drawn from a wide range of sources in many languages. Similarly, Jones, Bremer, and Singer (1996: 180–182) are even more detailed in listing fifteen languages within which primary sources were consulted. It remains possible that the data collection pathologies described by Maier operate on conflict data and systematically underreport African conflict, but I find no strong evidence that the possibility is reality.

However, a perhaps more likely, and certainly more difficult to correct, source of region-specific measurement error may exist. I refer to potential problems introduced by only observing "states" as the uniformly relevant political actors in the world.[24] All standard sources of data in world politics research, from the COW project, to information provided by the UN, to the Penn World Tables, and elsewhere, aggregate information at the societal level of the state/nation/country. Membership in the United Nations is the most common rule delineating which social aggregations qualify as "states." There is a presumption in these data sources that the *legal* political entities thereby included as observations in the datasets are *empirical* political entities. Jackson and Rosberg offer a trenchant discussion characterizing many of Africa's states as legal but not empirical entities. They write (1982: 9): "The modern 'administrative state' image of government is of questionable applicability in many

[24] This tendency is strongly inculcated in empirical international conflict studies by the widespread assumption, originating in realist theory, that states are the most important actors in world politics. See Jackson (1990) and Clapham (1996) for persuasive arguments invalidating this assumption in the Third World generally and in Africa specifically. For an interesting effort to move beyond state-centrism in international politics theorizing, see Lake's discussion of polities as political actors (1999: ch. 2).

parts of the world, but Black African governments are even less likely than others to be rational agencies." And then: "It is evident that the term 'empirical state' can only be used selectively to describe many states in Black Africa today" (p. 12). The term "empirical state" is adapted from Weber's "*de facto* state" conceptualization, in which a state truly exists only if there is a centralized, effective government supervising interactions within a clearly delineated territory. Later, Jackson (1990) coins the term "quasi-state" to designate juridical but not empirical political entities.

It may be that in Africa (and other parts of the Third World), the parallel to interactions between developed states is not interactions between the legal entities that enjoy membership in the United Nations, but rather is interactions between sub-national groups. Perhaps Biafra's "war" against the Nigerian federal government, or Mobutu's relations with regional power brokers in eastern Zaire during his long rule, are more like interactions between France and Germany than are interactions between African quasi-states. Since the legal entities enjoying UN membership are widely recognized as independent states, information is gathered about them. Various data collections report how many soldiers there are in Sudan (for instance), how much money is spent on the "Sudanese" army, the gross national product of "Sudan," etc. What these summary figures do not indicate is how many of those soldiers are loyal to the Sudanese central government, whether those military expenditures are motivated by internal or external threats, and how much of the economic activity occurring within the legal borders of "Sudan" is taxable by the central government. The assumption that summary characteristics of an entire state are relevant indicators of what the "state" can bring to bear in interactions with its neighboring "states" simplifies data collection, but it may distort reality.

My point is obvious, but has profound consequences for any analysis aggregating observations of developed and underdeveloped dyads into a global whole. If the legal entities defined as states in our datasets are not the empirical interacting entities our theories describe, then our research designs will be indeterminate because we are observing, in the underdeveloped cases, the wrong actors. It may be that Biafra and the Federal Government of Nigeria fought each other when they were at parity and Biafra was dissatisfied with the local status quo. If these sub-national political entities are the "true" African political actors, the multiple hierarchy model would, given the above, expect the Nigerian "Civil" War to have been fought when it was. Unfortunately, this confirming evidence would never be observed, because data on Biafra were never collected. Similarly, data on Zairean provinces, on Sudanese warring groups, and on other similar situations were not collected. I may be observing cross-regional variation and an African Peace in this book only because my naïve designation of what is a political actor leads me systematically to observe the "wrong" units in regions comprised primarily of underdeveloped states.[25] Imagine a scenario in which I have a theory generating an hypothesis that birds tend to build nests while other animals do not. If, when I turned to empirical analysis of my theory, my classification scheme defined all flying animals as birds, I would be inappropriately including both bats and flying insects in the bird category. If I then observed that "birds" are not disproportionately likely to build nests, I might conclude that my theory is wrong. This would be unfortunate because if I removed the myriad species of bats and flying insects from my bird category, it might well be that birds do disproportionately build nests compared to other animals. I fear that when it comes to analysis of political interactions in Africa, the entire community of empirical international relations scholars has a lot of bats mixed in with its birds. Unfortunately, this possibility cannot be easily diagnosed or remedied unless very different datasets are collected.

One way in which we might at least speculate about remedying the problem of observing the "wrong" actors in the underdeveloped world is suggested by consideration of why empirical states are uncommon where development is absent. Such consideration reminds us that Africa's weak states (and weak states in the rest of the Third World, of course) are weak *because* they are in the early stages of the process of developing. A number of authors (for example, Ayoob 1991, 1995; Weede 1996) make plausible connections between the issue of juridical vs. empirical states in the developing world and the processes of development. In so doing they explicitly connect Tilly's (1975, 1985) arguments about war- and state-making in Europe to current African and

[25] Even if I am wrong about who the political actors are, something representing international politics is going on. Consider Clapham's (1996: 266) claim:

> In areas of Africa where the state was no more than a fiction, the activities in which international relations essentially consisted still continued to take place: goods were imported and exported; external NGOs provided medical help or famine relief, and were sometimes even protected by outside powers; local rulers sought to control the exchanges between domestic and external resources, and in the process to maintain their own power and security. The connection between statehood and international relations was ultimately a contingent one.

wider Third World experience. The disunity, corruption, violence, lack of cooperation and other problems plaguing the fragmented states of the less-developed parts of the Third World seem directly comparable to the emerging states in Europe's Middle Ages. In this regard, the political puzzle of assembling a unified, coherent, effective "Nigeria" out of various regional and tribal pieces is exactly parallel to the earlier puzzle of creating an "England" out of Mercian, Northumbrian, Anglian, and Danelaw kingdoms.[26]

According to Tilly (1975, 1985), war and violence are important parts of the process of putting states together. Political elites use violence against each other to determine who will control the territory. Those who emerge victorious continue to use violence to centralize their control over the resources of a territory and thereby cement their authority. In order to do so they often develop an infrastructure to facilitate the mobilization of the resources necessary to retain their privileged positions. Political elites use violence and make war in order to make states in the first place.[27]

If we allow this argument, then we must allow the possibility that warfare serves different purposes at different times over the course of a state's development. In the early phases of a state's developmental history, warfare (even when it involves actors physically external to the territory) may tend to be about control of the territory that eventually becomes the "state." After these preliminary conflicts are resolved, wars may be fought to establish the new state's place in the international system, or to otherwise improve its international position. Multiple hierarchy model arguments clearly seem applicable to the later stage, but may also apply, in modified form, to the earlier. It may be that the various

[26] But see Widner (1995) for a less enthusiastic appraisal of the parallels between contemporary African and early European state-building experiences. Widner argues the African experience differs in terms of the impact of extended family structure, the existence of parallel political authorities the ruthless suppression of which is prevented by the international community, the widespread availability of weapons, international factor mobility, and international aid regimes. Other authors questioning the European past as a model for the Third World's future include Centeno (1997) for Latin America and Herbst (2000) for Africa. An interesting point is made by Weiner (1971) in his argument that the only part of Europe relevant to the Third World's situation is the Balkans, where states emerged from colonialism, did so with externally imposed borders, did so in a context involving external developed states interested in their affairs, and were characterized by much ethnic division.

[27] For empirical evaluation of Tilly's arguments, see Cohen, Brown, and Organski (1981), and Rasler and Thompson (1985, 1989). For a specific application of Tilly's argument to modern Africa, see Kirby and Ward (1991). My argument here is clearly foreshadowed by theirs.

competitive political elite groups within a state fight wars of national consolidation when they are roughly equal with each other and disagree about what the domestic status quo should be.[28] Unfortunately though, if we use datasets aggregating the various local elite groups into a national total, we cannot evaluate such possibilities.

It may also be the case that at the earlier stages of state development, wars are fought, perhaps often involving actors from other "states," for reasons and under conditions very different from those identified by the multiple hierarchy model. It could be that in these "young-state" wars neither parity nor status quo evaluations are especially relevant. If this is true, then we should certainly expect a weaker relationship between *any* given covariates (such as parity and dissatisfaction, or joint democracy for that matter) and war. This is similar to the argument advanced in the preceding section, and suggests we might actually theorize about causes of region-specific measurement error that subsequently "cause" an observation of cross-regional variation and an African Peace. Further, if these speculations are valid, then we should observe an increasingly stronger association between parity, dissatisfaction, and war among the great powers over time as we move through the millennium just ended.[29] At the start of this thousand-year period, political territories were coalescing into what became the great powers. Over time, internal power struggles were resolved, political and economic infrastructures developed, and warfare evolved from the "young-state" to the "established-state" variety. Unfortunately, I do not have any data with which to evaluate this proposition, and thus leave it as a suggestion for future research. But, I am encouraged in this line of argument because the positive coefficients on underdevelopment and coups in table 7.3 are inconsistent with the loosely theoretical story justifying them. That story is plausible and thus the positive coefficients are unexpected. However, if high values on these variables do represent newly emerging states, since they are positively associated with war, a possible interpretation is that wars are part of the process of state emergence.

[28] For an intriguing empirical hint that power-transition-like arguments may offer insight into such domestic conflicts, see Benson and Kugler (1998). McFaul (2002) offers an interesting application of power-transition-like arguments in his discussion of domestic conflict revolving around Russia's democratic transition in the 1990s.

[29] Statistically this amounts to an hypothesis that the relationship between parity, dissatisfaction, and war is heteroskedastic, where the heteroskedastic factor is time. If this is true, then all longitudinal analyses of war (such as those undertaken in this book) are incorrect because the data would violate the assumption of homoskedasticity.

Conclusions

Is there an African Peace? Does cross-regional variation exist in analyses of the multiple hierarchy model? The answer is "yes and no." On the one hand there very definitely is statistically and substantively significant variation in the fit of the multiple hierarchy model across various regions. At the same time, there is statistically and substantively significant variation in the propensity of dyads within different regions to be involved in interstate wars regardless of the presence of parity and dissatisfaction with the status quo. These answers suggest there is an African Peace and there is cross-regional variation.

However, it seems to me inappropriate to conclude this means there is something different about underdeveloped regions, or about regions more generally, that cautions against attempts to apply what we know about the developed world to analysis of interactions within the developing world. Mindless aggregation for the sake of increasing sample size strikes me as a bad idea, but mindless abandonment of the effort to pool regional analyses strikes me as equally unwarranted. There is important information to be gained by thoughtfully piecing the regions together. Doing so demonstrates an underlying similarity coexisting with persistent cross-regional variation. This chapter offers some elaborate speculation about what might cause such cross-regional variation to exist. I do not think it is coincidental. Rather, I think there are characteristics of some regions causing the observed cross-regional variation and its extreme manifestation dubbed the African Peace. Rather than toss our hands in the air and relegate these characteristics to something nebulous like "political culture" or "colonial legacy," I think a more productive path is to try to theorize about what might cause the regions to vary. Interestingly, it seems to me the process of development by which territories become organized into centralized states likely causes us to mismeasure political activity in underdeveloped regions, and to observe those regions as somehow "different" from the developed world. Earlier in this chapter I demonstrated that controlling for some factors likely involved in this process of development attenuates how substantively different the most underdeveloped region is from the developed world. Subsequently I speculated about how the process of development more broadly might affect war, and mused about what this might mean for how we should study war. An African Peace may sound absurd, but simply being open-minded enough to speculate about it may tell us something interesting about Africa, or about development and war, or about problems applying developed-world concepts and research practices to the developing world.

Of course, the most productive path to pursue might be to recognize that my political development → conflict process is only part of the story. Introducing variables designed to represent parts of that process (underdevelopment, instability) do improve the statistical model's fit to the data. They seem to tell part of the story. But I cannot ignore the fact that the regional variables remain statistically significant. Widner (1995), Centeno (1997), and Herbst (2000) all question how relevant Tilly's story of European development is for development in Africa and Latin America. If only because the Europeans did not develop within borders dictated to them by already-developed states, nor try to develop in the presence of stronger already-developed competitors, it seems prudent to heed their informed warnings (they are recognized experts on the politics of their regions, after all). What this might amount to is a strategy of specifying variables they identify as relevant (family structure, multiple authority structures, weapons transfers, factor mobility, and aid for Widner; the delegitimation of political authority, fragility of elite coalitions, and lack of national identity for Centeno; and demographic and geographical factors for Herbst), as well as variables I identify as relevant, in an effort to account for cross-regional variation. Such is not undertaken in this exploratory analysis, but it seems a promising direction for continued research.

Our own writings often strike us as more important or more profound than they do our readers, and thus this last paragraph might best be read as conceited musings. It seems to me power transition theory has come full circle in the course of the multiple hierarchy model extension to minor power regions. The central factor distinguishing Organski's theorizing from that which preceded him was his concentration on processes of political and economic development in the construction of power transition theory's argument. Only if and when states develop, according to his theory, do they come to be contenders for control of the international system. The very process of a state's development, how its elite organizes domestic society in terms of resource aggregation and allocation, determines whether the state is satisfied or dissatisfied with the status quo.[30] Power transition theory made the first international relations

[30] Readers interested in tracing this central element in Organski's thought are referred to part 1 of his *World Politics* (1958; 2nd edn. 1968), all of his *The Stages of Political Development*

argument explicitly linking state development and subsequent "high" politics on the world stage. My extension of this theory to minor power regions, and my discovery of variation in how well it fits in different regions, suggests that not only was Organski right to argue development sets the stage for subsequent wars, but he was also extremely, and uniquely, prescient in foreseeing development and war as inextricably linked. If my speculations in this chapter are correct, not only does development set the stage for subsequent war, but war and development interact with and condition each other in setting that stage.

(1965), chapter 2 and appendix 1 of Organski and Kugler's *The War Ledger* (1980), and Organski *et al.*'s *Births, Deaths and Taxes* (1984).

8 Conclusions, implications and directions for continued research

The need for a weaving together of the strands of this book seems greater than is the case with most volumes. The reason for this is that I address three interrelated tasks in this book. The first is an evaluation of the multiple hierarchy model extension of power transition theory to minor power regions, necessitating consideration of whether such an extension is justifiable. The second task is empirical identification of what a regional sub-system is. Unless regional sub-systems of the international system are objectively identified, extensions of great power theories to the minor power level cannot be empirically evaluated. The final task is an exploration of possible sources of persistent cross-regional variation in the relationships between power parity, status quo evaluations, and war onset. All three of these tasks have been accomplished, at least partially, in the preceding chapters. However, my book offers only a first perspective on each, and more can clearly be done to address all three. The third section below lays out steps likely to help any effort to move beyond my preliminary achievements.

Summary

Power transition theory was created to account for great power interactions. No clearer statement of this is needed than Organski and Kugler's own recognition that their work could:

> not claim to establish connections between changes in the international power structure and the outbreak of wars among small nations, or among large and small nations; nor do the models explain colonial wars . . . The hypotheses in question can be tested fairly only if we locate conflicts whose outcomes will affect the very structure and operation of the international system. (1980: 45)

I elaborate power transition theory with the multiple hierarchy model (introduced in chapter 3) by extending this avowedly great power theory of international politics to the more localized interactions of minor powers. There are various motivations for doing so. As described in chapter 2, power transition theory is an especially good candidate for continuing theoretical elaboration because so much empirical support for it has been amassed over the years. Moreover, there are a variety of arguments consistent with power transition theory which suggest it might account for a number of empirical phenomena beyond the hypothesis of when world wars are fought. The motivation for an extension specifically to minor power interactions also arises from a pair of sources. First, a larger empirical domain is evidence of a better theory. Thus, on epistemological grounds such elaboration is desirable. Second, practically speaking, great power interactions comprise only a fraction of exchanges between states (although the fraction is a disproportionately significant one). Consequently, there seems to be simply too much international politics operating beyond the theory's original purview to justify claims it is truly useful for those who would base policy on its arguments (see Tammen *et al.* 2000 for a policy-relevant application).

In order to be able to evaluate the multiple hierarchy model's hypothesis about the importance of power parity and status quo dissatisfaction for war onsets among both the great powers and within localized minor power sub-systems, I have to know what a minor power local international system, or local hierarchy, is. This leads to chapter 4 in which I explain in detail how I define local hierarchies, and why I use the definition I do. I believe my definition is better than immediately available alternatives, and more generally that objective efforts such as presented in chapter 4 offer a useful way for anyone to identify regions. In chapter 3, I speculate about how Morgan and Palmer's "two-good theory of foreign policy" might be improved by regional elaboration. The procedure for identifying regions described in chapter 4 would allow evaluation of such minor power regional elaboration for the two-good theory, or for any other theory that might be similarly extended to account for minor power interactions.

Of course, in any such effort to transplant what we "know" about the developed world to interactions within the underdeveloped world, questions of whether such interactions are fundamentally similar enough for the transplant to take root and grow must be addressed. If interstate politics in the Third World are fundamentally different from those among developed states, the extension of power transition theory would be about as productive as transplanting trees from the Amazon to the Antarctic. Such questions are central to caricatured debates between area specialists and political science generalists. I review such arguments in chapter 1, and return to detailed consideration of them in the analyses presented in chapter 5. My results suggest the extension offered by the multiple hierarchy model is fruitful. There is enough underlying similarity between developed-, developing-, and underdeveloped-world interactions to make unified analysis of interactions within all three meaningful.

That said, however, there are still important differences across regions, just as the caricatured area specialists would anticipate. I find the inclusion of region-specific variables improves the fit of my statistical model to the data on war onsets. Moreover, I then discover interesting cross-regional variation in how much impact parity and status quo dissatisfaction have on the probability of war. These variables have their largest substantive effects among Great Power, Middle Eastern, and Far Eastern dyads, and have much smaller substantive effects in South America and Africa. These findings persist even after great power interference is considered.

I offer a detailed follow-up analysis of the cross-regional variation. I try to diagnose why such cross-regional variation exists. I offer a preliminary effort at the development of a theoretical explanation of what causes the cross-regional variation. I provide some evidence substantiating my claim of political and economic underdevelopment affecting the conditional probability of war onset. I speculate this would be the case if the process of development is intertwined with both the timing of war and the purposes for which wars are fought.

In sum, I find the multiple hierarchy model produces meaningful and empirically substantiated expectations about when both great powers and minor powers will and will not make war on one another. In coming to this finding I offer a new empirical procedure for identifying regional sub-systems of the international system. I argue this designation of regions is useful in its own right, and encourage others to make use of it in regional extensions of their arguments. Additionally, I find in my evaluation of the multiple hierarchy model that while there is much consistency in war behavior across all five regions studied, there are also important and interesting differences. These region-specific effects may be important hints that the process of development complicates questions about the conditions under which states fight wars and about the purposes they pursue when they go to war. At a more fundamental level, I see hints that the process of development affects our ability to observe international interactions accurately. The successful extension of power transition theory to minor power regional interactions via the multiple hierarchy model, the empirical delineation of minor power localized international systems, and the discovery of persistent, and theoretically important, cross-regional variation are the three interrelated accomplishments of my book.

Implications for policy and research

The most immediate implications of the foregoing analyses for policymakers concern how they might more profitably view the world. If the United States, for example, would prefer peace to obtain in the Third World, its foreign policy decision-makers might pay more attention to local power relationships and indications of discontent between minor powers. My analyses suggest very unequal minor powers without substantial disagreements about their local status quo are unlikely to wage war on each other. Crises between such minor powers might thus take lower priority than those between relatively equal dyads with dissatisfaction. The prospects for peace in Third world local hierarchies will, according to my analyses, be enhanced by diplomatic efforts to serve as an honest broker seeking to rectify fundamental disagreements between minor powers about their local relations. If these differences are intractable, it may be impossible to preserve peace diplomatically. Also, efforts to "preserve a balance" between such implacably opposed minor power states will more likely increase the probability of war than of peace.[1]

The foregoing analyses also offer implications for how we might better study international politics. The discussion in chapter 7 suggests it might be valuable to re-consider definitions of who the main actors in world politics are. We might be very well served by trying to gather data on effective/actual political actors rather than on quasi-states. Most members of the United Nations might satisfy the criteria of empirical statehood (effective, sovereign authorities supervising interactions

[1] Exactly this sort of "mistake" may have been made by the United States and Soviet Union in the Middle East during the Cold War. According to Kinsella (1994, 1995) American military assistance to Israel, and Soviet military assistance to Egypt and Syria, approximately complemented each other. If the assistance was intended to make each side strong enough to deter conflict, obviously the policies failed. A more sinister view might be that great powers sometimes intentionally foment wars by striving to maintain parity between minor powers.

within a defined territory), but some are merely juridical states (legal fictions lacking an effective centralized authority). The assumption that all juridical states are empirical states greatly simplifies data collection and reinforces the traditional assumption that states are the most relevant actors in international politics. However, almost all of our theories are about the behavior of international actors. I am aware of no theory of international politics that specifically applies only to legally defined states. Most of the legal entities are actors on the international stage, but other legal entities may actually encompass two or more tribal, ethnic or other sub-state aggregations of individuals, *each* of which is an effective international actor approximating an empirical state. If we continue to restrict ourselves to unquestioned analysis of juridical states as *the* actors in world politics, we run the risk of inappropriately observing the wrong groups of people.

Similarly, my analyses suggest we might rethink what international conflict is. Perhaps standard definitions such as that offered by the Correlates of War project should be supplemented with instances of violent interaction between any international actors. Had the federal government forces lost the Nigerian Civil War, few would object to calling this Biafran war of independence an interstate war. Theories like the multiple hierarchy model seem to suggest the conflicts that should be of interest to us are those between any two or more international actors. If we redefine the actors in world politics, we need also to redefine what constitutes conflict and other interactions in world politics.

There is yet a third way in which the foregoing analyses and arguments suggest we might have to change how we study international conflict. If the process of development affects not only when wars are fought but also what they are fought about, then it seems likely patterns of conflict and war will vary systematically over the course of a state's, or dyad members', development. This suggests series of data relevant to war and conflict will be heteroskedastic, with progress toward development being the factor associated with that heteroskedasticity. I am aware of no current international conflict research program that diagnoses whether such heteroskedasticity exists (with the possible exception of Maoz 1989). My arguments may be too preliminary at this stage to justify dramatic changes in research design along these lines. But if subsequent evidence bears out the possible interrelationship between development and conflict, changes in estimation procedures to incorporate this heteroskedasticity will have to be made.

A final implication from my analyses concerns the large epistemological question of whether we should pool disparate evaluations into unified, global wholes. Over-stated and caricatured all-or-nothing debates between area specialists and generalists obscure the possibility (strongly supported here) that both positions are partially correct. I suspect likelihood ratio tests such as those undertaken in chapter 5 would confirm the statistical appropriateness of pooling for most studies of international conflict. But I also suspect such tests would indicate the inclusion of region-specific dummy variables within such pooled analyses is also statistically appropriate. I do not think these results are specific only to evaluation of the multiple hierarchy model. What this means is that while pooling is not wrong, it does obscure the fact that there are differences across regions. We need to be sensitive to such questions of aggregating observations while allowing for region-specific effects. We need then to produce theoretical explanations for the cross-regional differences we might thereby uncover.

Directions for continued research

As mentioned above, the analyses throughout this book offer only first attempts to answer the questions raised in pursuit of the three intertwined tasks. There are quite a few directions in which continued research could improve upon what I accomplish here.

First, and perhaps most obviously, the loosely theoretical explanation for cross-regional variation offered in chapter 7 is simply inadequate. It does not satisfactorily express how development and conflict might affect each other, nor is it specific enough to provide clear guidelines as to what theoretical variables should or could account for the regional effects. I believe the expectation that the correlates of war will vary with the process of development is plausible. I think the pseudo-typology of wars of national consolidation early on, followed by wars of national advancement within the international system later, has a certain appeal, but am aware how underdeveloped it is. Moreover, it could well be that some other factors, perhaps suggested by research programs of which I am unaware, offer clues about what better variables would account for the cross-regional variations. I offer hints from work by Widner, Centeno, and Herbst, but much more research on the sources of cross-regional variation lies ahead.

Of course, this suggestion for better theoretical elaboration of the sources of region-specific differences in the substantive importance of parity and dissatisfaction for the probability of war is moot if the cross-regional variation is not robust. I believe it is, based on Barro's similar findings, the replication by Bill Reed discussed in chapter 7, and the wider literature involving similar "specific ignorance" variables in American politics research. But a second direction in which the foregoing analysis would be improved is to offer many more, and more varied, sensitivity analyses to see how truly robust are the relationships reported here. Throughout the text I recognize that others might object to my specific designation of cases to be included in the analysis. Changing the definition of military reachability (perhaps to a different threshold at which a target state is unreachable, or replacing inter-capital distances with the distances between capital cities and the borders of putative foes) would change the identity of cases in the dataset. Similarly, other researchers might believe different operationalizations of critical variables, or different estimation techniques, would be more appropriate. Any one of these changes might produce results different from those in chapters 5–7. These potentially different results might not include cross-regional variation. If a compelling case could be made for such changes in case selection, variable measurement, or estimation procedure, then the robustness of my results might be undermined. Thus, whether time, effort, and money should be expended on theoretical elaboration might best wait until more sensitivity analyses, or at least more consideration of such reanalyses, have been undertaken. I have exhausted my intellectual resources in producing the results here, and am persuaded that better measures of my variables, better procedures for case selection, or more appropriate estimation techniques are not readily available. But social science is a social enterprise, and I leave it to others to express their opinions on these matters.

I evaluate relations between states in most of the world. I include dyads in South America, the Middle East, the Far East, Africa and among the very strongest of the great powers. I think this a reasonably broad spatial domain, and am proud of my accomplishment. However, broad as my spatial domain may be, it does omit a substantial number of dyads. The most obvious omissions are Central America, interactions among European states apart from the Great Powers, and Oceania.[2] These regions are omitted from the analyses here because I was concerned about the extent to which interactions in Central America

[2] It is interesting to note that in his elaboration of regional security complexes, Buzan (1991) omits, or treats as subordinate to higher-order security complexes, many of the same states and sub-regions I omit.

might be non-independent owing to massive American interference, and that European Great Powers might have similarly compromised how independent European lesser-power interactions might be. Finally, aside from the extension of the World War II Pacific theater into Oceania, there is virtually no international conflict in that region to draw attention. Thus, these regions are omitted for reasons – but the reasons may not be especially good ones. Omission of America's or Britain, France, Russia/Soviet Union and Germany's potential spheres of influence in Central America or Europe simplifies my analysis. Any future research claiming to be an advance over this book, however, would clearly be bolstered by more inclusive consideration of these omitted regions.

The analyses above suggest the multiple hierarchy model allows anticipation of when wars will and will not occur among great powers and among minor powers. This encompasses a great deal of the conflict occurring in the international system. However, it misses an embarrassingly large number of wars pitting great powers against minor powers. A quick perusal of the detailed COW list of sixty-seven interstate wars through 1980 (Small and Singer 1982: 82–95), uncovers twenty-three (one-third!) fought between a great power and a non-great power. Eleven of these latter wars were fought in Europe, nine in the Far East, two in the Middle East, and one in North America.

The problem these wars pose for the multiple hierarchy model is broader than the simple failure to anticipate their occurrence. It is that the multiple hierarchy model suggests the probability such wars will be fought is so low that we only very rarely would expect them to occur. According to the theory, when a disproportionately powerful actor makes a demand of a much weaker state, the weaker state can be virtually certain it would lose any military conflict arising from failure to satisfy that demand, and thus the expectation is that in virtually every instance the minor power will simply cede whatever point is in question without recourse to warfare. How many such wars should occur can only be calculated if we know how often great powers make demands of minor powers, but even in the absence of such data I wonder whether we should expect twenty-three of these wars to have occurred between 1816 and 1980?

This discussion might lead to an expectation that the twenty-three wars between great powers and non-great powers should disproportionately be characterized by low fatality levels. We might surmise that most of these wars are mistakes in which the minor power miscalculates the great power's willingness to go to war over whatever issue is at stake. In such a situation the minor power might resist, a battle would occur, and then the minor power would concede defeat in order to avoid continued death and destruction in pursuit of a lost cause.[3]

This reasonable expectation is contradicted by the fact that the average number of battle fatalities in the twenty-three wars is just over 40,000. Recall from the previous chapter that the average number for all COW wars excluding the extreme cases of 1,000,000+ is around 35,000. There are no million-plus fatality wars among the twenty-three, but there are a few extreme cases (interestingly, all involved Russia). If these are removed the average drops significantly to slightly more than 10,000. This may be lower than the overall average excluding the high extreme cases, but it still seems a good bit higher than what should suffice to convince minor powers to concede defeat.

In a fascinating essay, Carlos Escudé (1998: 55) distinguishes between two types of minor powers: "states that obey, the majority of the interstate community, including the Third World and advanced but militarily weak industrialized states, and rebel states (a small number of Third World states that choose to be part of the anarchical system of the Great Powers by challenging the right of the Great Powers to dominate)." Escudé's examples of "rebel states," Iraq under Saddam Hussein, Libya under Khadaffi, and Argentina in the early 1980s under Galtieri, are consistent with an expectation that it might be rebel states pitted against great powers in wars. This suggests there are two types of non-great powers: those operating within their localized international sub-systems, and those bucking the trend and acting as though they were great powers. Their attempts to do so may draw unfavorable great power reactions, expressed in the twenty-three wars mentioned above. It would likely be promising to develop theory about which states will be the "rebels" and under what circumstances their rebellions will generate war with a true great power.[4]

[3] Regardless of what the theory might lead us to expect, it could logically, and just as easily, be the great power that underestimates the resolve of the minor power in the dispute. If this were the case it might take a *higher* number of fatalities to convince the great power the minor power is resolved than vice versa. There is some evidence minor powers in these wars are more resolved than their great power opponents. In the twenty-three asymmetric wars referred to here, the minor power suffered 2.84 times as many casualties as the great power, on average. In nineteen of the twenty-three wars minor power fatalities were higher than great power fatalities, and often drastically higher (as high as one hundred times in one instance).

[4] Such wars might be an especially consequential omission from power transition research because it could be they are the very preventive wars far-sighted dominant powers fight, namely wars against much weaker, but in the future much stronger, states.

Escudé's argument suggests the action of "rebel" states being disciplined by attacking/avenging great powers is a description of asymmetric war. In contrast, T. V. Paul (1994) investigates conditions associated with war initiations by the weak against the strong. Paul's analysis is based on detailed consideration of six wars initiated by weak states. He suggests such conflicts may be more likely when the initiator's politico-military strategy offsets the power disparity, when the initiator possesses offensive weapons and/or enjoys support from great power allies, and when domestic political conditions within the weaker state make war initiation favorable. Escudé's argument might offer hints about when and where the strong wage war on the weak, while Paul's might suggest clues about when the weak wage war on the strong. Combining such arguments, if possible, might offer an account of asymmetric conflicts. The multiple hierarchy model as currently developed is inconsistent with the existence of each of the twenty-three asymmetric wars described above. This does not mean necessarily that the multiple hierarchy model should be abandoned, but rather that efforts to further elaborate it so it more accurately reflects the reality of great power versus non-great power interactions are needed. Escudé's and Paul's work might aid such elaboration.

Finally, as discussed in chapter 2, one of the problems critics of power transition theory have highlighted is the failure to define the status quo and the benefits it confers on satisfied states. This concept is central to the theory, but only loosely represented by the empirical measures employed in statistical evaluations thereof. This is equally true of the local status quos central to the multiple hierarchy model. In chapter 3 I speculate about what local status quos might be, and how the ability to influence these status quos would confer benefits on those doing the influencing. Unfortunately, I did not represent these plausible considerations directly in my statistical models. I attempted to do so while constructing the datasets employed in this book by specifying a variable indicating the existence of a territorial disagreement between local hierarchy members. The problem I encountered is that for the years in which I have data on this potential alternate indicator of status quo dissatisfaction, there is perfect identification between it and wars fought in local hierarchies. The development of a scale indicating the intensity of territorial disagreements (ranging from no disagreement at all to extreme situations such as in the cases of Palestine, Kashmir, etc.) might offer a technical way to side-step the statistical problem of perfect identification. As yet, unfortunately, no such scale exists.

A more fundamental question might profitably be addressed before other empirical elaboration is undertaken. Specifically, what if models of war as fought in the great power past are inapplicable to the minor powers, not because the great powers and minor powers differ in terms of levels of development, but because the nature of war has fundamentally changed? What if the types of wars central to theories like power transition simply are no longer fought? Such speculation lies at the heart of Holsti's *The State, War, and the State of War* (1996). In this study he claims "wars of the third kind," wars not related to specific crises, without specific starting points, declarations of war, decisive battles, or peace treaties, have predominated since 1945. He thinks we need new theories to account for them because he claims they are a new phenomenon. I disagree with his oft-stated claim that "Wars within and between communities are not the same as wars between states" (p. 18) because it is offered as an untested assertion. I would offer, in contrast, research such as that by Benson and Kugler (1998) which finds power-transition-like dynamics underlying some civil wars. But I admit no definitive empirical evaluation has been offered to either support or refute Holsti's claims. Further, I agree that if he is right, attempts to understand wars in the Third World based on a theory about wars in the First World's past are bound to fail. Thus, a good direction for future research might be definitively to investigate Holsti's provocative claim.

Final thoughts

The longest section of this concluding chapter discussed ways in which the analyses I offer could be improved or otherwise better addressed in future research. I suggest this section was as long as it was because the issues attendant upon any effort to analyze the multiple hierarchy model are complicated. Consequently, there are many ways in which the analysis could be recast and many ways in which it could be elaborated (a sign of fertility?). I trust readers will grant that a reasonably sound base for the later improvement and elaboration hinted at in the previous section has been constructed in the foregoing chapters. I conclude that the effort expended in this book to address the three interrelated tasks has been productive. It seems reasonably clear there are important similarities in patterns of war onset among great powers interacting atop the overall international system, and among minor powers interacting within smaller, local hierarchies nested within that overall international system. At the same time, there are region-specific differences in the frequency of war onset and in the effect of power parity and status quo dissatisfaction on the probability of war onset. These differences do not deny the claim of fundamental similarity; rather, they qualify it. They suggest we might profitably think broadly about the issues associated with aggregating our analyses into unified, global wholes. We are statistically justified in doing so, I believe, but if we then conclude the whole is the sum of identical parts, we prevent ourselves from discovering useful information about region-specific effects. If we fail to allow for these region-specific effects in our unified analyses, we increase the probability we will remain ignorant of them. I prefer the lesser evil of specific ignorance: knowledge that the regions vary somewhat, but ignorance as to why they should do so. The next step along this path from general ignorance through specific ignorance to knowledge is to construct theoretical explanations for the cross-regional variation to help understand how and why the whole is the sum of differently shaped parts.

In *World Politics,* Ken Organski introduced power transition theory as a persuasive explanation of great power interactions. He wrote:

> We are all bound by our own culture and our own experience, social scientists no less than other men. We frame our theories to explain the past and blithely project them into the future as "universal laws," assuming that the assumptions on which our theories are based will continue to be true. Social theories may be adequate for their day, but as time passes, they require revision. (1958: 307)

In this book I have revised power transition theory in an attempt to account for minor power interactions. I have offered suggestions for future revisions to similarly enlarge the theory's explanatory capacity. I have approached these tasks with keen awareness that those who preceded me constructed a theory accurate enough, fertile enough, and flexible enough to both demand and deserve such revisions.

Appendix: Replications with Correlates of War capabilities data

As mentioned in chapter 4, the Correlates of War composite capabilities index is a very widely used indicator of national power. I rely primarily upon GDP as a measure of national power resources, because of greater agreement between GDP and the conceptualization of national power within the power transition research tradition, but present this appendix with replications of all of my analyses using COW power. In general, all of the results presented in chapters 5 and 7 are reproduced quite closely in the tables below.

The first result in chapter 5 is the likelihood ratio test investigating the statistical appropriateness of pooling the five regions into one unified analysis. When power is measured with the COW index, the difference in log likelihoods between the pooled model and the sum of the five individual regional models is just below 21. With the same twelve degrees of freedom used in chapter 5, this value is almost statistically significant at the $p < 0.1$ level. Consequently, one might want to be more cautious in pooling with the COW power variable than with GDP as the measure of power. However, given that the difference in log likelihoods here is essentially insignificant, and that the GDP power model clearly can and should be pooled, I pool.

The next statistical model regressed the onset of war against parity and dissatisfaction controlling only for possible consequences of duration dependence by inclusion of time-interval dummy variables in line with Beck, Katz, and Tucker's (1998) procedure. Table A5.1 presents these estimates (tables in this appendix are indicated with the letter "A" to distinguish them from tables in the main text).

As was the case when power was measured with GDP, both parity and dissatisfaction increase the probability of war. Unlike in the GDP-based model, however, the multiplicative interaction term is not statistically

Table A5.1. *Logistic regression estimates*

Dependent variable is War Onset	
Covariate	Coefficient (Probability)
Constant	−3.833***
Parity	1.698** (0.0391)
Dissatisfaction	1.754*** (0.0068)
Parity* Dissatisfaction	−1.038 (0.1961)
Observations: 326; model χ^2: 19. 573; correct predictions: overall: 94.48%, wars: 0%, non-wars: 100%	

Notes: Twelve time-interval dummy variables to control for duration dependence are included but not reported in order to preserve space.

$^{*}p < 0.10$ $^{**}p < 0.05$ $^{***}p < 0.01$

significant when power is measured with the COW index. Thus, the joint presence of parity and dissatisfaction is gauged by the additive combination without the multiplicative version. These results are similar to those in chapter 5 in terms of substantive significance, and indeed the presence of parity and dissatisfaction increases the probability of war even more when power is measured by the COW index.

The next statistical analysis in chapter 5 was a second likelihood ratio test, this time indicating the statistical appropriateness of including region-specific dummy variables along with the theoretically important parity and dissatisfaction variables. The difference in log likelihoods between models with and without regional dummies,

Table A5.2. *Substantive effects of Parity and Dissatisfaction for model reported in table A5.1*

Neither Parity nor Dissatisfaction	2.1%
Parity, no Dissatisfaction	10.6%
Dissatisfaction, no Parity	11.1%
Parity and Dissatisfaction	40.5%

when measuring power with the COW index, is just over 7. With the appropriate four degrees of freedom, this is statistically significant at the $p < 0.10$ level. Adding region-specific dummy variables is statistically appropriate when measuring power with the COW index.

The next step is to report the statistical model including the region-specific dummies. This is offered in table A5.3 with the substantive effects of the coefficients produced therein reported in table A5.4. Once again we see parity and dissatisfaction increasing the probability of war onset (although the multiplicative term is again not statistically significant). Also similar is the fact that the Africa and South America dummies are statistically significant. A difference here is that the dummy representing the Far East region is also statistically significant. As was the case in table 5.3, all the regional dummies have the anticipated negative sign and, also paralleling chapter 5's results, Africa's coefficient is the absolutely largest. The substantive effects of parity and

Table A5.3. *Logistic regression estimates with regional variables*

Dependent variable is War Onset	
Covariate	Coefficient (Probability)
Constant	−2.53**
Parity	1.436* (0.0758)
Dissatisfaction	1.947*** (0.0055)
Parity* Dissatisfaction	−1.064 (0.2017)
Africa	−2.452*** (0.0068)
Far East	−1.426** (0.0444)
Middle East	−0.983 (0.1360)
South America	−1.340* (0.0853)

Observations: 326; model χ^2: 27.130*; correct predictions: overall: 94.79%, wars: 5.56%, non-wars: 100%

See notes to table A5.1.

Table A5.4. *Substantive effects of Parity and Dissatisfaction for model reported in table A5.3*

	Great Powers	Middle East	Far East	S. America	Africa
Neither Parity, nor Dissatisfaction	7.4	2.9	1.9	2.0	0.7
Parity, no Dissatisfaction	25.1	11.1	7.4	8.1	3.0
Dissatisfaction, no Parity	35.8	17.3	11.8	12.8	4.6
Parity and Dissatisfaction	44.7	23.3	16.3	17.5	6.5

Cell entries are the estimated conditional probability of war (expressed as a percentage) given the conditions specified in each row in the region designated in each column.

dissatisfaction across the regions are nearly identical in the COW-based model to those previously reported for the GDP-based model. Again, parity and dissatisfaction have large substantive effects.

The final set of analyses in chapter 5 added four control variables. Table A5.5 presents the estimates, while table A5.6 offers the substantive effects.

Once again the COW-based models nearly identically replicate the GDP-based models. Not only do all coefficients have the same signs across the two versions of the model, but all the variables that are statistically significant in one are statistically significant in the other. The only exception is that the South America dummy variable is statistically significant in the GDP-based model while it is insignificant in the COW-based model and the Far East dummy is significant in the COW-based model but not in the GDP-based one. As reported in chapter 5, the substantive effects of parity and dissatisfaction across all five regions, and controlling for temporal dependence as well as the four additional control variables, are large and positive.

In sum, there are only tiny differences between the results from models using COW's capabilities index and those using GDP. The multiple hierarchy model is robustly supported regardless of which power measure is employed.

In chapter 7 I shifted focus somewhat from analysis of the multiple hierarchy model *per se* to analysis of the African Peace. When I measure

Table A5.5. *Logistic regression estimates with regional and control variables*

Dependent variable is War Onset	
Covariate	Coefficient (Probability)
Constant	−2.764**
Parity	1.499* (0.0712)
Dissatisfaction	1.764** (0.0145)
Parity* Dissatisfaction	−1.022 (0.2186)
Alliance	−0.374 (0.6142)
Joint Democracy	0.123 (0.2130)
Dominant Power's Militarization	−0.145 (0.3140)
Challenger's Militarization	0.202* (0.0626)
Africa	−1.984** (0.0500)
Far East	−1.594** (0.0536)
Middle East	−1.144 (0.1336)
South America	−1.191 (0.1305)
Observations: 316; model χ^2: 30.702*; correct predictions: overall: 94.3%, wars: 5.88%, non-wars: 99.33%	

See notes to table A5.1.

power with the COW index I also consistently generate a large negative coefficient for the Africa dummy variable. This coefficient is absolutely larger than those for the other regions, and consequently there is an African Peace based on the COW index of power as there is based on the GDP measure.

The first statistical results reported in chapter 7 were of the differences between expected and observed frequencies of international conflict

Table A5.6. *Substantive effects of Parity and Dissatisfaction for model reported in table A5.5*

	Great Powers	Middle East	Far East	S. America	Africa
Neither Parity, nor Dissatisfaction	7.6	4.0	1.6	2.1	0.9
Parity, no Dissatisfaction	27.0	15.8	6.8	8.6	4.0
Dissatisfaction, no Parity	32.5	20.0	8.6	10.9	5.1
Parity and Dissatisfaction	68.3	52.3	29.7	35.4	19.4

Cell entries are the estimated conditional probability of war (expressed as a percentage) given the conditions specified in each row in the region designated in each column. Control variables are set at their regional means.

in Africa. Those results do not involve power calculations, and consequently are not relevant here. I also presented table 7.3 in which I introduced three variables anticipated to erase the African Peace. Table A7.3 presents the same statistical model as in chapter 7, but with power measured by the COW index.

Once again quite similar results are produced. Both parity and dissatisfaction continue to increase the probability of war (providing one is flexible about how close to the $p < 0.10$ level one must adhere). As was the case in table 7.3, the underdevelopment variable is large and statistically significant while challenger's militarization is small and statistically significant. The Africa and South America dummies remain negative and statistically significant as well. However, when I measure power with the COW index, the coups variable is also positive and statistically significant. Most surprisingly, in table A7.3 *all* of the region-specific dummies are negative and statistically significant. Table A7.4 presents the substantive effects of the coefficients estimated in table A7.3, which very closely mirror those reported for the GDP-based model in chapter 7.

Finally, table A7.5 reports the substantive effects of parity and dissatisfaction on the probability of war for the great powers and a hypothetical, although not extraordinary, underdeveloped African dyad with three

Table A7.3. *Logistic regression estimates with additional control variables*

Dependent variable is War Onset	
Covariate	Coefficient (Probability)
Constant	−4.847**
Parity	1.285 (0.1108)
Dissatisfaction	2.184*** (0.0048)
Parity* Dissatisfaction	−1.185 (0.1788)
Alliance	−0.194 (0.8171)
Joint Democracy	0.332 (0.1190)
Dominant Power's Militarization	−0.010 (0.4830)
Challenger's Militarization	0.219* (0.0593)
Joint Autocracy	0.161 (0.2394)
Coups	0.633*** (0.0043)
Underdevelopment	2.2549* (0.0551)
Africa	−3.234*** (0.0098)
Far East	−1.991** (0.0238)
Middle East	−1.563* (0.0920)
South America	−3.281** (0.0155)

Observations: 308; model χ^2: 41.860**; correctly predicted: overall: 95.13%, wars: 17.65%, non-wars: 99.66%

See notes to table A5.1.

Table A7.4. *Substantive effects of Parity and Dissatisfaction for model reported in table A7.3*

	Great Powers	Middle East	Far East	S. America	Africa
Neither Parity, nor Dissatisfaction	4.2	1.2	0.5	0.4	0.2
Parity, no Dissatisfaction	13.6	4.4	1.8	1.5	0.6
Dissatisfaction, no Parity	27.9	10.1	4.3	3.5	1.5
Parity and Dissatisfaction	58.3	28.8	14.1	11.6	5.2

Cell entries are the estimated conditional probability of war (expressed as a percentage) given the conditions specified in each row in the region designated in each column. Control variables are set at their regional means.

coups in the decade in question. Under these circumstances the African Peace substantively disappears. There is virtually no difference in the probability of war given changes in parity and dissatisfaction between the great power and African dyads in this example. This suggests the region-specific variables in table A7.3 might be statistically significant, but perhaps not substantively significant.

Table A7.5. *Substantive effects of Parity and dissatisfaction for hypothetical African dyad with Coups = 3 and Underdevelopment = 1*

	Great Powers	African dyads
Neither Parity, nor Dissatisfaction	4.2	4.6
Parity, no Dissatisfaction	13.6	14.9
Dissatisfaction, no Parity	27.9	30.1
Parity and Dissatisfaction	58.3	60.9

Cell entries are the estimated conditional probability of war (expressed as a percentage) given the conditions specified in each row in the region designated in each column.

In this appendix I have reported results of statistical analyses of hypotheses drawn from the multiple hierarchy model. All of these results are successful replications, many of them virtually exact replications, of the GDP-based analyses that provide the structure of chapters 5 and 7. This book's results are *not* sensitive to how power is measured.

References

Agyeman-Duah, Baffour, and Olatunde B.J. Ojo. 1991. "Interstate Conflicts in West Africa." *Comparative Political Studies* 24(3): 299–318.

Alsharabati, Carole. 1997. "The Dynamics of War Initiation." Ph.D. dissertation, Claremont Graduate University, Claremont, California.

Alt, James, Randall Calvert, and Brian Humes. 1988. "Reputation and Hegemonic Stability." *American Political Science Review* 82(2): 445–467.

Altfeld, Michael. 1983. "Arms Races? – And Escalation? A Comment on Wallace." *International Studies Quarterly* 27(2): 225–231.

Anderson, John. 1997. *The International Politics of Central Asia*. Manchester: Manchester University Press.

Arbetman, Marina, and Jacek Kugler, eds. 1997. *Political Capacity and Economic Behavior*. Boulder, CO: Westview Press.

Aron, Raymond (translated from French by Richard Howard and Annette Baker Fox). 1966. *Peace and War*. Garden City, NY: Doubleday and Company.

Ayoob, Mohammed. 1991. "The Security Problematic of the Third World." *World Politics* 43(2): 257–283.

1995. *The Third World Security Predicament*. Boulder, CO: Lynne Rienner.

Banks, Arthur. 1971. *Cross-Polity Time-Series Data*. Cambridge, MA: MIT Press.

Banks, Michael. 1969. "Systems Analysis and the Study of Regions." *International Studies Quarterly* 13(4): 335–360.

Barro, Robert. 1991. "Economic Growth in a Cross Section of Countries." *Quarterly Journal of Economics* 106(2): 407–443.

1997. *Determinants of Economic Growth*. Cambridge, MA: MIT Press.

Bates, Robert. 1997. "Area Studies and the Discipline." *PS: Political Science and Politics* 30(2): 166–169.

Beasley, W. G. 1987. *Japanese Imperialism 1894–1945*. Oxford: Clarendon Press.

Beck, Nathaniel, Jonathan Katz, and Richard Tucker. 1998. "Taking Time Seriously." *American Journal of Political Science* 42(4): 1260–1288.

Bennett, D. Scott, and Allan Stam. 1996. "The Duration of Interstate Wars, 1816–1985." *American Political Science Review* 90(2): 239–257.

1998. "The Declining Advantages of Democracy." *Journal of Conflict Resolution* 42(3): 344–366.

2000. "A Universal Test of an Expected Utility Theory of War." *International Studies Quarterly* 44(3): 451–480.

Benson, Michelle, and Jacek Kugler. 1998. "Power Parity, Democracy, and the Severity of Internal Violence." *Journal of Conflict Resolution* 42(2): 196–209.

Bernstein, Steven, Richard Ned Lebow, Janice Gross Stein, and Steven Weber. 2000. "God Gave Physics the Easy Problems." *European Journal of International Relations* 6(1): 43–76.

Berton, Peter. 1969. "International Subsystems." *International Studies Quarterly* 13(4): 329–334.

Bethell, Leslie, ed. 1984–1991. *The Cambridge History of Latin America*. Cambridge: Cambridge University Press.

Binder, Leonard. 1958. "The Middle East as a Subordinate International System." *World Politics* 10(3): 408–429.

Block, Fred. 1977. *The Origins of International Economic Disorder*. Berkeley, CA: University of California Press.

Boulding, Kenneth. 1962. *Conflict and Defense*. New York: Harper and Brothers Publishers.

Bowman, Larry. 1968. "The Subordinate State System of Southern Africa." *International Studies Quarterly* 12(3): 231–261.

Brace, Paul, and Barbara Hinckley. 1992. *Follow the Leader*. New York: Basic Books.

Brecher, Michael. 1963. "International Relations and Asian Studies." *World Politics* 15(2): 213–235.

Brecher, Michael, and Jonathan Wilkenfeld. 1997. *A Study of Crisis*. Ann Arbor, MI: University of Michigan Press.

Bremer, Stuart. 1980. "National Capabilities and War Proneness." In J. David Singer, ed. *Correlates of War II*. New York: The Free Press.

1992. "Dangerous Dyads." *Journal of Conflict Resolution* 36(2): 309–341.

1993. "Democracy and Militarized Interstate Conflict, 1816–1965." *International Interactions* 18(3): 231–249.

Brooks, Lester. 1971. *Great Civilizations of Ancient Africa*. New York: Four Winds Press.

Bueno de Mesquita, Bruce. 1975. "Measuring Systemic Polarity." *Journal of Conflict Resolution* 19(2): 187–216.

1981. *The War Trap*. New Haven, CT: Yale University Press.

1985a. "The War Trap Revisited." *American Political Science Review* 79(1): 156–177.

1985b. "Toward a Scientific Understanding of International Conflict." *International Studies Quarterly* 29(2): 121–136.

1989. "The Contribution of Expected Utility Theory to the Study of International Conflict." In M. Midlarsky, ed. *Handbook of War Studies*. Boston: Unwin Hyman.

1990a. "Big Wars, Little Wars." *International Interactions* 16(2): 159–169.
1990b. "Pride of Place." *World Politics* 43(1): 28–52.
Bueno de Mesquita, Bruce, and David Lalman. 1992. *War and Reason*. New Haven, CT: Yale University Press.
Bueno de Mesquita, Bruce, James Morrow, and Ethan Zorick. 1997. "Capabilities, Perception, and Escalation." *American Political Science Review* 91(1): 15–27.
Bull, Hedley. 1977. *The Anarchical Society*. New York: Columbia University Press.
Burden, Barry, and David Kimball. 1998. "A New Approach to the Study of Ticket Splitting." *American Political Science Review* 92(3): 533–544.
Burr, Robert. 1955. "The Balance of Power in Nineteenth-Century South America." *Hispanic American Historical Review* 35(1): 37–60.
1970. "International Interests of Latin American Nations." In L. Cantori and S. Spiegel, eds. *The International Politics of Regions*. Englewood Cliffs, NJ: Prentice-Hall.
Buzan, Barry. 1991. *People, States and Fear*, 2nd edn. Boulder, CO: Lynne Rienner.
Cantori, Louis, and Steven Spiegel. 1969. "International Regions." *International Studies Quarterly* 13(4): 361–380.
Carment, David. 1993. "The International Dimensions of Ethnic Conflict." *Journal of Peace Research* 30(2): 137–150.
Carment, David, and Patrick James, eds. 1997. *Wars in the Midst of Peace*. Pittsburgh, PA: University of Pittsburgh Press.
1998. *Peace in the Midst of Wars*. Columbia, SC: University of South Carolina Press.
Centeno, Miguel Angel. 1997. "Blood and Debt." *American Journal of Sociology* 102(6): 1565–1605.
Chan, Steve. 1997. "In Search of Democratic Peace." *Mershon International Studies Review* 41(1): 59–92.
Clapham, Christopher. 1996. *Africa and the International System*. Cambridge: Cambridge University Press.
Clark, David, and Robert Hart, Jr. 1998. "Controlling Duration Dependence in Conflict Analysis." *American Journal of Political Science* 42(4): 1335–1342.
Clarke, Harold, Marianne Stewart, and Paul Whiteley. 1998. "New Models for New Labour." *American Political Science Review* 92(3): 559–575.
Cohen, Raymond. 1994. "Pacific Unions." *Review of International Studies* 20(3): 207–223.
Cohen, Youssef, Brian Brown, and A. F. K. Organski. 1981. "The Paradoxical Nature of State Making." *American Political Science Review* 75(4): 901–910.
Cook, Chris, and David Killingray. 1983. *African Political Facts since 1945*. New York: Facts on File, Inc.
Cooper, James Fenimore. 1993 [1826]. *The Last of the Mohicans*. New York: Book-of-the-Month Club.
Coser, Lewis. 1961. "The Termination of Conflict." *Journal of Conflict Studies* 5(4): 347–353.
David, Steven. 1989. "Why the Third World Matters." *International Security* 14(1): 50–85.

1992/1993. "Why the Third World Still Matters." *International Security* 17(3): 127–159.

Davis, David, and Will Moore. 1997. "Ethnicity Matters." *International Studies Quarterly* 41(1): 171–184.

Davis, H. E., and L. C. Wilson. 1975. *Latin American Foreign Policies*. Baltimore, MD: Johns Hopkins University Press.

Davison, R. H. 1960. "Where is the Middle East?" *Foreign Affairs* 38(4): 665–675.

Desch, Michael. 1996. "Why Realists Disagree About the Third World (and Why They Shouldn't)." *Security Studies* 5(3): 358–381.

de Soysa, Indra, John Oneal, and Yong-Hee Park. 1997. "Testing Power Transition Theory Using Alternative Measures of National Capabilities." *Journal of Conflict Resolution* 41(4): 509–528.

DiCicco, Jonathan, and Jack Levy. 1999. "Power Shifts and Problem Shifts." *Journal of Conflict Resolution* 43(6): 675–704.

Diehl, Paul. 1983. "Arms Races and Escalation." *Journal of Peace Research* 20(3): 205–212.

1985. "Contiguity and Military Escalation in Major Power Rivalries, 1816–1980." *Journal of Politics* 47(4): 1203–1211.

1991. "Geography and War." *International Interactions* 17(1): 11–28.

Diehl, Paul, and Mark Crescenzi. 1998. "Reconfiguring the Arms Race – War Debate." *Journal of Peace Research* 35(1): 111–118.

Diehl, Paul, and Jean Kingston. 1987. "Messenger or Message?" *Journal of Politics* 49(3): 801–813.

du Chaillu, Paul. 1861. *Explorations and Adventures in Equatorial Africa*. London: T. Werner Laurie, Ltd.

Dupuy, R. E., and R. N. Dupuy. 1986. *The Encyclopedia of Military History*, 2nd rev. edn. New York: Harper and Row.

Economist. 2000a. "Hopeless Africa." 355(8170): 17 (May 13).

Economist. 2000b. "The Trouble with Africa." 355(8170): 22–24 (May 13).

Erikson, Robert, Michael MacKuen, and James Stimson. 1998. "What Moves Macropartisanship?" *American Political Science Review* 92(4): 901–912.

Escudé, Carlos. 1998. "An Introduction to Peripheral Realism and Its Implications for the Interstate System." In S. Neuman, ed. *International Relations Theory and the Third World*. New York: St. Martin's Press.

Facts on File. 1967. *Facts on File*, vol. XXVII. New York: Facts on File, Inc.

French, Howard. 1997. "Opposition Strike Turns Zaire's Capital into 'Dead City'." *New York Times* www.nytimes.com accessed on April 15, 1997.

Gardiner, Robert, ed. 1979. *Conway's All The World's Fighting Ships, 1860–1905*. London: Conway Maritime Press.

Gardiner, Robert, ed. 1983. *Conway's All The World's Fighting Ships, 1947–1982*. London: Conway Maritime Press.

Gartner, Scott Sigmund, and Randolph Siverson. 1996. "War Expansion and War Outcome." *Journal of Conflict Resolution* 40(1): 4–15.

Gartzke, Erik. 1998. "Kant We All Just Get Along?" *American Journal of Political Science* 42(1): 1–27.

Garver, J. B., ed. 1990. *National Geographic Atlas of the World*, 6th edn. Washington, DC: National Geographic Society.

Geller, Daniel. 1993. "Power Differentials and War in Rival Dyads." *International Studies Quarterly* 37(2): 173–194.

1998. "The Stability of the Military Balance and War among Great Power Rivals." In P. Diehl, ed. *The Dynamics of Enduring Rivalries*. Urbana, IL: University of Illinois Press.

Geller, Daniel, and J. David Singer. 1998. *Nations at War*. New York: Cambridge University Press.

Gelpi, Christopher. 1997. "Democratic Diversions." *Journal of Conflict Resolution* 41(2): 255–282.

Gleditsch, Kristian, and Michael Ward. 1997. "Double Take." *Journal of Conflict Resolution* 41(3): 361–383.

1999. "A Revised List of Independent States Since the Congress of Vienna." *International Interactions* 25(4): 393–413.

Gochman, Charles. 1990. "Capability-Driven Disputes." In C. Gochman and A. Sabrosky, eds. *Prisoners of War?* Lexington, MA: Lexington Books.

1991. "Interstate Metrics." *International Interactions* 17(1): 93–112.

Gochman, Charles, and Zeev Maoz. 1984. "Militarized Interstate Disputes, 1816–1976." *Journal of Conflict Resolution* 28(4): 585–616.

Goertz, Gary, and Paul Diehl. 1995. "The Initiation and Termination of Enduring Rivalries." *American Journal of Political Science* 39(1): 30–52.

Goldsmith, Arthur. 1987. "Does Political Stability Hinder Economic Development?" *Comparative Politics* 19(3): 471–480.

Green, Donald, Soo Yeon Kim, and David Yoon. 2001. "Dirty Pool." *International Organization* 55(2): 441–468.

Green, Donald, Bradley Palmquist, and Eric Schickler. 1998. "Macropartisanship: A Replication and Critique." *American Political Science Review* 92(4): 883–900.

Grosvenor, M. B., ed. 1966. *National Geographic Atlas of the World*, 2nd edn. Washington, DC: National Geographic Society.

Gujarati, Damodar. 1995. *Basic Econometrics*, 3rd edn. New York: McGraw Hill.

Gulick, Edward Vose. 1955. *Europe's Classical Balance of Power*. New York: W. W. Norton and Company.

Gurr, Ted Robert, Keith Jaggers, and Will Moore. 1989. *Polity II Codebook*. Boulder, CO: Department of Political Science, University of Colorado.

Haas, Michael. 1968. "Social Change and National Aggressiveness, 1900–1960." In J. D. Singer, ed. *Quantitative International Politics: Insights and Evidence*. New York: Free Press.

1970. "International Subsystems." *American Political Science Review* 64(1): 98–123.

1973. "Societal Development and International Conflict." In J. Wilkenfeld, ed. *Conflict Behavior and Linkage Politics*. New York: David McKay Company.

Hardy, Melissa. 1993. *Regression with Dummy Variables*. Beverly Hills, CA: Sage.

Hellman, Donald. 1969. "The Emergence of an East Asian International Subsystem." *International Studies Quarterly* 13(4): 421–434.

Henderson, Errol, and J. David Singer. 2000. "Civil War in the Post-Colonial World, 1946–92." *Journal of Peace Research* 37(3): 275–299.

Hensel, Paul. 1994. "One Thing Leads to Another." *Journal of Peace Research* 31(2): 281–297.

1996. "Charting a Course to Conflict." *Conflict Management and Peace Science* 15(1): 43–73.

1998. "Reliability and Validity Issues in the ICOW Project." Paper presented at the Annual Meeting of the International Studies Association, Minneapolis, MN.

Herbst, Jeffrey. 2000. *States and Power in Africa.* Princeton, NJ: Princeton University Press.

Hibbert, Christopher. 1982. *Africa Explored.* London: Allen Lane.

Holsti, Kalevi. 1996. *The State, War, and the State of War.* New York: Cambridge University Press.

1998. "International Relations Theory and Domestic War in the Third World." In S. Neuman, ed. *International Relations Theory and the Third World.* New York: St. Martin's Press.

Houweling, Henk, and Jan Siccama. 1988. "Power Transitions as a Cause of War." *Journal of Conflict Resolution* 32(1): 87–102.

Hudson, Valerie, Robert Ford, and David Pack, with Eric Giordano. 1991. "Why the Third World Matters, Why Europe Probably Won't." *Journal of Strategic Studies* 14(3): 255–298.

Huth, Paul. 1996. *Standing Your Ground.* Ann Arbor, MI: University of Michigan Press.

Huth, Paul, D. Scott Bennett, and Christopher Gelpi. 1992. "System Uncertainty, Risk Propensity, and International Conflict." *Journal of Conflict Resolution* 36(3): 478–517.

Huth, Paul, and Bruce Russett. 1993. "General Deterrence Between Enduring Rivals." *American Political Science Review* 87(1): 61–73.

Iida, Keisuke. 1988. "Third World Solidarity." *International Organization* 42(2): 373–395.

Intriligator, Michael, and Dagobert Brito. 1984. "Can Arms Races Lead to the Outbreak of War?" *Journal of Conflict Resolution* 28(1): 63–84.

Jackson, Robert. 1990. *Quasi-States.* Cambridge: Cambridge University Press.

Jackson, Robert, and Carl Rosberg. 1982. "Why Africa's Weak States Persist." *World Politics* 35(1): 1–24.

Jacobson, Harold, Dusan Sidjanski, Jeffrey Rodamar, and Alice Hougassian-Rudovich. 1983. "Revolutionaries or Bargainers?" *World Politics* 35(3): 335–367.

Jaggers, Keith, and Ted Robert Gurr. 1995. "Transitions to Democracy." *Journal of Peace Research* 32(4): 469–482.

1996. "Tracking Democracy's Third Wave with the Polity III Data." *Journal of Peace Research* 32(4): 469–482.

James, Patrick, Michael Brecher, and Tod Hoffman. 1988. "International Crises in Africa, 1929–1979." *International Interactions* 14(1): 51–84.

Jansen, Marius. 1975. *Japan and China*. Chicago: Rand McNally.

Johnson, Chalmers. 1997. "Preconception vs. Observation, or the Contributions of Rational Choice Theory and Area Studies to Contemporary Political Science." *PS: Political Science and Politics* 30(2): 170–174.

Jones, Daniel, Stuart Bremer, and J. David Singer. 1996. "Militarized Interstate Disputes: 1816–1992." *Conflict Management and Peace Science* 15(2): 163–213.

Kacowicz, Arie. 1995. "Explaining Zones of Peace." *Journal of Peace Research* 32(3): 265–276.

1998. *Zones of Peace in the Third World*. Albany, NY: State University of New York Press.

Kaiser, Karl. 1968. "The Interaction of Regional Subsystems." *World Politics* 21(1): 84–107.

Kaplan, Robert. 1994. "The Coming Anarchy." *The Atlantic Monthly* 273(2): 44–76.

Karnow, Stanley. 1983. *Vietnam*. New York: Penguin Books.

Kaufman, Robert, and Leo Zuckermann. 1998. "Attitudes toward Economic Reform in Mexico." *American Political Science Review* 92(2): 359–376.

Keesing's. 1967. *Keesing's Contemporary Archives*, vol. XVI. London: Keesing's Publications, Ltd.

Kende, Istvan. 1971. "Twenty-Five Years of Local Wars." *Journal of Peace Research* 8(1): 5–22.

1978. "Wars of Ten Years (1967–1976)." *Journal of Peace Research* 15(3): 227–241.

Kennedy, Paul. 1984. "Arms Races and the Causes of War." In P. Kennedy, ed. *Strategy and Diplomacy*. London: Fontana Press.

Key, V. O., with Alexander Heard. 1949. *Southern Politics in State and Nation*. New York: Knopf.

Kim, Woosang. 1989. "Power, Alliance, and Major Wars, 1816–1975." *Journal of Conflict Resolution* 33(2): 255–273.

1991. "Alliance Transitions and Great Power War." *American Journal of Political Science* 35(4): 833–850.

1992. "Power Transitions and Great Power War from Westphalia to Waterloo." *World Politics* 45(1): 153–172.

1996. "Power Parity, Alliance and War from 1648 to 1975." In J. Kugler and D. Lemke, eds. *Parity and War*. Ann Arbor, MI: University of Michigan Press.

Kim, Woosang, and James Morrow. 1992. "When Do Power Shifts Lead to War?" *American Journal of Political Science* 36(4): 896–922.

Kinsella, David. 1994. "Conflict in Context." *American Journal of Political Science* 38(3): 557–581.

1995. "Nested Rivalries." *International Interactions* 21(2): 109–125.

Kirby, Andrew, and Michael Ward. 1991. "Modernity and the Process of State Formation." *International Interactions* 17(1): 113–126.

Krasner, Stephen, ed. 1983. *International Regimes*. Ithaca, NY: Cornell University Press.

Kugler, Jacek. 1973. "The Consequences of War." Ph.D. dissertation, University of Michigan, Ann Arbor, Michigan.

1996. "Beyond Deterrence." In J. Kugler and D. Lemke, eds. *Parity and War*. Ann Arbor, MI: University of Michigan Press.

Kugler, Jacek, and Marina Arbetman. 1989a. "Choosing Among Measures of Power." In R. Stoll and M. D. Ward, eds. *Power in World Politics*. Boulder, CO: Lynne Rienner.

"Exploring the Phoenix Factor with the Collective Goods Perspective." *Journal of Conflict Resolution* 33(1): 84–112.

Kugler, Jacek, Michelle Benson, Andy Hira, and Dimitry Panasevich. 1997. "Political Capacity and Violence." In M. Arbetman and J. Kugler, eds. *Political Capacity and Economic Behavior*. Boulder, CO: Westview Press.

Kugler, Jacek, and William Domke. 1986. "Comparing the Strength of Nations." *Comparative Political Studies* 19(1): 39–96.

Kugler, Jacek, and Douglas Lemke, eds. 1996. *Parity and War*. Ann Arbor, MI: University of Michigan Press.

Kugler, Jacek, and Douglas Lemke. 2000. "The Power Transition Research Program." In M. Midlarsky, ed. *Handbook of War Studies II*. Ann Arbor, MI: University of Michigan Press.

Kugler, Jacek, and A. F. K. Organski. 1989. "The Power Transition." In M. Midlarsky, ed. *Handbook of War Studies*. Boston: Unwin Hyman.

Kugler, Jacek, and Frank Zagare. 1990. "The Long-Term Stability of Deterrence." *International Interactions* 15(3/4): 255–278.

Kydd, Andrew. 2000. "Arms Races and Arms Control." *American Journal of Political Science* 44(2): 222–238.

Lake, David. 1999. *Entangling Relations*. Princeton, NJ: Princeton University Press.

Lake, David, and Patrick Morgan, eds. 1997. *Regional Orders*. University Park, PA: Pennsylvania State University Press.

Langer, William, ed. 1948. *An Encyclopedia of World History*. Boston: Houghton Mifflin.

Lawrence, T. E. 1927. *Revolt in the Desert*. New York: George K. Doran.

1938. *The Seven Pillars of Wisdom*. New York: Garden City Publishing Company.

Lebovic, James. 1986. "The Middle East." *International Interactions* 12(3): 267–289.

1998. "Consider the Source." *International Studies Quarterly* 42(1): 161–174.

Leeds, Brett Ashley, and David Davis. 1997. "Domestic Political Vulnerability and International Disputes." *Journal of Conflict Resolution* 41(6): 814–834.

Lemke, Douglas. 1993. "Multiple Hierarchies in World Politics." Ph.D. dissertation, Vanderbilt University, Nashville, Tennessee.

1995. "The Tyranny of Distance." *International Interactions* 21(1): 23–38.

1996. "Small States and War." In J. Kugler and D. Lemke, eds. *Parity and War*. Ann Arbor, MI: University of Michigan Press.

1997. "The Continuation of History." *Journal of Peace Research* 34(1): 23–36.

Lemke, Douglas, and William Reed. 1996. "Regime Types and Status Quo Evaluations." *International Interactions* 22(2): 143–164.

1998. "Power Is Not Satisfaction." *Journal of Conflict Resolution* 42(4): 511–516.
2001a. "The Relevance of Politically Relevant Dyads. *Journal of Conflict Resolution* 45(1): 126–144.
2001b. "War and Rivalry Among Great Powers." *American Journal of Political Science* 45(2): 457–469.
Lemke, Douglas, and Suzanne Werner. 1996. "Power Parity, Commitment to Change, and War." *International Studies Quarterly* 40(2): 235–260.
Levy, Jack. 1983. *War in the Modern Great Power System*. Lexington, KY: University of Kentucky Press.
1987. "Declining Power and the Preventive Motivation for War." *World Politics* 40(1): 82–107.
1989. "The Diversionary Theory of War." In M. Midlarsky, ed. *Handbook of War Studies*. Boston: Unwin Hyman.
Lieske, Joel. 1993. "Regional Subcultures of the United States." *Journal of Politics* 55(4): 888–913.
Lijphart, Arend. 1963. "The Analysis of Bloc Voting in the General Assembly." *American Political Science Review* 57(4): 902–917.
Lustick, Ian. 1997. "The Disciplines of Political Science." *PS: Political Science and Politics* 30(2): 175–179.
Luttwak, Edward. 1969. *Coup d'Etat*. New York: Alfred A. Knopf.
Maddison, Angus. 1989. *The World Economy in the 20th Century*. Paris: OECD.
Maier, Mark. 1991. *The Data Game*. Armonk, NY: M. E. Sharpe, Inc.
Mansfield, Edward, and Helen Milner, eds. 1997. *The Political Economy of Regionalism*. New York: Columbia University Press.
Mansfield, Edward, and Helen Milner. 1999. "The New Wave of Regionalism." *International Organization* 53(3): 589–627.
Maoz, Zeev. 1989. "Joining the Club of Nations." *International Studies Quarterly* 33: 199–231.
1998. "Realist and Cultural Critiques of the Democratic Peace." *International Interactions* 24(1): 3–89.
Maoz, Zeev, and Nasrin Abdolali. 1989. "Regime Types and International Conflict." *Journal of Conflict Resolution* 33(1): 3–35.
Maoz, Zeev, and Bruce Russett. 1993. "Normative and Structural Causes of the Democratic Peace, 1946–1986." *American Political Science Review* 87(3): 624–638.
Marin-Bosch, Miguel. 1987. "How Nations Vote in the General Assembly of the United Nations." *International Organization* 41(4): 705–724.
Mastanduno, Michael. 1992. *Economic Containment*. Ithaca, NY: Cornell University Press.
Maugham, William Somerset. 1938. *The Summing Up*. New York: Literary Guild of America.
McFaul, Michael. 2002. *Russia's Troubled Transition from Communism to Democracy*. Ithaca, NY: Cornell University Press.
Mearsheimer, John. 1990. "Back to the Future." *International Security* 15(1): 5–56.

Merritt, Richard, and Dina Zinnes. 1989. "Alternative Indexes of National Power." In R. Stoll and M. Ward, eds. *Power in World Politics*. Boulder, CO: Lynne Rienner.

Midlarsky, Manus. 1990. "Systemic Wars and Dyadic Wars." *International Interactions* 16(2): 171–181.

Miller, Benjamin. 1995. *When Opponents Cooperate*. Ann Arbor, MI: University of Michigan Press.

Modelski, George, and William Thompson. 1996. *Leading Sectors and World Powers*. Columbia, SC: University of South Carolina Press.

Moon, Bruce. 1998. "Regionalism is Back! Now What?" *Mershon International Studies Review* 42(2): 338–342.

Morgan, T. Clifton, and Kenneth Bickers. 1992. "Domestic Discontent and the External Use of Force." *Journal of Conflict Resolution* 36(1): 25–52.

Morgan, T. Clifton, and Glenn Palmer. 1997. "A Two-Good Theory of Foreign Policy." *International Interactions* 22(3): 225–244.

1998. "Room to Move." In R. M. Siverson, ed. *Strategic Politicians, Institutions, and Foreign Policy*. Ann Arbor, MI: University of Michigan Press.

Morgenthau, Hans. 1948. *Politics Among Nations*, 1st edn. New York: Alfred A. Knopf.

1960. *Politics Among Nations*, 3rd edn. New York: Alfred A. Knopf.

Morley, James William, ed. 1983. *The China Quagmire*. New York: Columbia University Press.

Morris, Donald. 1965. *The Washing of the Spears*. New York: Simon and Schuster.

Morrow, James. 1988. "Social Choice and System Structure in World Politics." *World Politics* 41(1): 75–97.

1991. "Alliances and Asymmetry." *American Journal of Political Science* 35(4): 904–933.

1996. "The Logic of Overtaking." In J. Kugler and D. Lemke, eds. *Parity and War*. Ann Arbor, MI: University of Michigan Press.

2000. "The Ongoing Game-Theoretic Revolution." In M. Midlarsky, ed. *Handbook of War Studies II*. Ann Arbor, MI: University of Michigan Press.

Moul, William. 1988. "Balances of Power and the Escalation to War of Serious Disputes Among European Great Powers." *American Journal of Political Science* 32(2): 241–275.

Mueller, John. 1989. *Retreat From Doomsday*. New York: Basic Books.

Myers, David, ed. 1991. *Regional Hegemons*. Boulder, CO: Westview Press.

Neuman, Stephanie, ed. 1998. *International Relations Theory and the Third World*. New York: St. Martin's Press.

New York Times. 1968. *The New York Times Index for 1967*. Current series vol. 55. New York: The New York Times Company.

Nish, Ian. 1977. *Japanese Foreign Policy 1869–1942*. London: Routledge and Kegan Paul.

Olson, Mancur. 1982. *The Rise and Decline of Nations*. New Haven, CT: Yale University Press.

Oneal, John, Indra de Soysa, and Yong-Hee Park. 1998. "But Power and Wealth *Are* Satisfying." *Journal of Conflict Resolution* 42(4): 517–520.
Oneal, John, and Bruce Russett. 1997. "The Classical Liberals Were Right." *International Studies Quarterly* 41(2): 267–294.
Organski, A. F. K. 1958. *World Politics*. New York: Alfred A. Knopf.
1965. *The Stages of Political Development*. New York: Alfred A. Knopf.
1968. *World Politics*, 2nd edn. New York: Alfred A. Knopf.
Organski, A. F. K., and Jacek Kugler. 1977. "The Costs of Major Wars." *American Political Science Review* 71(4): 1347–1366.
1980. *The War Ledger*. Chicago: University of Chicago Press.
Organski, A. F. K., Jacek Kugler, Timothy Johnson, and Youssef Cohen. 1984. *Births, Deaths, and Taxes*. Chicago: University of Chicago Press.
Organski, A. F. K., with Alan Lamborn. 1972. "Effective Population as a Source of International Power." In J. Barratt and M. Louw, eds. *International Aspects of Overpopulation*. Cape Town: South African Institute of International Affairs.
Organski, Katherine, and A. F. K. Organski. 1961. *Population and World Power*. New York: Alfred A. Knopf.
Ortega, L. 1984. "Nitrates, Chilean Entrepreneurs and the Origins of the War of the Pacific." *Journal of Latin American Studies* 16(2): 337–380.
Pakenham, Thomas. 1991. *The Scramble for Africa*. New York: Random House.
Papadakis, Maria, and Harvey Starr. 1987. "Opportunity, Willingness, and Small States." In C. Hermann, C. Kegley, and J. Rosenau, eds. *New Directions in the Study of Foreign Policy*. London: Harper Collins Academic.
Paul, T. V. 1994. *Asymmetric Conflicts*. Cambridge: Cambridge University Press.
2000. *Power versus Prudence*. Montreal: McGill-Queen's University Press.
Powell, Robert. 1996. "Uncertainty, Shifting Power, and Appeasement." *American Political Science Review* 90(4): 749–764.
1999. *In the Shadow of Power*. Princeton, NJ: Princeton University Press.
Przeworski, Adam, and Henry Teune. 1970. *The Logic of Comparative Social Inquiry*. New York: Wiley-Interscience.
Rasler, Karen, and William Thompson. 1985. "War Making and State Making." *American Political Science Review* 79(2): 491–507.
1989. *War and State Making*. Boston: Unwin Hyman.
1999. "Predatory Initiators and Changing Landscapes for Warfare." *Journal of Conflict Resolution* 43(4): 411–433.
Ray, James Lee. 1995. *Democracy and International Conflict*. Columbia, SC: University of South Carolina Press.
1998. *Global Politics*, 7th edn. Boston: Houghton Mifflin.
2001. "Does Interstate War Have a Future?" Paper presented at the workshop on The Study of Future War and the Future Study of War, Pennsylvania State University, March 16–17.
Reed, William. 1998. "Selection Effects and Inference in World Politics." Ph.D. dissertation, Florida State University, Tallahassee, Florida.
2000. "A Unified Statistical Model of Conflict Onset and Escalation." *American Journal of Political Science* 44(1): 84–93.

Reiter, Dan. 1995. "Exploding the Powder Keg Myth." *International Security* 20(2): 5–34.

Reiter, Dan, and Allan Stam. 1998. "Democracy, War Initiation, and Victory." *American Political Science Review* 92(2): 377–389.

Richardson, James. 1994. *Crisis Diplomacy*. Cambridge: Cambridge University Press.

Richardson, Lewis F. 1960a. *Arms and Insecurity*. Pacific Grove, CA: Boxwood Publishers.

1960b. *Statistics of Deadly Quarrels*. Pittsburgh, PA: Quadrangle Press.

Rothstein, Robert. 1968. *Alliances and Small Powers*. New York: Columbia University Press.

Rousseau, David, Christopher Gelpi, Dan Reiter, and Paul Huth. 1996. "Assessing the Dyadic Nature of the Democratic Peace." *American Political Science Review* 90(3): 512–533.

Russett, Bruce. 1967. *International Regions and the International System*. Chicago: Rand McNally.

Russett, Bruce, J. David Singer, and Melvin Small. 1968. "National Political Units in the 20th Century." *American Political Science Review* 62(4): 932–951.

Sabrosky, Alan Ned. 1980. "Interstate Alliances." In J. D. Singer, ed. *The Correlates of War II*. New York: The Free Press.

Salisbury, Harrison. 1985. *The Long March*. New York: Harper and Row.

Sample, Susan. 1997. "Arms Races and Dispute Escalation." *Journal of Peace Research* 34(1): 7–22.

Schweller, Randall. 1992. "Domestic Structure and Preventive War." *World Politics* 44(2): 235–269.

Shepsle, Kenneth, and Barry Weingast. 1981. "Structure-Induced Equilibrium and Legislative Choice." *Public Choice* 37(3): 503–519.

Sigler, John. 1969. "News Flows in the North African International Subsystem." *International Studies Quarterly* 13(4): 381–397.

Signorino, Curtis, and Jeffrey Ritter. 1999. "Tau-b or Not Tau-b." *International Studies Quarterly* 43(1): 115–144.

Singer, J. David. 1988. "Reconstructing the Correlates of War Data Set on Material Capabilities of States, 1816–1985." *International Interactions* 14(1): 115–132.

1991. "Peace in the Global System." In C. Kegley, ed. *The Long Postwar Peace*. New York: Harper Collins.

Singer, J. David, Stuart Bremer, and John Stuckey. 1972. "Capability Distribution, Uncertainty, and Major Power War, 1820–1965." In B. Russett, ed. *Peace, War and Numbers*. Beverly Hills, CA: Sage.

Singer, J. David, and Melvin Small. 1966. "Formal Alliances, 1815–1939." *Journal of Peace Research* 3(1): 1–32.

Singer, Max, and Aaron Wildavsky. 1993. *The Real World Order*. Chatham, NJ: Chatham House Publishers.

Siverson, Randolph, and Paul Diehl. 1989. "Arms Races, the Conflict Spiral, and the Onset of War." In M. Midlarsky, ed. *Handbook of War Studies*. Boston: Unwin Hyman.

Siverson, Randolph, and Ross Miller. 1996. "The Power Transition." In J. Kugler and D. Lemke, eds. *Parity and War*. Ann Arbor, MI: University of Michigan Press.

Small, Melvin, and J. David Singer. 1969. "Formal Alliances, 1816–1965." *Journal of Peace Research* 3(3): 257–282.

1982. *Resort to Arms*. Beverly Hills, CA: Sage.

Smith, Alastair. 1995. "Alliance Formation and War." *International Studies Quarterly* 39(4): 405–426.

1996a. "To Intervene or Not to Intervene." *Journal of Conflict Resolution* 41(1): 16–40.

1996b. "Diversionary Foreign Policy in Democratic Systems." *International Studies Quarterly* 40(1): 133–153.

Solingen, Etel. 1998. *Regional Orders at Century's Dawn*. Princeton, NJ: Princeton University Press.

Stam, Allan. 1996. *Win, Lose or Draw*. Ann Arbor, MI: University of Michigan Press.

Stanley, Henry. 1890. *In Darkest Africa*. New York: Charles Scribner's Sons.

Starr, Harvey. 1978. "'Opportunity' and 'Willingness' as Ordering Concepts in the Study of War." *International Interactions* 4(4): 363–387.

Starr, Harvey, and Benjamin Most. 1976. "The Substance and Study of Borders in International Relations Research." *International Studies Quarterly* 20(4): 581–620.

1978. "A Return Journey." *Journal of Conflict Resolution* 22(3): 442–467.

1983. "Contagion and Border Effects on Contemporary African Conflict." *Comparative Political Studies* 16(1): 92–117.

1985. "The Forms and Processes of War Diffusion." *Comparative Political Studies* 18(2): 206–227.

Stimson, James. 1985. "Regression in Space and Time." *American Journal of Political Science* 29(4): 914–947.

Stoll, Richard, and Michael Ward, eds. 1989. *Power in World Politics*. Boulder, CO: Lynne Rienner.

Summers, Robert, and Alan Heston. 1991. "The Penn World Tables (Mark 5): An Expanded Set of International Comparisons, 1950–1988." *Quarterly Journal of Economics* 106(2): 327–368.

Tammen, Ronald, Jacek Kugler, Douglas Lemke, Allan Stam, Mark Abdollahian, Carole Alsharabati, Brian Efird, and A. F. K. Organski. 2000. *Power Transitions*. New York: Chatham House Publishers.

Taylor, A. J. P. 1954. *The Struggle for Mastery in Europe*. Oxford: Oxford University Press.

Thompson, William. 1973a. "The Regional Subsystem." *International Studies Quarterly* 17(1): 89–118.

1973b. *The Grievances of Military Coup-Makers*. Sage Professional Papers in Comparative Politics, series #01-047. Beverly Hills, CA: Sage.

1981. "Delineating Regional Subsystems." *International Journal of Middle Eastern Studies* 13(2): 213–235.

1983. "Succession Crises in the Global Political System." In A. Bergesen, ed. *Crises in the World-System*. Beverly Hills, CA: Sage.

1988. *On Global War*. Columbia, SC: University of South Carolina Press.

1990. "The Size of War." *International Interactions* 16(2): 183–199.

Tilly, Charles. 1975. "Reflections on the History of European State-Making." In C. Tilly, ed. *The Formation of National States in Western Europe*. Princeton, NJ: Princeton University Press.

1985. "War Making and State Making as Organized Crime." In P. Evans, D. Rueschemeyer, and T. Skocpol, eds. *Bringing the State Back In*. New York: Cambridge University Press.

Timpone, Richard. 1998. "Structure, Behavior, and Voter Turnout in the United States." *American Political Science Review* 92(1): 145–158.

Tomlin, Brian. 1985. "Measurement Validation." *International Organization* 39(1): 189–206.

Tucker, Richard. 1998. "The Robustness of the Dyadic Democratic Peace Result." Unpublished mimeo., Harvard University.

UNCTAD (United Nations Conference on Trade and Development). Various years. *Handbook of International Trade and Development Statistics*. New York: United Nations.

Vagts, Alfred. 1956. *Defense and Diplomacy*. New York: King's Crown Press.

van Chi-Bonnardel, Regine. 1973. *The Atlas of Africa*. New York: The Free Press.

Van Evera, Stephen. 1990. "Why Europe Matters, Why The Third World Doesn't." *Journal of Strategic Studies* 13(2): 1–51.

Vasquez, John. 1993. *The War Puzzle*. New York: Cambridge University Press.

1996. "When Are Power Transitions Dangerous?." In J. Kugler and D. Lemke, eds. *Parity and War*. Ann Arbor, MI: University of Michigan Press.

1997. "The Realist Paradigm and Degenerative versus Progressive Research Programs." *American Political Science Review* 91(4): 899–912.

1998. *The Power of Power Politics*. New York: Cambridge University Press.

Voeten, Erik. 2000. "Clashes in the Assembly." *International Organization* 54(2): 185–215.

Wallace, Michael. 1975. "Clusters of Nations in the Global System, 1865–1964." *International Studies Quarterly* 19(1): 67–110.

1979. "Arms Races and Escalation." *Journal of Conflict Resolution* 23(1): 3–16.

Waltz, Kenneth. 1979. *Theory of International Politics*. New York: McGraw Hill.

1981. "The Spread of Nuclear Weapons." *Adelphi Papers*, no. 171. London: International Institute of Strategic Studies.

Waugh, Evelyn. 1960. *A Tourist in Africa*. London: Chapman and Hall.

Wayman, Frank Whelon. 1996. "Power Shifts and the Onset of War." In J. Kugler and D. Lemke, eds. *Parity and War*. Ann Arbor, MI: University of Michigan Press.

Weede, Erich. 1976. "Overwhelming Preponderance as a Pacifying Condition Among Contiguous Asian Dyads." *Journal of Conflict Resolution* 20(3): 395–411.

1980. "Arms Races and Escalation: Some Persisting Doubts." *Journal of Conflict Resolution* 24(2): 285–287.
1996. *Economic Development, Social Order and World Politics*. Boulder, CO: Lynne Rienner.
Weiner, Myron. 1971. "The Macedonian Syndrome." *World Politics* 23(4): 665–683.
Werner, Suzanne. 2000. "The Effects of Political Similarity on the Onset of Militarized Disputes, 1816–1985." *Political Research Quarterly* 53(2): 343–374.
Werner, Suzanne, and Jacek Kugler. 1996. "Power Transitions and Military Buildups." In J. Kugler and D. Lemke, eds. *Parity and War*. Ann Arbor, MI: University of Michigan Press.
Werner, Suzanne, and Douglas Lemke. 1997. "Opposites Do Not Attract." *International Studies Quarterly* 41(3): 529–546.
Widner, Jennifer. 1995. "States and Statelessness in Late Twentieth-Century Africa." *Dædalus* 124(3): 129–153.
Wight, Martin. 1946. *Power Politics*. Looking Forward Pamphlets, no. 8. London: Royal Institute of International Affairs.
Wilson, Dick. 1971. *The Long March 1935: The Epic of Chinese Communism's Survival*. New York: Viking Press.
Winter, Harold. 1998. *Battling the Elements*. Baltimore, MD: Johns Hopkins University Press.
Wohlstetter, Albert. 1968. "Theory and Opposed-System Design." *Journal of Conflict Resolution* 12(3): 302–331.
Woods, Randall Bennett. 1990. *A Changing of the Guard*. Chapel Hill, NC: University of North Carolina Press.
Woodward, Bob. 1991. *The Commanders*. New York: Simon and Schuster.
Wright, Quincy. 1942. *A Study of War*. Chicago: University of Chicago Press.
Zagare, Frank, and D. Marc Kilgour. 2000. *Perfect Deterrence*. Cambridge: Cambridge University Press.
Zimmerman, William. 1972. "Hierarchical Regional Systems and the Politics of System Boundaries." *International Organization* 26(1): 18–36.
1981. "Soviet–East European Relations in the 1980s and the Changing International System." In M. Burnstein, Z. Gitelman, and W. Zimmerman, eds. *East–West Relations and the Future of Eastern Europe*. London: George Allen & Unwin.

Index

CAMBRIDGE STUDIES IN INTERNATIONAL RELATIONS

68 *Molly Cochran*
Normative theory in international relations
A pragmatic approach

67 *Alexander Wendt*
Social theory of international politics

66 *Thomas Risse, Stephen C. Ropp and Kathryn Sikkink (eds.)*
The power of human rights
International norms and domestic change

65 *Daniel W. Drezner*
The sanctions paradox
Economic statecraft and international relations

64 *Viva Ona Bartkus*
The dynamic of secession

63 *John A. Vasquez*
The power of power politics
From classical realism to neotraditionalism

62 *Emanuel Adler and Michael Barnett (eds.)*
Security communities

61 *Charles Jones*
E. H. Carr and international relations
A duty to lie

60 *Jeffrey W. Knopf*
Domestic society and international cooperation
The impact of protest on US arms control policy

59 *Nicholas Greenwood Onuf*
The republican legacy in international thought

58 *Daniel S. Geller and J. David Singer*
Nations at war
A scientific study of international conflict

57 *Randall D. Germain*
The international organization of credit
States and global finance in the world economy

56 *N. Piers Ludlow*
Dealing with Britain
The Six and the first UK application to the EEC

55 *Andreas Hasenclever, Peter Mayer and Volker Rittberger*
Theories of international regimes

54 *Miranda A. Schreurs and Elizabeth C. Economy (eds.)*
The internationalization of environmental protection

53 *James N. Rosenau*
Along the domestic–foreign frontier
Exploring governance in a turbulent world

52 *John M. Hobson*
The wealth of states
A comparative sociology of international economic and political change

51 *Kalevi J. Holsti*
The state, war, and the state of war

50 *Christopher Clapham*
Africa and the international system
The politics of state survival

49 *Susan Strange*
The retreat of the state
The diffusion of power in the world economy

48 *William I. Robinson*
Promoting polyarchy
Globalization, US intervention, and hegemony

47 *Roger Spegele*
Political realism in international theory

46 *Thomas J. Biersteker and Cynthia Weber (eds.)*
State sovereignty as social construct

45 *Mervyn Frost*
Ethics in international relations
A constitutive theory

44 *Mark W. Zacher with Brent A. Sutton*
Governing global networks
International regimes for transportation and communications

43 *Mark Neufeld*
The restructuring of international relations theory

42 *Thomas Risse-Kappen (ed.)*
Bringing transnational relations back in
Non-state actors, domestic structures and international institutions

41 *Hayward R. Alker*
Rediscoveries and reformulations
Humanistic methodologies for international studies

40 *Robert W. Cox with Timothy J. Sinclair*
Approaches to world order

39 *Jens Bartelson*
A genealogy of sovereignty

38 *Mark Rupert*
Producing hegemony
The politics of mass production and American global power

37 *Cynthia Weber*
Simulating sovereignty
Intervention, the state and symbolic exchange

36 *Gary Goertz*
Contexts of international politics

35 *James L. Richardson*
Crisis diplomacy
The Great Powers since the mid-nineteenth century

34 *Bradley S. Klein*
Strategic studies and world order
The global politics of deterrence

33 *T. V. Paul*
Asymmetric conflicts: war initiation by weaker powers

32 *Christine Sylvester*
Feminist theory and international relations in a postmodern era

31 *Peter J. Schraeder*
US foreign policy toward Africa
Incrementalism, crisis and change

30 *Graham Spinardi*
From Polaris to Trident: the development of US Fleet Ballistic Missile technology

29 *David A. Welch*
Justice and the genesis of war

28 *Russell J. Leng*
Interstate crisis behavior, 1816–1980: realism versus reciprocity

27 *John A. Vasquez*
The war puzzle

26 *Stephen Gill (ed.)*
Gramsci, historical materialism and international relations

25 *Mike Bowker and Robin Brown (eds.)*
From Cold War to collapse: theory and world politics in the 1980s

24 *R. B. J. Walker*
Inside/outside: international relations as political theory

23 *Edward Reiss*
The Strategic Defense Initiative

22 *Keith Krause*
Arms and the state: patterns of military production and trade

21 *Roger Buckley*
US–Japan alliance diplomacy 1945–1990

20 *James N. Rosenau and Ernst-Otto Czempiel (eds.)*
Governance without government: order and change in world politics

19 *Michael Nicholson*
Rationality and the analysis of international conflict

18 *John Stopford and Susan Strange*
Rival states, rival firms
Competition for world market shares

17 *Terry Nardin and David R. Mapel (eds.)*
Traditions of international ethics

16 *Charles F. Doran*
Systems in crisis
New imperatives of high politics at century's end

15 *Deon Geldenhuys*
Isolated states: a comparative analysis

14 *Kalevi J. Holsti*
Peace and war: armed conflicts and international order 1648–1989

13 *Saki Dockrill*
Britain's policy for West German rearmament 1950–1955

12 *Robert H. Jackson*
Quasi-states: sovereignty, international relations and the Third World

11 *James Barber and John Barratt*
South Africa's foreign policy
The search for status and security 1945–1988

10 *James Mayall*
Nationalism and international society

9 *William Bloom*
Personal identity, national identity and international relations

8 *Zeev Maoz*
National choices and international processes

7 *Ian Clark*
The hierarchy of states
Reform and resistance in the international order

6 *Hidemi Suganami*
The domestic analogy and world order proposals

5 *Stephen Gill*
American hegemony and the Trilateral Commission

4 *Michael C. Pugh*
The ANZUS crisis, nuclear visiting and deterrence

3 *Michael Nicholson*
Formal theories in international relations

2 *Friedrich V. Kratochwil*
Rules, norms, and decisions
On the conditions of practical and legal reasoning in international relations and domestic affairs

1 *Myles L. C. Robertson*
Soviet policy towards Japan
An analysis of trends in the 1970s and 1980s